TALES TO NOSES OVER BERLIN

THE 8th AIR FORCE MISSIONS

RAY BOWDEN

USAAF
NOSE ART RESEARCH PROJECT

Published in England By
Design Oracle Partnership
in association with
USAAF Nose Art Research Project
98 West Bay Road, Bridport, Dorset DT6 4AX

"Here's a toast to the host of those who fly...
To the ones who will live and to those who die...
Drink a toast, say a prayer for the next of kin...
For the target today is the heart of Berlin."

Extract from poem by S/Sgt Preston Clark, 94BG
Veteran of two missions to Berlin in May 1944

USAAF
NOSE ART RESEARCH PROJECT

First published 1996

ISBN 1 898575 02 9

We recognise that some words, product names and
designations, for example, mentioned herein are the
property of the trademark holder. We use them for
identification purposes only.

The author would be pleased to have the opportunity to
study and copy any photographs relating to the subject of
WWII aviation nose art or personalisation of aircraft of the
USAAF, any group, any theatre of operation; or hear from
any person who has information relating to named aircraft,
their crews or service record.
USAAF NOSE ART RESEARCH PROJECT
50 Argyle Road, Ealing, London W13 8AA, England

Published in England by
Design Oracle Partnership, 50 Argyle Road, Ealing
London W13 8AA, England

Printed in England by Printkings Ltd, London NW10

381BG Fortress passes over Tempelhof on 3rd February 1945

ACKNOWLEDGEMENTS

Ernest Aita, Don Almon, Paul Andrews, John Archer, David Armstrong, Mike Banta, Ralph Beggs, Charles Bell, Gil Bradley, Ralph Brant, Jesse Brashers, Richard Braun, Charlie Busa, Walter Byrne, Preston Clark, Byron Cook, Harry Culver, Dave Dahlberg, Earl Dahlgren, Abel Dolim, Dale Darling, Denis Dufield, Roy Edney, Vince Edwards, Jeff Ethell, Ken Everett, Mrs Pat Everson, Mike Faley, Bob Fickley, Don Freer, Frank Frison, Dan Hagedorn, M Hall, Frank Halm, David Hanst, Evan Harris, Mike Harvey, Ian Hawkins, Bill Heller, Cliff Hermann, John Hey, Doug Hiley, Rick Janicki, Asay Johnson, Al Keeler, Mrs Joan Kirwan, Ed Kueppers, Louis LaHood, James Lantz, Gerda Laumann, William Lawson, Howard Leech, Jim Long, Rena Sargis Lovell, Charles Lubicic, Floyd Mabee, Arthur Mack, Philip Mack, Sam Markz, John Massol, Jim McDonald, Marshall McKew, Mac McKenzie, Ed McKay, J McPartlin, George Miller, Jack Miller, John Mills, Arnold Moselle, Michal Mucha, R Murphy, Stephen Najarian, Tony North, John Page, Mike Pappas, Walter Pickard, Art Pickens, George Odenwaller, Jerry Ramaker, Eric Ratcliffe, Wilbur Richardson, Bob Roach, Dick Rock, Perry Row, Mark Samson, Cliff Schultz, J Schwarz, Dick Scroxton, Sam Sox, Asa Sprengler, Bob Stachel, Mrs Jackie Starcer, Hans-Heiri Stapfer, Ed Stern, Merrill Stiver, Russell Strong, Bill Thompson, Duane Vieth, Bob Vollmer, Don Wellings, G Williams, R R Williams, Mervyn Wilson, Mrs Kay White, John Whorton, Samuel Wilensky, John Winslett, Doug Wright, Ernie Zapf

BERLIN — The very name burned a deep impression on the memories of almost every one of the 140,000 or more USAAF aircrew who flew the daylight raids to targets in the city. Some flew several missions to Berlin, others only one. Many never returned — for them, the reality more than equalled the nightmare. For some it would not prove to be the ogre they had feared, not the worst target they would have to endure. For some it was an anti-climax, a milk run, but for all it had an unenviable and unfailing psychological effect.

"Big B", the very heart of the Nazi war machine, was protected by the cream of the Luftwaffe in the air and thousands of anti-aircraft weapons on the ground. The Royal Air Force was brought almost to a standstill in its Battle for Berlin which it fought through the night skies in the autumn and winter of 1943-44. As the RAF prepared its final heavy bomber night raid on the city, the US 8th Air Force began its daylight campaign which lasted until the closing days of the war in Europe and saw an even greater number of sorties flown against Berlin.

This book, limited by its size, can only encompass a few of the stories relating to those Berlin missions — merely scratch the surface. Every one of the 140,000 men involved has a story to tell, each would fill a book in its own right. Perhaps this volume will stimulate more veterans to record their story, their perspective, before it is too late. Some of those approached were reluctant to recount their memories, the scars still too deep. Some were regretful of their role, for Berlin became a controversial target as the war dragged on. The initial pinpoint attacks on war factories became an all out massed attack on the city centre. Many an airman manning his station in the massed ranks of B17s and B24s as they ploughed through the flak and fighters towards Berlin must have recalled famed words: "Ours not to reason why, ours but to do or die". Many did. And of those who returned, few would ever forget they had been. This book is respectfully dedicated to them all.

RAY BOWDEN, London 1996

"On one of the Berlin missions I remember the German fighters coming right thru the flak over the target, it was unusual for them to do that.... I have a first cousin who had to enter the German army at the start of the war... The ironic part is that he was in charge of an anti-aircraft battery in Berlin when I was bombing it! Here were two first cousins who had never met and were trying their best to kill each other."

Ernie Zapf, pilot 100BG

ABBREVIATIONS

a/c	Aircraft	FG	Fighter Group	PFF	Radar Pathfinder aircraft
AD	Air Division	F/O	Flight Officer	RAF	Royal Air Force
ASR	Air Sea Rescue	FS	Fighter Squadron	RCM	Radio Countermeasures
ATF	Air Task Force	FW	Focke Wulf		aircraft
(B)	Bombardier	GP	Group	SHAEF	Strategic Headquarters
BBC	British Broadcasting	He	Heinkel		Allied Expeditionary
	Corporation	HE	High Explosive		Force
BD	Bomb Division	HSL	High Speed Launch	S/Sgt	Staff Sergeant
BG	Bomb Group	H2S	Airborne Radar	(TG)	Tail gunner
BS	Bomb Squadron	H2X	Airborne Radar	(Tog)	Togglier
(BT)	Ball turret gunner	IB	Incendiary Bombs	T/Sgt	Technical Sergeant
CBW	Combat Wing	INTOPS	Intelligence Summary	(TT)	Top turret gunner
Col	Colonel	IP	Initial Point on bomb run	V1, V2	German rocket weapons
Cpl	Corporal	JG	Luftwaffe Jagdgeswader	WIA	Wounded in Action
(CP)	Copilot	KIA	Killed in Action	(WG)	Waist gunner
Do	Dornier	Maj	Major	WWI, II	World War I, II
e/a	Enemy Aircraft	Me	Messerschmidt	1Lt	First Lieutenant
ETO	European Theatre	MIA	Missing in Action	2Lt	Second Lieutenant
	of Operation	(N)	Navigator	8AF	US 8th Air Force
FD	Luftwaffe Fighter	(NG)	Nose Gunner	9AF	US 9th Air Force
	Division	Oblt.	Luftwaffe Oberleutnant	#	Number

BERLIN

Berlin's fate was sealed on the day that the first shot of World War Two was fired. In spite of the pronouncements of the head of the Luftwaffe, Reichsmarshal Herman Goering, and his colleague in the Propaganda Ministry, Dr Goebbels, it was inevitable that the capital of the Fatherland would receive the attention of the Allied Air Forces. Although not a target of great strategic value, it was one of immense political and psychological importance.

Goering had made his wild claim that "no bomb shall fall on German soil" to the Krupp workers in 1938, in the days before hostilities had commenced. In the days when it seemed that the Luftwaffe, built up in such secrecy during the 1930s, would have no difficulty in ruling the skies over Europe. As the war developed, and America joined in, the Allied air forces ranged further and further into Germany seeking targets which would hit the Nazi war machine where it hurt most. During post-war interrogation, Goering remarked that he knew the war was lost the day he saw Allied fighter escorts over Berlin in daylight.

In 1939, at the start of WWII, Berlin was the prime industrial and commercial centre on the European continent, ranking sixth in the world. Its pre-war population was over four million people and a city of that size inevitably spawned significant industrial targets. Being the capital of Germany, it also housed the Ministries controlling the Wehrmacht, Kriegsmarine and Luftwaffe as well as those governing the civil administration and the headquarters of the SS. Evacuation began in 1942 and by the end of 1943 almost all schools had been closed, their pupils having

been despatched to camps far away from the city. By 1945, a million and a half had been evacuated.

The 8AF planners considered that the main reasons for striking Berlin were its legitimacy as a top military and governmental target, the effect on German morale and the opportunity it presented to break the Luftwaffe once and for all. The USAAF was taking delivery of its new long range escort fighter — the P51 Mustang, which along with the twin-engined P38 Lightning could

"If bombers appear over Berlin you can call me Meier" Reichsmarshal HERMANN GOERING

accompany the vulnerable daylight formations to the very heart of Germany. It was felt that the German fighters would be forced into the air in a bid to stop any raid on the capital. Once in the air, the Luftwaffe could be confronted and defeated. So, as a result of the directives of early 1944 to strike at the heart of the Nazi Germany, the bombers were to be the bait — the long range fighters, the trap.

8AF crews were briefed for Berlin missions as early as 23rd November 1943, again on 14th December, but these and other early attempts were scrubbed due to poor weather. In addition to the completed missions detailed in this volume, there were several other scheduled raids throughout the remaining months of war which were scrubbed or diverted as a result of poor weather. A half dozen missions were planned, then cancelled, during February as tension mounted among the crews.

It would be March 1944 before the first raids got airborne. Weather again caused a turn-about on the 3rd March, although a few P38 Lightnings from 55FG

pressed on and became the first Americans over Berlin in daylight. The following day a handful of bombers and escorts finally made it to the city.

It was 6th March 1944 before the citizens of Berlin received their first real taste of daylight bombing. The results were less than substantial and the resulting loss of 69 American bombers from the force of almost 700 again brought the viability of daylight raids into question. However, to put these losses into perspective, consider that

on 19th February 1944 the RAF sent 823 heavies to attack Leipzig at night and lost 78! — an almost identical loss ratio. The cloak of darkness was no longer proving to be an effective shield against the Luftwaffe's defences.

Initial plans for the raid of 21st June 1944 were for a massive assault on Berlin with 900 RAF Lancasters and the entire 15AF heavy bomber force adding their weight to the 8th's three Bomb Divisions. In the final event neither the RAF nor the 15AF joined the effort, mainly due to fears over insufficient fighter escort cover. The RAF bomber crews were not trained to fly in the tight defensive box formations considered to be so vital by the Americans for effective defence against fighters. With an inadequate escort the result might easily have been carnage on scale not previously seen.

Perhaps the most extraordinary, and unscheduled, daylight raid on the capital occurred on

12th September 1944. A late take-off by David Armstrong's 100BG Fort forced it to join the 351BG formation en route for Ruhland. Having become detached from them, the plane made a lonely and solitary strike on the outskirts of Berlin before joining the 457BG to return home to England.

The USAAF's first 1000-bomber Berlin raid on 3rd February 1945 caused massive damage to the capital, a city by then packed with refugees. The civilian casualties were considerable and were reported by journalists from neutral countries like Sweden, fed by German statistics. Secret records from German archives suggest that the actual loss of life was not as catastrophic as was reported at the time — although it was still very substantial. Public opinion amongst the Allies, however, began to waver and editorial discontent began to appear, questioning the need to bomb German cities full of refugees. Certainly the change of emphasis in targeting did not go unnoticed by the pilots, navigators and bombardiers of the 8AF who had always prided themselves of the fact that they bombed military targets with considerable precision. Dropping hundreds of tons of bombs onto a city centre did not sit easily on their shoulders or in their minds.

The arguments for and against bombing Berlin as a means to crack open civilian morale had ranged long and hard. Sir Arthur Harris, commander of RAF Bomber Command, had written to Winston Churchill on 3rd November 1943 stating

"I take my hat off to the pilot who bombed Berlin alone and returned safely to England." Reported comment made by President Roosevelt in radio broadcast

"American attacks on the capital clearly indicate to the Nazis that no target is now safe by day or night"

Sec. of War, Henry L Stimson, Washington, 9th March 1944

"We can wreck Berlin from end to end if the USAAF will come in on it. It will cost 400-500 aircraft. It will cost Germany the war." In fact, by the end of hostilities, RAF Bomber Command alone had lost more than six hundred heavy night bombers in the Battle for Berlin. The Americans, even though they did not "come in on it" until March 1944, also lost about 450 heavy bombers raiding Berlin by the end of the war.

Lt General Carl Spaatz, commanding the US air forces, shared Harris's belief that air power might win the war. The differences came in the application and target choice. The Combined Chiefs of Staff returned control of the strategic bomber forces back to their British and American commanders in mid-September 1944 after the campaign to support the D-Day invasion. Sir Charles Portal, who had commanded the combined bomber offensive prior to Eisenhower taking over in preparation for D-Day, favoured an assault on Berlin using every available heavy bomber in an operation code-named "Thunderclap". The idea was not well received at this time but nevertheless, Hap Arnold requested Spaatz to prepare a plan which would involve a week long "all-out widespread attack" against Germany by both British and US air forces. It was suggested that Berlin should be one of the recipients of such attention though not exclusively. In subsequent discussions with Eisenhower, Spaatz was instructed not to just plan to hit definite military objectives but also be ready to drop bombs in to the centre of the city when ordered to do so. In August, Eisenhower had written that such a raid might be executed if a sudden and devastating blow held a real promise of ending the war quickly.

This constituted a major change of tactics and planning but it should not be forgotten that it was at a time when German V2 rockets were beginning to fall on London and the southeast of England. The V2 was far more potent than its predecessor the V1 but equally as indiscriminate. By mid-summer of 1944 the V1 had already destroyed more than 15,000 houses in London alone and damaged another 690,000; a quarter of million people had been evacuated and another half million had simply moved out. Hospitals were being prepared for the 4,000 casualties per day expected from V2 attacks. The Allies were also shaken, later in 1944, by the unexpected level of German resistance. The audacious attack through the Ardennes just before Christmas was a stunning blow and use of the overwhelming might of the heavy bomber force against German morale was back on the agenda.

On 30th January 1945, meeting on the island of Malta, the Joint Chiefs of Staff put Berlin, Leipzig and Dresden high on the list of targets to "cause great confusion in civilian evacuation from the east and hamper reinforcement from other fronts." The transport network had become a top priority and Berlin was an important rail and communications centre — the destruction of which would yield considerable benefits in assisting the Russian advance into eastern Germany. Coincidentally, it might also serve to remind the Russians of the enormous destructive power of the Allied air forces. A higher targeting priority other than transportation would only be accorded to German synthetic oil production.

The validity of this decision to continue to hammer transportation facilities and bottlenecks is reinforced by statements made during post-war interrogation of Field Marshal Kesselring. "The attack on transportation was the decisive blow that completely disorganised the German economy", he stated. "It reduced war production in all categories and made it difficult to move what was produced to the front.... also limited the tactical mobility of the German Army."

But while the official view was that raids on major population centres were not retaliatory, that they were legitimate strikes against transport and communication bottlenecks, which just happened to be within cities, many aircrew began to feel otherwise. Diary notes and recollections reflected "after initial attacks on Berlin silenced Luftwaffe boasts, the general feeling was not fear but anger. Berlin missions were retaliatory, not tactical or strategic." Others pondered the fact that they were loaded "with demolition bombs and incendiaries, followed by delayed action anti-personnel bombs and that the bomb train was usually controlled by a 500ft intervalometer setting — one bomb every 500ft on the ground." Not a bomb load intended for precision targeting. After the 21st June mission one veteran wrote in his diary, "The demolition bombs used on today's mission were fused to explode from one to 72 hours after impact. These coupled with the incendiaries create the maximum hazardous situation for the enemy firefighting and 'UXB' demolition crews.... Some thermite bombs have anti-personnel fragmentation devices to discourage countermeasures. They explode in contact with water.... there are many among us who are not proud of today's accomplishment."

The crippling attack on Berlin on 3rd February was followed by others elsewhere including an even more devastating raid on Dresden on 14th February by the combined forces of the RAF and USAAF. An Associated Press despatch announced that the Allies had adopted "deliberate terror bombing... as a ruthless expedient to hasten Hitler's doom." The despatch was widely published across America but was banned in Britain. The highest authorities began a scramble to distance themselves from the horrors of city area bombing, of which it seemed the 8AF had now become a part, but another devastating daylight attack was made on Berlin on 26th February. A month later, a further attack was made against the tank and armament plants on the western outskirts of the city at the same time as an attack against the rail targets in the centre.

On 28th March 1945, as public concern grew, the 8AF yet again visited Berlin with a precision attack on the armament plants. On that same day, Allied Supreme Commander General Eisenhower informed Stalin of his intent to turn his advancing ground forces away from the city. The 8AF continued to pound at oil plants, marshalling yards and airfields across Germany in the closing days of war but never again raided Berlin en masse.

BERLIN – THE TARGETS

The 8AF planners and target selecters considered Berlin and its sprawling suburbs to have an abundance of military targets of significance. There were an estimated 1500 factories within the city limits, employing at least 600,000 people. 375 of these factories were considered big plants and sixty of them were listed as priority targets.

The VKF plant at Erkner was considered a most important target. Located 16 miles southeast of the centre, it was the sixth largest producer of ball bearings in Germany, following plants at Schweinfurt, Steyr and Stuttgart. However, whereas these latter factories produced the bulk of the standard size general purpose ball bearings, Erkner was known to specialise in special sizes required in the production of high performance aircraft and aero engines. The entire output from the plant went to the Luftwaffe. Since one of the aims of striking Berlin was to assist in the elimination of the

Luftwaffe, the Erkner plant was a very important target indeed. Its elimination would reduce the enemy's ability to replace its lost fighters. There was also another smaller ball bearing plant in the east of the city at Lichtenberg which, when combined with the VKF facility, brought Berlin production of ball bearings up to an estimated 13% of total German capacity.

Much of the German electrical industry was headquartered in the Berlin area. The Robert Bosch plant at Klein Machnow made vital ignition equipment used in a wide range of military vehicles. AEG had plants at Kopenick, Henningsdorf and Moabit. Telefunken made radio and radar equipment at a plant located at Tempelhof. The huge electrical equipment manufacturer, Siemens, was concentrated in a self-contained complex in Seimenstadt with other plants across the city.

At Henningsdorf and Tegel, the Rheinmetall Borsig plant turned out guns, bombs and

torpedoes while the Borsig Lokomotiv works, which covered an area of 120 acres, produced a range of armoured vehicles and artillery as well as locomotives and rolling stock. The Alkett plant at Spandau was the biggest single tank factory in Germany and produced self-propelled guns and much of the Wehrmacht's field artillery. Hitler considered this plant to be of such importance that on the night of 26 November 1943, when the RAF set it ablaze, he ordered every available fire engine in Berlin to attend the scene — leaving other fires in the city to burn.

bombers. In the north of the city at Reinickendorf was a factory producing jet engines for V1 rockets. At Genshagen, to the south, was the huge Daimler Benz plant producing aero engines with the Heinkel assembly and aero engine plant located close by. Another Daimler Benz aero engine plant was positioned at Marienfelde in the south of the city and the Brandenburgisen Motor Works at Basdorf, 15 miles to the north, employed 8000 workers manufacturing 300 aircraft engines every month. Another important Heinkel factory making wings for Ju88s and

> ## "The sheet went up and the moan went out – Big B! We never called it Berlin, always Big B"
> Jerry Ramaker, 385BG ball gunner, *Well's Cargo* (42-31778)

Halftracks and other military vehicles were assembled at the Demag factory near Falkensee and the Auto Union plants at Halensee and Spandau.

Located within the city limits were several airfields, one at Staaken to the west and two major fields at Tempelhof and Johannisthal. The latter was also the site of a Henschel assembly plant which was producing attack aircraft and Ju88

assembling He177 heavy bombers, Germany's equivalent to the Flying Fortress, was located beyond the north of the city at Oranienburg.

In the very centre of Berlin were the ministerial buildings for the three armed forces as well as important administrative buildings such as the Reichstag and Hitler's bunker at the Chancellery. Hitler personally administered the war from the Reichstag — up until the 8th Air Force raid of 3rd February 1945 which severely damaged the building. Thereafter he withdrew to his infamous underground bunker. The Propaganda Ministry, Foreign Office and Gestapo headquarters were all close by. Just to the west of the centre in Charlottenburg, close to the giant flak tower at Zoo park, was the headquarters of the 1st Flak Division coordinating the anti-aircraft defences for Berlin. To the southwest, at Steglitz, was the SS

> ## "Last August, as a gag, someone put up the red ribbon across to Berlin, and no return route was indicated. Now it was no gag and there was a return route." Yank, 28th April 1944

Friedrichstrasse in central Berlin, the target for many USAAF raids.

BERLIN

0 MILES 10

Heinkel Aircraft Plant

Aero Engines

ORANIENBURG

BASDORF

V1 Jet Engine Plant

Rheinmetall Borsig AG
Tank Assembly Plant

Borsig-Lokomotiv
Armoured Vehicles

HENNINGSDORF

Demag AFVs

Auto Union AG –
Alkett Tank Plant

Spandau Neustadt
Ordnance depot

TEGEL

SPANDAU

REINICKENDORF

PANKOW

FALKENBERG

HQ 1st Flak
Division

River Spree

WEDDING

WEISSENSEE

HORST WESEL

MAHLSDORF

CHARLOTTENBURG

MITTE

LICHTENBERG

Telefunken
Lorenz

Lake Havel

TIERGARTEN

FRIEDRICHSHAIN

KREUZBERG

SCHONEBERG

WILMERSDORF

TREPTOW

Mueggel See

ERKNER

ZEHLENDORF

STEGLITZ

TEMPELHOF

MARIENDORF

KOEPENICK

JOHANNESTHAL

MARIENFELDE

KLEIN
MACHNOW TELTOW

POTSDAM

SS Barracks
Hitler Bodyguard

GENSHAGEN

WILDAU

Robt. Bosch AG

Daimler Benz

Aero Engine Plant

Buessing – Henschel
Nationale Automobile – AEG

Torpedo Components

Reichstag – Propaganda Ministry
Air Ministry – Foreign Office
OKW Army HQ – Government Bldgs
Kriegsmarine (Navy) HQ

NKF Ball Bearings

Telefunken
Lorenz – Maybach

VKF Ball Bearings

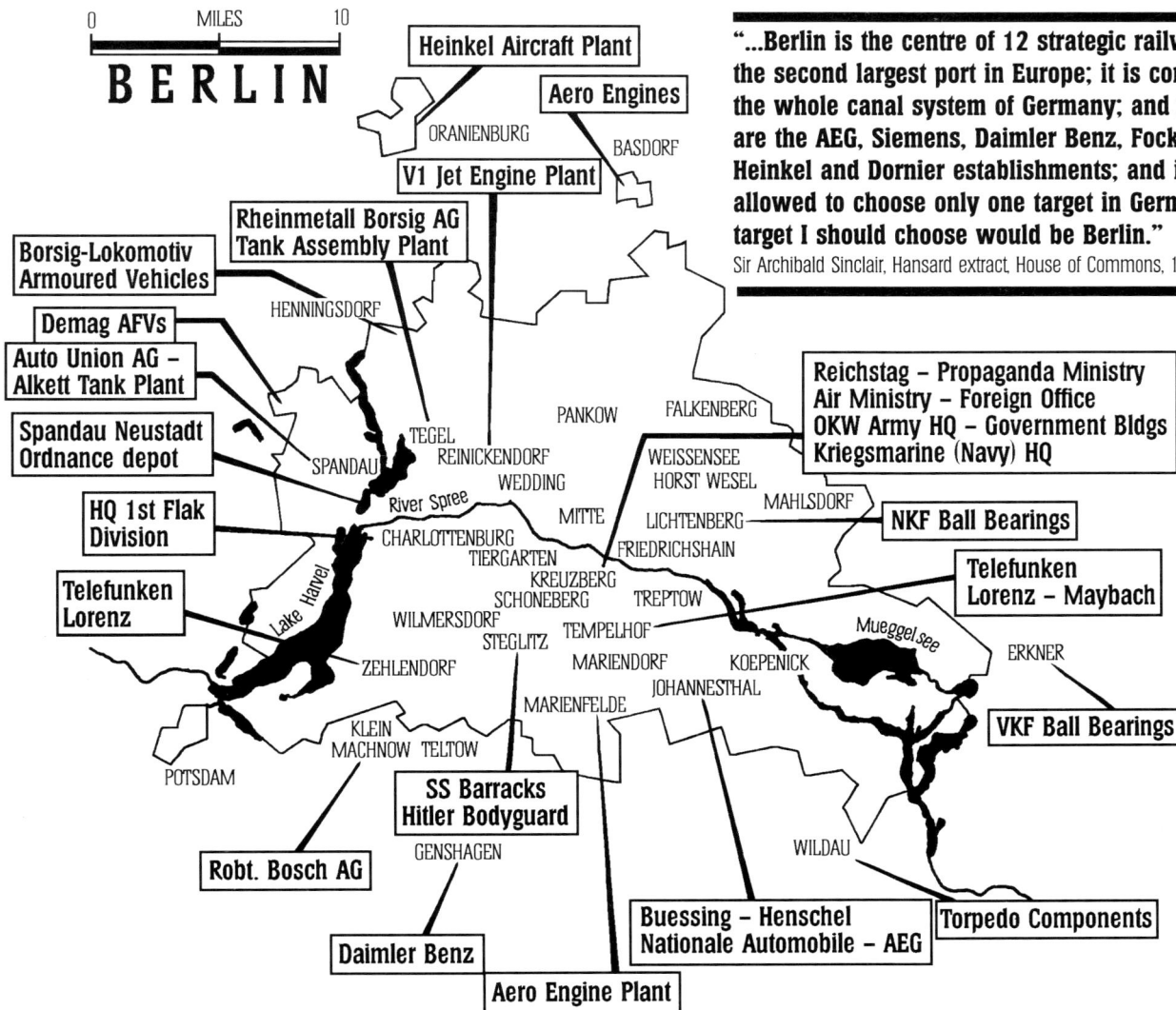

> "...Berlin is the centre of 12 strategic railways; it is the second largest port in Europe; it is connected with the whole canal system of Germany; and in that city are the AEG, Siemens, Daimler Benz, Focke Wulf, Heinkel and Dornier establishments; and if I were allowed to choose only one target in Germany, the target I should choose would be Berlin."
> Sir Archibald Sinclair, Hansard extract, House of Commons, 1st December 1943

barracks for Hitler's personal bodyguard, the Hauptkadettansteldt. The Berlin Garrison was barracked in a large camp beyond the northern edge of the Tiergarten. In all, there were almost one hundred military head-quarters, barracks and depots based within the confines of the city.

Berlin's Friedrich-strasse Station, the hub of the rail and subway network, lay dead centre with the important Potsdamer and Anhalter Stations and goods yards located not far to the south and the Stettiner (Berlin-

Nord) depot less than a mile to the north. Numerous other passenger stations, rail junctions and goods yards were located throughout the city. Berlin was in fact the focal point of a massive rail network in which twelve main rail lines converged. Its subway functioned throughout the war, much as did London's, as an effective transit system for military and civilian personnel.

An extensive canal system also linked the city to the Ruhr, Germany's industrial heart, and to Hamburg and Stettin. This

impressive network of roads, rail and canals became the recipient of much attention by the 8AF in the closing months of the war. Berlin was considered a key communications bottle-neck for transferring Wehrmacht troops, armour and munitions between the battle fronts as the Allied and Russian armies pushed closer to the city.

Although many of these important military sites were assigned as primary targets, crews were invariably given a secondary, in the event of bad weather, as the centre of the city. Having hauled their loads of bombs and incendiaries so far into the heart of the Fatherland they could hardly have been expected to bring them home again if cloud, haze or smoke obscured

their pinpoint targets. The 389BG diary, for example, notes on 8th March 1944 "target already destroyed so we bombed the centre." Thus more than one Berlin raid saw hundreds of B17s and B24s drop their loads through the undercast to fall "somewhere in the city". Whenever possible, bombardiers struggled to identify military targets of opportunity through the breaks in the cloud hoping to hit something of significance rather than just the densely packed domestic suburbs. German records reveal the results to be generally of mixed value militarily with inevitable hits on hospitals, school buildings and housing estates as well as the targeted government offices, factories, rail yards, barracks and transport facilities.

> "Heartiest congratulations on first US bombing of Berlin. It is more than a year since they were attacked in daylight but now they have no safety there by day or night. All Germany learns the same lesson."
> Air Chief Marshal of the RAF, Arthur Harris

7

THE DEFENCES

Four elements conspired in the defence of Berlin against the daylight aerial onslaught of the Eighth Air Force. The Luftwaffe fighter force located across northwest Europe, the heavy flak artillery positioned around all the major targets, the radar which was vital to guiding both onto their victims and, last but not least, the weather.

Arguably the weather did more to disrupt the attempts at daylight bombing of the German capital than any of the other three elements. Missions planned in late 1943 were scrubbed time and again as a result of deteriorating weather as the winter came on. In early 1944, when things improved, it was still able to turn back the formations of bombers completely on the 3rd March and all but a handful on the 4th. Other missions throughout 1944 were scrubbed when the weather closed in or were considerably disrupted by thick cloud forming over the target by the time the formations reached the city. A major raid was turned back on 27th August, for example, as a result of poor weather. Although thousands of tons of ordnance were still dropped onto the city when cloud obscured it, rarely could it be accurately dropped onto the chosen primary targets even when PFF radar guidance was at hand. On 6th March for example, in spite of the huge publicity afforded to the mission as the first major daylight raid on the capital, none of the primary targeting was hit — largely due to the cloud cover and obscured visibility. An unknown number of the aircraft which failed to return were claimed by the weather conditions. Mid-air collisions, icing and disorientation in dense cloud or contrails all claimed victims.

The aerial defence of Berlin was largely the responsibility of the Luftwaffe's 1st Fighter Corps, headquartered at Zeist in Holland, and its component 1st, 2nd, 3rd and 7th Fighter Divisions. The headquarters of the 1st Fighter Division was located just west of Berlin at Doeberitz, the 2FD HQ was just west of Hamburg at Stade and the 3FD HQ was located at Deelen near Arnhem, Holland. To the south was 7FD with its headquarters near Munich. The 2nd Fighter Corps' 4th Division, located at Metz, also contributed to the defence of Berlin.

Two fighter aircraft dominated the defence, the Me109 and FW190. The latter was the most formidable opponent of the USAAF escorts, carrying four 20mm cannon, two 13mm machine guns and a rugged engine that could take a lot of punishment in combat. The older Me109 was increasingly outpaced by the Allied fighters but its 20mm cannon and machine guns still proved highly effective in the right hands. The aircraft intended as the main defence against heavy bomber formations was in fact the twin-engined Me110 'destroyer' with two 30mm and four 20mm cannon. Many also carried four 210mm rocket launchers. This formidable fire power was highly effective on those occasions when it could be brought to bear on the dense formation of bombers. This however was rarely achieved since the lumbering twin-engine machines were totally out matched by the Allied fighters and subjected to grievous losses whenever they were caught by them.

In March 1944, when the USAAF began its first raids on the capital, the five Luftwaffe Fighter Divisions could muster an estimated 560 serviceable single engined and 92 twin-engined day fighters. These were supplemented by a further 348 night fighters but their pilots had little experience of day fighting. A proportion of these were brand new and still under test and others were assigned to pilot training schools. By mid-January 1945, Luftflotte 3, responsible for the defence of western Germany and Holland, could muster 871 serviceable single engined fighters plus a further 21 night fighters and 37 Me262 jets. Luftflotte Reich, in central Germany, could contribute another 225 day fighters and 19 Me163 jets as well as more than 700 night fighters, mainly twin-engined.

This increase in available fighters bears witness to the ability of the German aviation industry to withstand the bombing of its production facilities through dispersion and rationalisation. In May 1944, the Luftwaffe took delivery of 1065 Me109s and 841 FW190s. In September these figures had increased to 1605 and 1391 respectively. However, many of the Luftwaffe's best and most skilled fighter pilots were lost during the aerial battles of early 1944 when the 8AF set out to lure them up to destruction. This was one of the prime reasons for selecting Berlin as a target and it had succeeded, at least in part.

Several combat reports recorded by returning Allied pilots reveal them catching large formations of Luftwaffe fighters, slavishly following their leader in spite of being under attack. The Luftwaffe was having to field inexperienced pilots with woefully inadequate training. They could, and did, do immense damage to a bomber box if they got through in a massed attack but increasingly the escorts prevented them from getting anywhere near.

The arrival of high speed jets, which could outrun the Allied escorts in their effective hit and run tactics, proved to be a major problem for the bombers and fighters of the 8AF in the closing months of the war. But there were never enough of them available to make a real difference. Had the policy of the German High Command been different, development of the Jumo 004 engine been quicker

> ## "The Me262, manufactured in appropriate numbers, would have been death to the four-engine bomber."
> Extract from US Strategic Bombing Survey Report
> post war interview with Field Marshal Albert Kesselring

> **"We were going in to Berlin at altitude and could see this bank of clouds from the ground up to heaven, just as high as you could see. We saw other formations coming back and I remember our pilot checking in a couple of times with our radio operator asking 'Have we had a recall, have we had a recall?' 'No, sir!' 'No, sir!' came back the reply. So we headed into this cloud bank and then the pilot ordered 'Everyone put on your chutes, put them on now!' We headed into this stuff and we got the recall soon after. We hit the prop wash of another plane and it almost turned us upside down but our pilot got control of the plane and brought us out of it."**
> Lynn White, 385BG photographer on *Roger the Dodger*, 27th August 1944

and had fighter production been given a much higher priority sooner, then the jets could have proved to be a difficult threat to counter. Several bomber crews returning from the 18th March 1945 mission recorded a belief that it was only the sheer numbers of bombers in their formations which had prevented a slaughter by the jets which had attacked with great skill — they had met their match and they knew it! But it was too little, too late.

As the threat from aerial defences reduced the same was not true of the ground fire thrown up by the heavy flak guns which covered all the major targets throughout Germany and occupied Europe. Many crews feared flak more than fighters. There was nothing they could do against it but sit and take it. Careful routeing avoided the heaviest flak areas but Berlin was ringed by anti-aircraft defences and as the formations closed on their targets they could not be avoided. It has been estimated that during May 1944 the Luftwaffe had in total 17,500 heavy flak guns under its command; with a further 4000+ heavy AA weapons manned by Army and Navy personnel.

It has proved difficult to establish precisely the strength of the flak around Berlin. In any case it varied almost from day to day as a result of mobile units being moved around by road and rail. Some briefing documents reveal an estimated 2500 guns surrounding the city but this may have included those positioned close to the approach routes across Germany. The 390BG briefing before the mission of 6th March referred to 1700 guns around Berlin, the briefing officer jokingly commenting that four of them were out of

commission! 94BG records indicate 1200 guns defending Berlin for the 3rd February 1945 mission. Other briefing documents reveal 480 guns defending the ball bearing plant at Erkner and a total of 500 guns within range of the Friedrichstrasse rail station in the centre of the city.

The defence of the city was controlled by the 1st Flak Division, whose headquarters were located in Charlottenburg. In March 1944 the division is believed to have had 78 batteries of heavy flak guns available, totalling 414 guns of 88mm, 105mm and 128 mm calibre. In addition there were a further 331 light flak weapons available in 14 batteries but these would have been ineffective against the high flying

bomber formations. They would, however, have been devastating against fighter escorts which streaked across the city at low level on strafing runs.

RAF intelligence documents reveal that on 19th April 1945, three weeks after the last major daylight raid on Berlin, the city contained 315 x 88mm guns, 55 x 105mm and 24 x 128mm weapons. Most of the heavier flak guns were static; the majority of the 88mm weapons were transportable but only 40% had trailers available.

Within the city were three huge flak towers.

One was at the Zoo park in Charlottenburg, another in Friedrichshain, a third was located in Humboldthain. Each tower mounted four of the Luftwaffe's most powerful twin-128mm guns on top of their huge concrete structures. The barrage from each tower could cover an area of 260 yards radius at 45,000ft. Circled around the city, and positioned within parks throughout, were the batteries of 88mm and 105mm guns. These were generally sited in Grossbatteries of 12, 18 or 24 guns which fired in salvoes to produce a concentrated pattern of bursts. The more powerful 105mm and 128mm batteries were usually in smaller groups of four or twelve. This grouping allowed the efficient use of radar prediction equipment to track the weapons onto their targets. At Duppel, near Klein Machnow, an experimental Mammuth Batterie was established. This massive flak complex comprised 36 x 88mm guns with three predictors and two Wurzburg Giant radars.

Earlier 88mm guns had a ceiling of 26,000ft but this was raised to 30,000ft as the war went on, forcing bomber formations to fly even higher in their attempts to escape. The Luftwaffe achieved significant results from flak, in spite of the countermeasures employed by the attackers to confuse their guidance systems with chaff and other RCM interference such as 'Carpet' radar jammers. Hitler is said to have been personally convinced that flak was the only way to defeat the day bomber and more than one million personnel were assigned to that particular armed force throughout Germany. In November 1944 Fuhrer Directives ordered war plants to sub-ordinate all other considerations to flak production. The Luftwaffe also believed that flak defence made an attacker as much as one third less effective in their bombing.

It became obvious to the 8AF commanders that the leading groups of bombers were suffering more severely from accurate flak because they did not have the benefit of a chaff screen released ahead of them. The lead crews were highly trained and experienced and their disproportionate losses were severely felt. This was countered by despatching a small force ahead of them purely to discharge bundles of chaff. By November 1944, Mosquito aircraft from 25BG had been specially modified to saturate and jam the ground radars with chaff. This became even more important as the Luftwaffe interlinked flak units enabling them to instantly utilise the radar from a neighbouring battery. Alternative bomber formations were also developed to reduce the damage caused by each flak burst whilst still maintaining a strong fighter defence.

Industrial and aviation industry sites in Berlin, Erkner and, to the north, Oranienburg were the primary targets for the first major daylight attempt on the German capital. Almost 750 heavy bombers from all three Divisions were despatched, supported by an equal number of fighter escorts. One of the 194 Liberators was lost on take off when it crashed and burned at Hardwick but fortunately the crew escaped without fatalities.

Poor weather conditions and dense, persistent contrails forced the mission to be abandoned although some leading formations reached as far as the Schleswig-Holstein coast where they circled waiting for instructions. Others found targets of

opportunity at Wilhelmshaven and elsewhere.

Assembly in the difficult conditions had not been easy and many aircraft used up excessive fuel in trying to get into their defensive formations. Once assembled, the formations struggled to try to get on top of the cloud front which towered over the continent. The 100BG, for example, had a briefed altitude of 22,000ft but did not climb out of the dense cloud until 27,000ft or more. With the formation totally disrupted, individual aircraft had no option but to turn about and head for home.

As the 1CBW received the recall message and turned on to a reciprocal course it encountered the dense and persistent contrails of following groups. It

First American pilots over Berlin

Twelve groups of Thunderbolts, four of Mustangs and three of Lightnings were assigned for the escort of the bomber force on 3rd March. The force included the 4FG and 357FG which had only converted to the P51 a few days before.

The red-nosed P51s of 4FG had been selected to lead the fighter escort but they too became victims of the deteriorating weather. Very severe icing conditions were encountered and several pilots were forced to abort. Dense cloud made it very difficult to keep the formation together but they did rendezvous with a ragged formation of Forts and Liberators near Neumunster. As the formations wheeled about as a result of the general recall , part of the 4FG ran straight into a large force of enemy fighters. Nine aircraft from one squadron confronted a 60 strong Luftwaffe force near Wittenberg.

The murky conditions made combat very difficult and the 4FG lost two of their planes while Don Gentile got two Fw190s and three other pilots each claimed an Me110. Gentile's combat report recorded "... bounced by ten Fw190s... I dove down and got on the tail of a twin-engined plane, but my canopy was so badly

frosted over that I couldn't see anything. I was scared of hitting him so I pulled up and turned my defroster on and when the canopy started to clear there was a 110 right beside me and firing at me..." One more 4FG aircraft was lost on the way out, to the flak over Boulogne. Another, Capt Philip Dunn, chased and brought down an Me210 but got lost as a result. With his radio out of action, he headed for Spain, encountered an He111, shot it down but then ran out of fuel and bailed out just 8 miles short of the border.

The 364FG 's Lightnings were taking the group on only its second combat mission , to cover

the withdrawal, but the bombers failed to rendezvous. Other Lightnings from 20FG and 55FG were intended to shepherd the bombers over the targets at Berlin. When the recall was sent at around 11.20, most of the fighter groups responded and turned for home.

The 55FG, led by Lt Col Jack Jenkins in his P-38J (42-67074) *Texas Ranger*, continued on to become the first American pilots to fly over Berlin in daylight. Struggling through the dense cloud, several of the Lightnings experienced difficulties and flak over Magdeburg added to their problems. Only about half of the group made it to the capital where they circled on the outskirts for about

15 minutes waiting for bombers who never came. Jenkins himself suffered from a faulty engine which impaired the fighter's ability considerably. However, he was still able to outrun a force of 15 Me110s which confronted them out of the murky sky over the southwestern edge of Berlin.

Although frustrated by the apparent failure of the mission, pilots of the 55FG were surprised and delighted to learn, on their return to Nuthampstead, that they had become the centre of considerable press interest — they were the first over Berlin! They had proved that fighters could accompany the bomber stream to the German capital.

55FG's Lt Col Jack Jenkins led the first American pilots over Berlin (USAF)

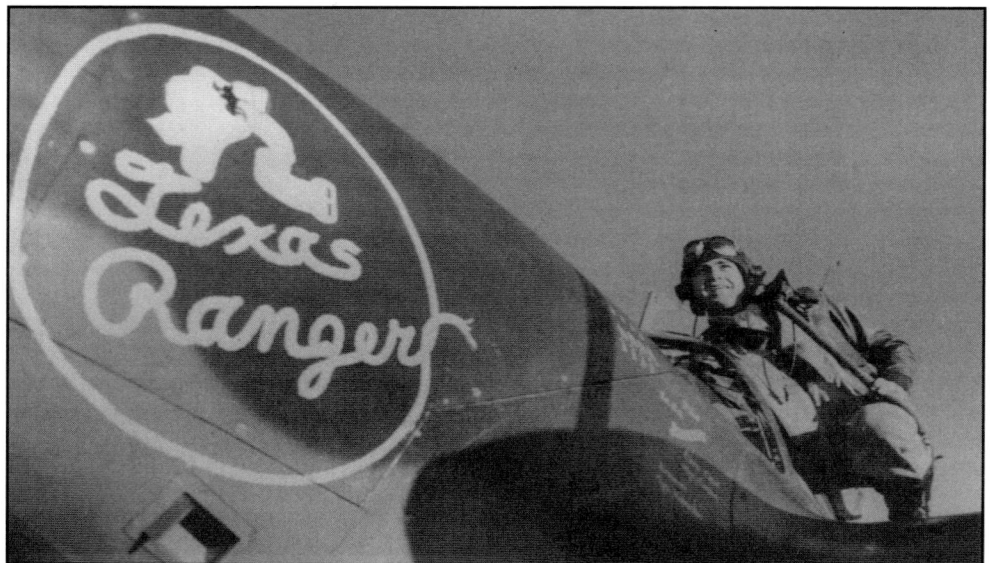

also encountered the 4CBW — head on. Fortress pilots struggled to maintain control in the turbulence of the prop wash and avoid the nightmare of a mid-air collision — but in a blinding flash some crews lost their desperate gamble. Eleven of the bombers were lost from various causes, including three ditched into the North Sea with only seven men recovered. Seven escort fighters were lost, two of them also ditching into the sea although one pilot was picked up by Air Sea Rescue.

"Now the fun and havoc began as the Forts turned right and the Libs went left... planes all over the sky. We flew through falling debris...."

The cruel sea claims *My Desire*

My Desire, a 91BG B17 (42-37965), had arrived at Bassingbourn just five days before Christmas 1943 and Lt Walter Pickard was flying it for the third time. The plane was on its thirteenth combat sortie on 3rd March and it would prove to be an very unlucky thirteenth mission.

Shortly after the war, Pickard filed a detailed report to the AAF headquarters on what happened. "As we circled over the coast, awaiting radio instructions from England, we ran into some fairly intense flak," he recorded. "One of the bursts hit the oil lines in my No.2 engine and I could not feather it. The added drag that this caused plus our extremely high altitude caused us to drop out of formation instantly. We salvoed the bombs immediately but by this time we had dropped into the undercast."

Unable to get enough power from the three good engines, *My Desire* set course towards England but the windmilling prop caught fire and Lt Pickard warned his crew to be ready to bail out. In a desperate attempt to extinguish the flames, the pilots put their plane into a steep dive and plummeted down through 21,000ft of thick cloud, finally dropping out into the clear over Holland.

"By this time we had been able to get the ship under better control," he continued. "We thought we were out of danger and relaxed slightly.... Then we ran into trouble that really put the finishing touch to our plane. We flew almost directly over a German flak battery that was not marked on our maps. At 8,000ft it is almost suicide to fly over a flak battery... we could not escape the guns and they shot the ship up very badly. They got an almost direct hit on No.3 engine.... shot out both the VHF and Liaison radio sets, and the plane looked like a sieve."

By the time it had got out of range of the flak, with two engines out and windmilling, *My Desire* was using full emergency power to make just 115mph. The crew jettisoned everything removable from their plane but finally, just 15 miles from the English coast, they were down to 1500ft. Any hope of making landfall was lost when No.1 engine burned out and seized up completely. Ditching was inevitable.

"About all I could do was stick the nose down and try to keep from stalling. The sea was rough that day... but I was lucky and made a comparatively smooth landing. The ship did not break up and none of the crew were injured." The final blow came when the crew found one of the rafts had been damaged and only one side would inflate, the other raft couldn't be removed from its storage box. *My Desire* floated for just six minutes before the crew were forced to take to the freezing waters, knowing they had only a little time before the numbing cold would claim them. Every passing minute drained the life from them. A trawler approached but the water was too shallow for it to get near. A small boat was launched but it could only pick up five men before the danger from capsizing forced it back to the trawler. 15 minutes later an Air Sea Rescue Walrus flying boat arrived and landed in the sea close to the sinking dinghy. Those aboard the trawler felt sure their comrades had been saved, but on reaching harbour they discovered that the Walrus crew had found all their colleagues floating face down. Those 15 minutes had proved too long for the five crew remaining in the freezing waters. The cruel North Sea had claimed yet more victims.

Hot reception for *Alice From Dallas*

On 3rd March, Ed McKay was flying on his eleventh mission, in what had become his regular plane *Alice From Dallas II* It was a replacement G model for a similarly named B17F which had been lost over Regensburg on 17th August 1943. One of the 100BG's original pilots, Captain Bill Desanders, named that aircraft after the wife he left behind in Dallas when they deployed to England.

Ed McKay noted that *Alice From Dallas II* was heavily laden with armour plate and was sluggish to control. "She also ran hot engines", he remembered. "*Alice* used more power to climb... and at 155mph it was easy to fall behind." Ed recalled the struggle to get above the towering cloud banks which confronted the formations as they headed towards Berlin on 3rd March. "The weather was bad and the 3rd Division was recalled. Before the recall we were trying to climb over a front already at 25-30,000ft but lost contact with all other aircraft. Maintaining a climbing straight-ahead course, we popped out at 32,000ft. There waiting for us were dozens of Fw190s and Me109s. Being alone, we virtually 'split-S'd' back into the clouds and safety. Before hitting the clouds, our gunners claimed three fighters — the tail gunner got one in our contrails and the ball and top turret gunners also made claims."

11

Fiasco and five sorties in seven days

Flying with the 100th Bomb Group from Thorpe Abbotts, bombardier Lt Ed Stern would have good reason to remember the name Berlin. On 3rd March 1944, as a member of John Massol's crew, he was on board a B17G which would become a record-breaker for the 100th — *Fever Beaver* (42-38047). Assigned to the group in mid-January 1944, the plane would eventually return to the USA with 125 combat markers painted on its nose but, on 3rd March, the majority of those missions had yet to be flown.

"One of the biggest fiascos I can remember took place on 3rd March, 1944," recalled Ed Stern. "We were assigned Berlin as the target for the first time. At briefing, I remember the combined gasp of surprise and dread that arose from the assembled airmen when the curtain was pulled back from the wall map, and that long, deadly red ribbon stretched from the English coast to Berlin across what seemed to be every Luftwaffe airbase in Germany. We were

informed later that these interminable cross-Deutschland missions were designed to suck-up the Luftwaffe so that we and our some-time fighter escort could eliminate them before the D-Day landings."

Ed continued, "We were flying about 24,000ft over Heligoland, on our way to Berlin, when the whole formation ran into stratospheric cumulus clouds so dense you could not see your wingman. When the word to abort finally came, turning planes began running into each other. Only with some luck and great skill by pilots Massol and Granger did we avert colliding with other aircraft. We got turned around and tried to climb above the clouds.... impossible! Massol then took us down to the deck where the props were whipping up the water. Again climbing to altitude, we broke out into the open only to be pursued by three FW190s. Recognising what seemed to be Holland, we dove back into the soup, changed course, and headed for

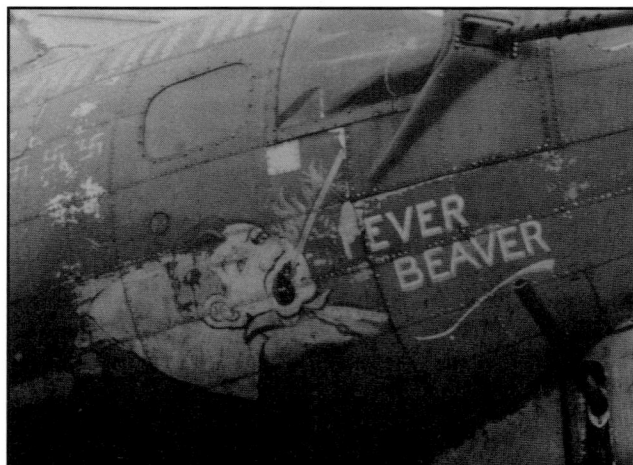

"One of the biggest fiascos I can remember took place on 3rd March 1944." Ed Stern, bombardier *Fever Beaver*, 100BG

Lowestoft. Eventually, we made it back to the base late in the day, short on fuel, and completely unnerved and exhausted. Berlin was spared but only for a day or two."

On the following day, 4th March, Lt Massol set out again in *Fever Beaver* and headed back to Berlin. Shortly before 11.00hrs, he was forced to turn for home with fire in the chin turret and two engines faltering. Two days later, *Fever Beaver* set out yet again for Berlin and this

time made it to the target. More importantly, the plane survived the terrible slaughter which would overtake the 100th Bomb Group. On the 8th March, and again on the 9th, *Fever Beaver* went back over Berlin — surviving five sorties to that same target in just seven days. Ed Stern also survived but it would be Berlin, two months later, which would leave a vivid mark on his memory when he was finally shot down in another ship, with another crew, on 24th May.

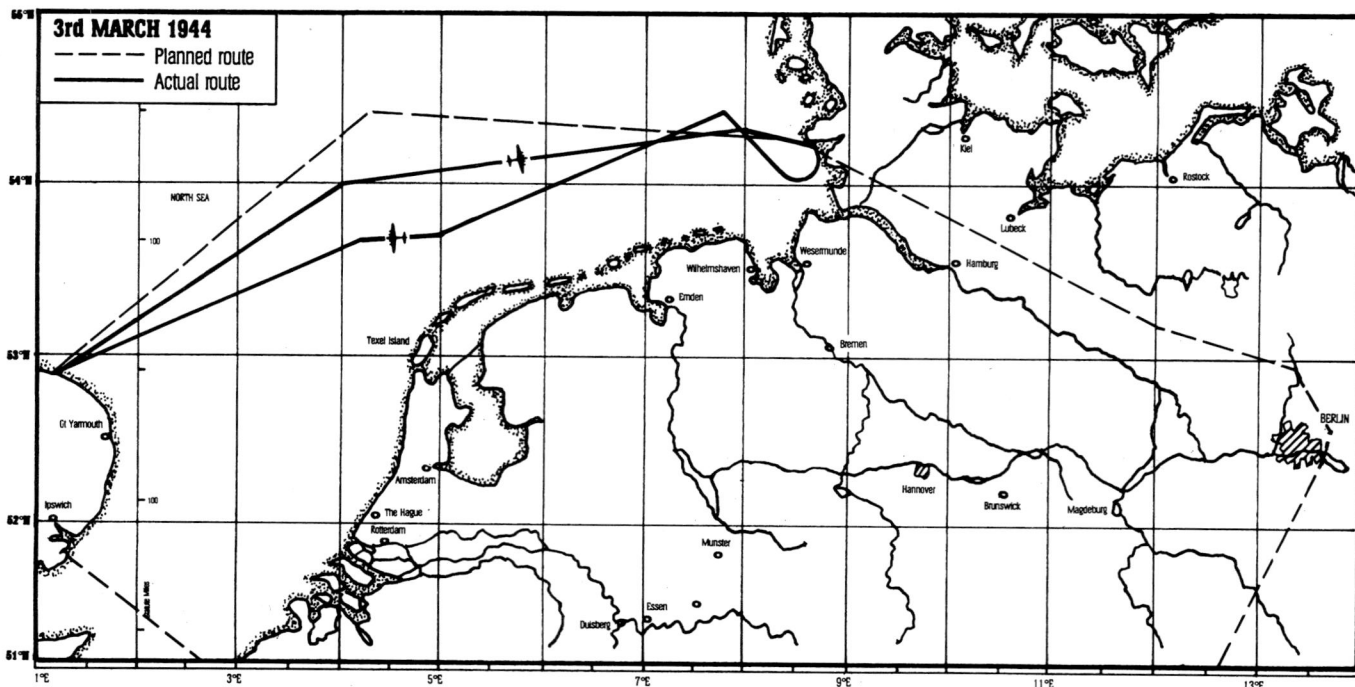

12

Who hit who at 5 miles high ?

Turning back on receipt of the recall, crews found that the weather had worsened behind them and their return routes soon became a nightmare of floundering aircraft clawing their way through a deepening gloom. Crewmen peered out to see shadowy shapes slide pass in slow motion within inches of each other. Worse was to come.

As the formation of the 1st Combat Wing, comprising the 91BG and 381BG, turned back along a reciprocal course they encountered the dense contrails of the entire 4th Combat Wing, 94BG, 447BG and 385BG. More than one hundred B17s from the two wings charged almost directly at each other at a closing speed of 5 miles per minute. Eyewitnesses later described the nightmare scenario of two groups meeting head-on. One 94BG airman experienced a Fortress roaring up over him at the same time as another dived below his ship. "Both so close I could see every detail... we were lucky to squeeze through but the ship and crew behind us were not so fortunate." A blinding flash illuminated the gloom high above the cold North Sea as two ships smashed into each other. Bomb loads and gasolene ignited, men and debris spewed out into the sky, catching a third plane, and leaving behind a huge pall of greasy smoke. After that many groups became severely disrupted and never recovered their integrity. Ships went home in ones and twos with men stunned and stressed to the limit by the nightmare of near misses.

For years it was thought that the 94BG ship of Lt Don Ahlwardt, 42-38075, had been rammed by a 91BG Fortress, *My Desire* flown by Walter Pickard. But Pickard's report on his loss, mouldering in the archives, made it clear that his ship was not involved. He was hit by flak and ditched later. Records of other units in the vicinity also make references to a "huge explosion in the sky" and the 100BG in the 13CBW recorded that it was three of their aircraft which were involved in the mid-air catastrophe. Investigation has established that the 100BG Forts, previously thought to have been involved, were in fact attacked by German fighters and shot down, with a loss of five members of Lt Vollmer's crew. "My radio operator

"a violent explosion.... produced a spectacular display of pyrotechnics" Interrogation Report, 457BG, 94CBW

did recognise the recall," affirmed Bob Vollmer, "and we repeatedly tried to notify Lohof in the lead plane by use of the lamp. I guess we should have used the radio and then got the heck out of there.... The first 20mm shells actually exploded in the cockpit, igniting hydraulic fuel and the oxygen system. The plane went through a series of dives and climbs.... I went out through the front hatch. It must have been about that time that *Murderer's Row* broke up, I can remember falling with debris all around me. Bob Lohof and John Gossage (the other 100BG crews previously thought to have been involved) were with me in Stalag Luft 1... so I did know that Gossage had landed because of his engineer's severe wound. I am pleased to confirm that there was no aerial collision between us."

German documents reveal that the wreckage of Vollmer's plane crashed to earth at Drage 8km north

"Two B17s collided, almost head-on at 11.32hrs, 5345-0910 alt. 20,000ft. No chutes seen and it was considered highly improbable that anyone escaped. The ships blew up completely and disintegrated. 2 crews reported the explosion disabled a 3rd B17 flying above." 385BG Intelligence Report, 3 March 1944

of Iztehoe in Holstein, at 11.40hrs scattered over a radius of about 3kms. These German records also became confused between this plane and Lohof's ship (42-31970) which came down in the same vicinity. They too had popped out of the cloud into clear blue sky and FW190s. The first pass by the fighters caught the ship and it went out of control, also crashing north of Iztehoe, after the crew had successfully abandoned it. The Germans incorrectly attributed its loss to flak from the naval batteries at Brunsbuettel.

The third 100BG ship to be brought down was John Gossage's (42-38017). The No.1 engine was damaged and the engineer badly wounded. With no hope of making it safely back to England Gossage headed for neutral Sweden. They never made it. In error they landed at the German airfield at Schleswig-Jagel to become prisoners.

Records from the two combat wings which met head-on indicate that a 381BG Fort from 1CBW , 42- 37985 flown by Lt Robert Rogers, also went down and this has always been thought to have been the third plane, hit by debris from a mid-air collision. Two other aircraft, from the 4CBW's 447BG were also lost that day. The 447BG and 94BG were flying in the same combat wing and surely too close to have turned to meet head-on as described by witnesses. However,

one witness did report seeing #112 "turn to the right with the Wing formation and collide with a plane from another Division which made a turn to the left." 92BG's Fort, the only other B17 unaccounted for, was hit by flak over Hamburg and crashed nearby.

The event is further confused by the 3BD Intelligence Report which indicated that there were apparently two separate mid-air collisions. "A/c 112 of 447BG - A Group - flying #6 position in lead squadron is believed to have collided with a/c having letter 'J' in Triangle on the tail at 1127hrs... both a/c exploded." Clouding this report is the fact that 351BG, Triangle J, did not record any losses on 3rd March. The report continues, "A/c 075 (Ahlwardt) of 94BG - B Group - collided with unidentified B17 in head on collision, a/c from 4CBW was believed observed in collision with a B17 from 1CBW at 1230hrs.... both a/c blew up and disintegrated completely."

This 3BD Intelligence Report conflicts with that of the 385BG (shown above) which indicated that the collision timed at around 11.30 was the one involving the third B17 caught by debris and not, therefore, the one which involved Lt Ahlwardt in #075 an hour later.

Whatever the true facts surrounding the tragic incident, a mystery still shrouds that "blinding flash, five miles up" which was observed through the gloom by so many of the crews that day.

The 8th Air Force's second major attempt on the German capital also proved to be something of an anti-climax. Severe weather caused some aircraft to take off in dangerous conditions of snow squalls and poor visibility. More seriously, it caused the entire 2BD to abort the mission during assembly and return to their bases.

The Fortress formations faired only slightly better and three groups turned back at the enemy coast as a result of failing to form up properly in the poor weather and expending vital fuel in the process. Other combat wings pressed on through the dense clouds and snow storms but turned back over the Koblenz-Bonn area and sought targets of oppor-

tunity at Dusseldorf, Cologne and Frankfurt. "It got to 58 degrees below zero and the clouds were so thick at times we could not see the planes that were flying only a few yards from us on either wing" recorded one airman.

The exception was part of the 13CBW, comprised of two squadrons from 95BG and one from 100BG, who pressed on to their primary target — Berlin. They became the first American heavy bombers to attack the German capital in daylight and both groups were awarded a Presidential Unit Citation for the day's action.

The Luftwaffe responded with brisk but short-lived opposition at the IP which continued through

Rubber Check claims a first

One gunner in the force which reached Berlin became the first American to down a German fighter over the city. Flying in 100BG's Rubber Check (42-39872), as top turret gunner, T/Sgt Harold Stearns gave the following report:

"An Me109 came in out of the sun at 12 o'clock high. He came barrelling straight at us and was attacking our nose. I got him in my sights at 800 yards and sweated him down to about 400, then I nailed him with a burst of 150 rounds. I could see bullets hitting into the front of the German plane which passed within twenty feet of our right waist window, then the German went into a crazy spin, on fire."

Harold Stearns description of the first fighter kill over Berlin was picked up by the press and given considerable coverage on

both sides of the Atlantic. Also given official credit for being 'first' over Berlin were several members of the crew of the PFF radar ship which led the meagre force over the city.

The honour of being officially accredited with the title of first man over 'Big B' was 2Lt Marshall Phixton, the bombardier in the 482BG pathfinder. He was flying his 13th mission that day, along with four other members of the crew. Crouched over the Norden bombsight in the nose of the B17 he had the edge on the other officers in the plane piloted by 1Lt William Owens. First enlisted man was the top-turret gunner T/Sgt Donald White.

The pilot to receive the official accolade of 'first American fighter pilot over Berlin while escorting heavy bombers' was 4FG's commanding officer Lt Col Donald Blakeslee (Below).

> **"The fighter came in through the contrails about 500 yards out, level and attacking alone. I gave him 50 rounds – the left wing came off at the fuselage and the plane started to smoke. The engine caught fire and the German fighter stalled, then went into a steep dive, about 200 yards out. Smoke and flames covered the entire ship."** COMBAT REPORT: S/Sgt Francis Kerin (BT), 100BG

Aerial heraldry – colourful foes

The USAAF was considered to be the master of airplane embellishment but the Luftwaffe also employed a colourful array of markings. Intended for identification rather than personalisation, their gaudy appearance was noted by aircrew at their de-briefing on 4th March.

Some aircrew reported Me109s, in the vicinity of the city, painted white underneath and dark on top. All black Me109s were also seen, others had the underside of wings and belly painted in yellow. Yellow noses together with yellow-orange patterned fuselages were also noted.

Grey camouflaged

German fighters displayed a variety of bars on their wings in white, blue or green; and one was reported as having red bulls-eyes between the landing gear. One escort group also reported seeing Luftwaffe fighters with white noses and trimmings, black fuselages with checker board markings. A few of the opposition were left unpainted, silver metal finish, factory fresh — gleaming like knights in armour — matching the thousands of American planes beginning to fill the skies over Germany with their similarly unpainted, shiny aluminium skins.

> **"As the fighters approached, I could see that most of them had yellow noses with the fuselage, in some cases, a mixed pattern of yellow and orange, a few were black. They all came in level heading right into our formation. They caught us with a blast of 20mm cannon shells. One shell ripped into the side of the ship and passed between the co-pilot's compartment and the top turret gunner's position. This shell smashed through our oxygen tanks and passed out the other side of the ship without exploding and without injuring anyone."** COMBAT REPORT Bombardier on Buffalo Gal, 100BG

until the Rally Point was reached. About 30 fighters, mainly Me109s, queued up to the right of the formation, weaving in the manner of the P51s until ahead of the formation and then boring in for head-on attacks. Barrel rolling in threes through the formations they then continued to attack singly, closely pursued by friendly fighters. Most assaults were pressed home aggressively, some to within 50 feet of their prey.

An estimated 31 bombers reached the city and broken cloud obscured much of the target but the PFF lead aircraft did identify western Berlin. The 13CBW had been briefed to hit the Robert Bosch electrical equipment factory at Klein Machnow in the southwest of the city and those over Berlin reported that their primary target had been attacked although the precision was not known. The German News Agency later claimed that "not a single bomb fell on Berlin itself, but some bombs were dropped on scattered targets in the surroundings." In fact, although no strikes were actually made on the target, Swedish press reports confirmed a scattering of bombs across the outer suburbs. The main force, in general, returned to their bases with their bomb load although some groups did

"We were all apprehensive on those first times we were briefed for Berlin, but once airborne it seemed almost like any other mission.... the pre-dawn takeoffs in fog and rain were about as scary as the flak at the target... we feared flak more than enemy fighters. It was nerve wracking when you turned on the IP and headed straight for the target.... you felt like a sitting duck. There were times when flying through a heavy box barrage you could hear the 88s going 'whoomp' and shrapnel hitting the plane sounding like a tin barn roof during a hail storm."

Art Pickens, pilot 92BG's *Lil Brat* (42-31921)

manage to locate targets of opportunity in other parts of Germany.

Flak defence around Berlin itself proved to be less than impressive on this day. Intense and accurate fire caught the formations over Magdeburg but over Berlin it was described as patchy — meagre to intense and very low. A combination of flak and fighters cut five Forts from the tiny force that had struggled all the way to the city outskirts.

Flagship flies the flag over Berlin

The wartime caption to the picture below reads: "Members of the crew of the battle-scarred Fortress *Flagship* examine their standard, the first American flag to fly over Berlin in the first American daylight raid over the German capital".

The crew shown is that of 1Lt Preston Dean who had taken the ship on its first mission with the 95BG on 29th January to Frankfurt. The crew completed eight of the plane's next twelve missions, including raids on Schweinfurt and Regensburg. On 3rd March they set out for Berlin but the foul weather forced a mission abandonment for the entire 8AF bomber force.

Finally, on 4th March, Lt Dean and crew were able to take *Flagship* (42-37988) over the German capital with the tiny force of 95BG and 100BG Forts to earn their accolade as the first US flag to fly over Berlin. Preston Dean's crew revisited the city on the following day and

survived the aerial slaughter which occurred. It was their last trip in *Flagship* before it was passed on to other combat crews.

The plane itself would return to bomb Berlin on the 9th March and go on to complete a further six missions. But on its 24th raid on the 29th April, returning for a fourth time to bomb the German capital, *Flagship* went down. It was last seen leaving the formation under control over the Dutch-German border near Enschede. All the crew of Lt J Vilberg survived as prisoners of war and the co-pilot successfully evaded capture altogether and returned to England.

4th MARCH 1944

Recall? What recall?

Leading the 13th Combat Wing on this maximum effort was a 95BG ship named *I'll Be Around* (42-31320). Lt Alvin Brown was accompanied by command pilot Lt Col Grif Mumford. It was the plane's 20th sortie and Al Brown's third trip in the ship which had joined the 95th back in November 1943.

High over Belgium, as the formations headed deeper into enemy territory, the ground below was totally shrouded by a solid floor of cloud. Further ahead that cloud towered up to over 29,000ft and as the formations struggled to gain altitude to clear the barrier the integrity of their tight defensive formations began to fall apart. Above the cloud layer, conditions conspired to create another hazard — dense contrails in the - 65°(F) temperature. As they crossed into Germany, radio operators picked up a VHF recall signal and hundreds of labouring bombers began to turn about and head back towards England.

But whether or not the recall, heard by all the formations, was in fact legitimate was hotly disputed by the radio operator on board *I'll Be Around*. The message, of course, was received in code but accurate decoding actually yielded an incorrect sequence. The message seemed correct — the sequence did not! The greeting had been used as the sign-off signature. The radio man, T/Sgt Frank Atterbury, reported the signal as not constituting Standard Operating Procedure or following the code for the day. On return to their base after the mission the 95BG Commander confirmed that to his knowledge no recall had been sent. Was it a phantom? Was it for real? It could easily have been a German ploy to divert the threatening strike away from the capital of the Third Reich. Bogus radio messages had been successfully used time and again by the Germans to mislead aircraft being ferried across the Atlantic from America. And the RAF had also employed the technique against the Luftwaffe. In the secret world of radio counter-measures, the stakes were high — especially when those stakes included Berlin.

On board *I'll Be Around*, Col Mumford and Al Brown had made their decision — they would carry on to the assigned target! Knowing that they would have been watched for many an hour on German radar screens and that they were already deep inside the enemy's territory, Col Mumford decided to use the extreme weather conditions to his advantage. To press on rather than turn back along the same route they had flown in on. The route along which German fighter controllers would vector in their attacks on the straggling formations, disrupted by weather and their sudden turn about. He gambled that his tiny force, then down to nineteen aircraft from 95BG and thirteen from 100BG, would surprise the Luftwaffe defences and score a massive propaganda coup. Berlin would reap its vengeance for such audacity.

As the tiny force closed on the designated target, the Lead Bombardier prepared for a visual approach. The undercast had begun to break up at last but the severe temperatures caused problems. Frozen shut, the bomb bay doors would not open and *I'll Be Around* was forced to lead the pass over the target without bombing. Supreme airmanship was called for as Col Mumford and Lt Brown kept up a constant dialogue with the path-finder ship which monitored the bomb run in conjunction with the visual sighting. Signal flares were used to indicate the moment of bombing in a co-ordinated manoeuvre that had never before been practiced. The first day-light bombs tumbled down toward Berlin since RAF Mosquitos had success-fully disrupted Goering's anniversary speech back in January 1943. Many more would follow.

After leaving the target behind them, with five more bombers trailing smoke and falling away, the dwindling force headed for home. As they dropped to a lower altitude, *I'll Be Around* finally got the bomb doors open and jettisoned their load towards a bridge. On landing, Lt Col Mumford anticipated a reprimand for his action but instead received the Silver Star, and Lt Brown the DFC, as they were debriefed, from no less a person than General LeMay himself.

Berlin bided its time for retribution. Exactly eight weeks later, to the day, *I'll Be Around* was lost — heading for Berlin again!

> **"The flak was very heavy where we dropped our bombs but that was the only trouble – that and frostbite, from which a lot of the boys suffered"**
> Sgt Thomas Dugan

Al Brown's 95BG crew pose for news photographers after their return from Berlin in *I'll Be Around* (A Keeler)

".... only the 95BG and twelve aircraft from one other group got through to the primary target and bombed it. At take off time, the weather conditions were so bad that one entire Division was forced to cancel the mission. The 95BG assembled in proper formation and departed the English coast as scheduled, despite local snowstorms and generally adverse weather.... One wing, led by the 95th Group, resolutely continued on to the objective. In the target area 20 to 30 single engine enemy aircraft pressed home vicious attacks... enemy ground positions fired heavy concentrations of anti-aircraft fire... Even after the target was bombed, enemy fighters continued to attack the formation until the rally point" Extract from Unit Citation to 95BG, signed by Maj Gen Partridge

Short lived celebration !

Although it is generally recorded that only Forts from the 95BG and the 100BG actually penetrated as far as Berlin on the 4th March, one 457BG aircraft also claimed to have accompanied them. When the recall was received by most units they turned about and headed home with their bombs still on board. Some aircraft, however, managed to locate targets of opportunity and bomb, including seven B17s from 457BG.

One of those 457BG aircraft, 42-31595 flown by Lt Gene Whelan, attached itself to the 13CBW's group which made it to Berlin and shed its load over the outskirts of the city. Whelan's subsequent post mission debriefing statement that he had reached and bombed Berlin was accepted by his interrogating officers as being factual.

The Whelan crew's elation at being the first 457BG men to have reached the "Big B" was, however, destined to be short lived. They became the victims of a cruel twist of fate over that same city just two days later.

On 6th March, the 457BG put 18 aircraft into the air and as they passed over the cloud-shrouded primary target of Erkner they were unable to release their load through the intermittent gaps — catching only brief glimpses of the ground. Just as they turned away, German fighters swept in with a vicious frontal assault. One Me410, piloted by Fw W Bonnecke of JG26, suddenly swung directly into Whelan's Fortress knocking off part of the tail. The damaged bomber swerved away, out of control, narrowly missing other B17s but smashed with terrific force into 42-31627, piloted by Roy Graves. So great was the mid-air impact and resulting maelstrom that wreckage from Whelan's Fort was strewn over four miles. Only one man survived from the two crews involved in the tragedy, nineteen died.

"28-30 Me109s and Fw190s – 27,000ft – 1250 to 1300hrs – 11, 12 and 1 o'clock. From above, came under formation. Me109 attacked at 9 o'clock. Two Fw190s plus one unidentified shot down by P-51 – over target area. One went down on fire, two went down smoking and in a spin." INTERROGATION REPORT: Lt F J Malooly Pilot, *Superstitious Aloysius*, 100BG

Highest escort loss on any Berlin raid

With the realisation that some of the bomber formations were pressing on towards Berlin, General Kepner had little option but to allow some of the escorts to continue also. Not all the planned escorts reached the target area but the 357FG did as well as one squadron from 354FG and one from 4FG — becoming the first single-engined US fighters over the capital. Not bad considering the 4FG had only converted to the Mustang a few days earlier on the 27th February. Their rapid conversion resulted from a promise made by 4FG's Col Blakeslee to General Kepner. So anxious was he to get the new fighter, Blakeslee promised that his group would be out of combat for no more than 24 hours for the changeover.

Some enemy fighters intercepted the meagre force, about 15 minutes before they reached their goal. About twenty Me109s and Fw190s attacked, two groups of four went head on straight through the bomber box and then dispersed while the others stayed topside. 4FG were bounced by this top cover but the effort lacked conviction. The P51s had little difficulty in out-manoeuvring their opponents, suffering greater problems from frosted windshields and frozen, jammed guns in the minus 55° temperatures.

One 4FG pilot, Lt Hugh Ward, went after an Me109 in a steep dive from 18,000ft. He was followed by another of the enemy, who in turn was followed by a second 4FG Mustang flown by Nicholas Megura. As the airspeed touched 550mph the canopy, wing and tail of Ward's P51 ripped away and smashed into the following Mustang, fortunately not seriously damaging it.

Ward was able to bail out and became a POW. One of the Germans also jumped after being chased by Megura down to 3000ft, no doubt to fly and fight another day.

4FG ended the day with four victories for the loss of three Mustangs — another crashed near Framlingham on return to England. Lt Col Blakeslee, who had led the group, returned delighted to have reached Berlin but fuming because his guns had jammed solid, leaving him unable to fire at the enemy.

Crossing the Channel on the way in, the 354FG had a rough time when they entered heavy cloud. Several aircraft went into a spin in the turbulent winds and two of their pilots were lost. Part of the group made the rendezvous point but could not find any bombers. While patrolling east of Berlin they were bounced by a lone Me109 which was promptly shot down.

The other group which escorted the bombers over Berlin itself was the 357FG. They lost one aircraft, the flight leader of their 364th Squadron, but claimed two Me109s downed and an He111 bomber.

9AF's 363FG was surprised by Me109s of II/JG1 with devastating results. The combined effect of the Luftwaffe and the weather cost them 11 Mustangs, one third of their despatched force. This would be the highest loss suffered by any P51 group escorting any 8AF bomber mission to any target. With only nine of the enemy destroyed, the USAAF had suffered its highest losses in fighters so far, twenty-three. Most losses were due to the weather rather than the enemy but the day would prove to be the most costly experienced by 8AF escorts on any of the Berlin raids.

The 8th Air Force finally made it to Berlin with a large force of heavy bombers on the 6th March — over 500 B17s and 200 B24s. Ten per cent of this force fell victim to the city's fighter and flak defences and caused the USAAF a severe blow. 1BD 's target was Erkner's ball bearing plant while the 3BD headed towards Klein Machnow. 2BD, originally destined for Oranienburg, were given the Daimler Benz plant at Genshagen as a result of last minute weather considerations. In the event of cloud cover all formations were to aim for the city centre.

During the penetration, the first seven CBWs led by the 91BG drifted south of their course as a result of inadequate correction for a 45mph wind. The 13CBW, in the trailing 3BD formation, lost sight of the preceding groups as it reached the Dutch coast. This created a stepped gap as the 13CBW continued along the prescribed route. A head-on assault was launched against the wing which was hit ferociously near Haseluenne. The 'Bloody Hundredth' spilled yet more blood in the skies over Germany, losing fifteen aircraft. Half of its lead and low squadrons were wiped out and the high squadron simply ceased to exist.

As the first three CBWs of 1BD approached the target they reported over one hundred fighters massed against them. While the remainder of the 1st Bomb Division fared a little better, this attack struck

The best life insurance for *Queenie* – a close formation!

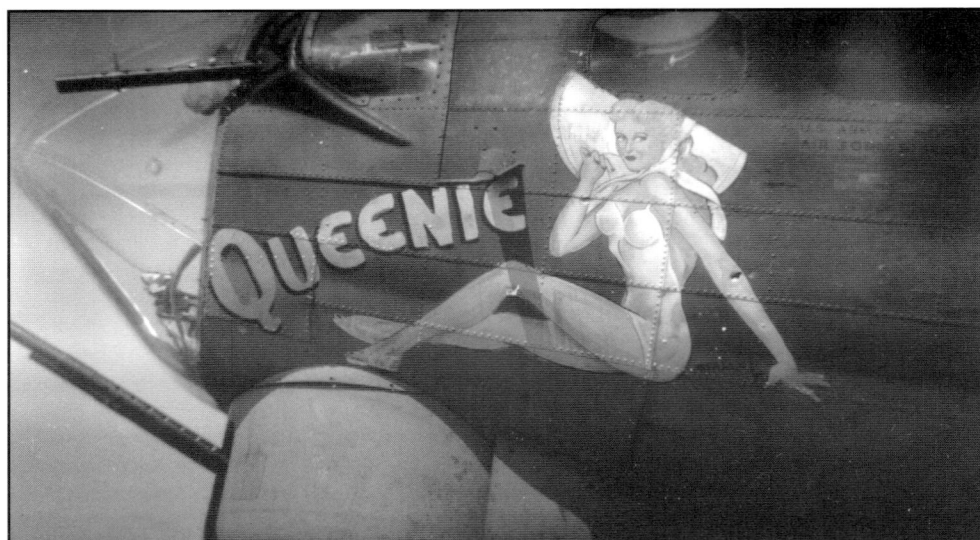

"We were flying at 21,000ft and everything was going great on the way in. We got a bit of flak only because we were off course. We were due at the target at 14.45hrs. It was a long ride in there. When you're over enemy territory, the time seems to go slow. You want to get the hell out of there. We had good fighter support until we were over Berlin and then I guess they were busy with individual dogfights.

"It was about 30 minutes from the target when we started getting hit by everything the Luftwaffe has left. We saw a bunch of planes in front of us and flying a little higher. They were crossing from right to left, out of range, and they were hard to recognize. Then we had it! They peeled off and came in at us head on. There were over 35 or 40 of them on the first attack and they came in all at once. I had looked away momentarily and when I looked back, they were on top of us and all were blazing away. I could see the flashes coming out of the wing guns. I called them out to the gunners and they started firing away at them. I grabbed the wheel and started some evasive action and kept bouncing the ship all around so they couldn't get a good shot at us. It makes me nervous to see a fighter line up at us for a shot.

"Joe and I were both on the controls. If he'd see one lining up, he'd dump the nose; then I'd see one and pull up. We stayed in a good formation though, regardless of all the evasive action. On the first attack, they hit a ship who was flying opposite us in our squadron. He had an engine smoking and went down. We were right up in front and they were trying to knock out the lead Group in a desperate attempt to halt the raid on their capital. They came round again, but there were a few missing this time. I guess our gunners knocked a few down. They peeled off again and came in and 20mm shells were bursting all around us and we started our evasive action again. Joe and I were really sweating. It wouldn't be so bad if we could fight back, but we have to keep right on thundering through, and your best life insurance is to stay in close formation. And we did exactly that!

"The Germans repeated their attacks two or three more times and we still didn't see any of our fighters... Anyway, we roared on around the city, heading for the factory. The clouds were broken and we could see Berlin. It's pretty big. There was also a lot of flak over the city.

"We got around to the target, but the bombardiers couldn't see because of the clouds, so they flew on over a part of the city and dropped the load and came out. I don't think the bombing results were too good.... I guess we broke a few windows.

"After we'd left, I looked back and saw the smoke and fires, and the sky was full of flak bursts, black smoke and white rocket trails and fighter planes smoking and spinning down. It was a tremendous air battle — something like you see in pictures... Today's raid made me realize that these Germans aren't beaten yet by a long shot... We lost six ships in our 18-ship group alone."

Diary extract, Louis Lahood, pilot 91BG, Queenie (42-31353) which was lost on a later mission to Berlin on 29th April 1944

the 1st, 41st and 94th Combat Wings just north of Magdeburg, and knocked twelve more Forts from the formations. Liberators of the tail-end 2nd Bomb Division reported opposition reduced to light or non-existent as they completed the bomber train.

In all, 69 bombers were lost, another ditched into the sea but was later beached. At least thirteen of these were brought down by the intense and accurate flak. Forty-two were known to have been shot down by enemy fighter action.

Fifteen hundred tons of bombs were unloaded over targets in the Greater Berlin area, together with 800,000 leaflets. The results, however, were disappointing and none of the primary industrial targets in the suburbs were effectively hit. The ignition equipment factory at Klein Machnow and the vital VKF ball bearing plant at Erkner escaped even a single bomb. The Daimler Benz plant at Genshagen had less than a quarter of the B24 force assigned pass over it and took not a single hit although official analysts logged 133 tons as dropped in the vicinity.

The Swedish press later reported that at least three bombers crashed into the city itself causing 'indescribable damage'. One was 93BG's *De-Icer* which came down at 13.52 hrs in Feldstrasse, Spandau, killing seven crew.

Cloud over the city was patchy and most groups began their bomb runs visually. In many cases, cloud patches obscured the aiming points at the last minute and lead bombardiers were left to find whatever target they could see. Some specific targets were hit, such as the Telefunken radar plant and an Army Depot but in general the bombs struck wide areas of the city: Koepenick to the southeast received 'a large number' of high explosive bombs and Spandau in the

> "We started out three days in a row for Berlin and each time had to turn back because of bad weather.... Now we were going back.... Now Hitler had a chance to get all his fighters and flak guns up to Berlin. They might as well have sent Adolph a telegram and told him we were coming." Diary extract, LOUIS LAHOOD, pilot of *Queenie*, 91BG

west with the Staaken housing estate suffering 110 bursts. Reconnaissance photos taken the next day showed fires still burning in Steglitz where at least 250 bombs had fallen and Zehlendorf in the southwest. Outside of Berlin itself, concentrations fell as far north as Oranienburg, on Potsdam in the southwest and Eggesdorf to the east of the city.

As the bombers reformed and withdrew they were hit again by a strong force of Luftwaffe fighters which caught them over the German-Dutch border. The 388BG lost five aircraft, a sixth was fatally rammed by a Fort as it went down out of control and a seventh limped to Sweden for safety. Four other B17s and five B24s were also shot down as a result of these fighter attacks.

Luftwaffe fighters and flak brought down more bombers on this day than ever before, almost ten percent of the attacking force — it would prove to be more than on any other day of the entire war. In excess of 700 American aircrew were either killed, captured, interned or on the run somewhere in Occupied Europe. But more crucially, the Luftwaffe had lost some of its most experienced fighter pilots in the aerial battles, with many others wounded and out of action. Unlike the USAAF, trained fighter pilots were losses the Luftwaffe could not readily replace.

> "The enemy's method of attack against the 3BD was skilfully executed. From both the offensive standpoint of the enemy fighters and from the escort standpoint... the bombers presented a column of combat wing pairs, covering from head to tail a distance of perhaps as much as 60 miles..." Mission Summary, 6th March 1944

Fortresses from 41CBW's 303BG and 384BG plough their way through Berlin's heavy flak. In the foreground, 384BG's *Tremblin Gremlin* (42-37982) which would later be lost over Hamm on the 19th September (USAF)

The fighter battle claims 82 victories

Eight Thunderbolts from 56FG confronted the Luftwaffe just as it emerged from the devastating attack on the 13th Combat Wing over Haseluenne and immediately shot down two Fw190s from JG 11. An Me109 was also shot up badly, the pilot wounded and forced to belly land his plane. Other P47s from 56FG then arrived on the scene, one of them Colonel Hub Zemke who promptly shot down an isolated Fw190. Another two were claimed soon after and the group finished the day claiming ten victories for one loss.

78FG also moved to intervene but were bounced by fifteen Me109s from JG11's II Gruppe which had been flying as top cover to the attackers. The Thunderbolts knocked down three but lost one.

Fifteen minutes later, at about 12.40hrs, another mass attack on the bombers by 110 German fighters developed twenty miles north of Magdeburg. A mixed formation of Me109s, Fw190s and twin-engined Me110s and Me410s slammed into the 1st and 41st CBWs. Mustangs from 4FG and 357FG had just taken over escort positions and, as the Germans raced in towards the bomber boxes, they moved to block the attack. 4FG manoeuvred head-on and fired directly into Me110s, just as they loosed their rockets, and brought down at least two. When

the dogfight was over 4FG claimed fourteen destroyed for the loss of four of their own. 357FG also hit the twin engined fighters, from behind, and shot down four in a battle which ranged from 23,000ft down to the deck. Going after Fw190s who were following up the attack, they brought down one more.

354FG were bounced by Me109s as a huge air battle developed, likened to a swarm of angry bees, and claimed eight destroyed for just one lost. The dogfights continued until the German planes began to run short of fuel and ammunition. Lasting about 25 minutes, isolated skirmishes continued for another half hour.

Four P51s were lost in the Berlin area but ten Me110s and six Me410s were destroyed together with five Me109s and two Fw190s. While the bombing was still in progress, some Mustangs from 4FG strafed the Henschel works airfield at Johannisthal, damaging one Ju88, and then went on to strafe a train. Other escorts chasing German fighters found themselves amidst the falling bombs and promptly broke off their attacks and headed for safer airspace. Returning pilots claimed fifteen victories but for the loss of four P51s.

As the 1BD went over its target and turned north of Berlin, several Me110 night fighters moved in to

pick off stragglers. 357FG escorts caught the lumbering attackers and shot down eleven of the sixteen without loss to themselves or to the bombers. An Fw190 was also chased into the ground by a flight from the group without them firing a shot. As the group withdrew, it strafed an airfield at Stendal and claimed an Me109 just as it was landing, damaged several He111s on the ground and caught another lone Me109 and shot it down. The pilot of this latter aircraft fell from his parachute harness and was killed. He was Oblt Gerhard Loos, JG54, a veteran with 92 victories. The 357FG claimed twenty destroyed at the end of the day, for no loss.

When the bombers reformed at the Rally Point, P38 Lightnings from 20FG and 364FG took over the escort for the withdrawal. Thunderbolts from 359FG tangled with four Me109s as they attempted to pick off a damaged B17, and shot down two of them, adding a third later.

As the formations crossed the German-Dutch

border another onslaught caught them. Thirty-five Me109s and eighteen Fw190s from JG1, JG2, JG11 and JG300 attacked from dead ahead. One Fw190 collided with a 388BG Fort and several others went down as the 45CBW suffered a savage assault. 361FG Thunderbolts intervened and shot down two Fw190s, and 355FG claimed three Me109s. When the day was over, between them, 361FG and 355FG claimed thirteen enemy fighters destroyed for no loss to themselves.

The planners' guess that the Luftwaffe must rise to defend its capital had been proved correct. The loss of the bombers and their aircrews was horrendous but the fighter battle had been won. Claims amounted to 82 destroyed and half that number again had been damaged or were judged as 'probables'. USAAF fighter losses amounted to just eleven aircraft. With such an apparent rate of attrition, the Luftwaffe would certainly be the more hard pressed to replace their losses of experienced pilots.

> "I took my wingman in front of the bombers and tacked onto the last of the Fw190s making the 3 or 4 o'clock attacks. I saw four blazing bombers as I passed... I lined up on the rear Fw190 and saw lots of hits on the wings and fuselage... I then closed on the next enemy aircraft.... and hit him first on the right wing then on the fuselage, and finally in the cockpit... it was impossible for the enemy aircraft to have pulled out"
>
> COMBAT REPORT, Major James Stewart, 56FG
> Destroyed FW190A flown by Fw H Neuendorf, KIA, JG II/1

56FG's *Lil Abner* (41-6347) escorts a formation of Fortresses (S. Sox)

> "The enemy employed new tactics, hitting the bombers as a mass in a formation similar to the ones the bombers use. Today the enemy, I'd say at least 100 of them in boxes of 40 -50, flew through the bombers head-on and then went to the stragglers and to the deck. It worked damned well.... a squadron on one side of the bombers.... 3-5 miles from the rest of the group, cannot stop this new attack."
>
> Combat Report, Major James Stewart, 56FG

Mission Briefing, 0500hrs!

"Have breakfast then slide over to non-com briefing for instructions on today's mission... before us, a small stage with map and ribbons attached to show route of flight to be taken. Attention! — At Ease! Smoke if you wish, announces the G-2 officer. He points out the target, how long the total flight should be, how many hours we will be on oxygen, where and when we will encounter enemy fighters, approx number of P51s and P47s that will accompany us, where we will pick them up, when they might leave us, flak areas are pointed out and a long route back (rarely the same route back). The navigator will advise us as to when these things will occur in flight, from his briefing.

Take off time is posted, as is bomb load, ETA over target... then comes weather along with bombing altitude and outside air temperature. Attention! — Good hunting, dismissed! We make mental notes and sometimes notes on the back of our hand, then outside again to head for the equipment shack to pick up our flight gear and equipment."

George Odenwaller, ball gunner 91BG, *Outhouse Mouse* (42-31636)

Col Eugene Romig, 351BG, announces the target for the day, 6th March 1944 – Berlin! (USAF)

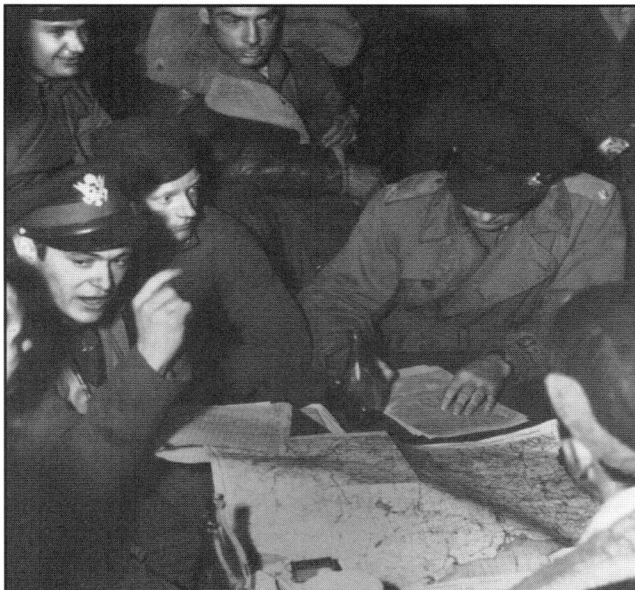

Interrogating Officer, Major Jessie Barrett, takes notes from the 379BG crew of Lt John Lawler. They lost an engine on the way to the target, jettisoned part of their load and then went over the city with just a few P38 escorts for company before limping home between two combat wings (USAF)

"The city was like Dante's Inferno after the bombing"
S/Sgt James Young, 458BG's *Little Shepherd*, 41-29359

"We really set that place on fire... it will take the Atlantic Ocean to put out those fires"
S/Sgt John Brown, gunner 447BG, *Sunrise Serenader*

"... they didn't give a damn about anything. One FW came so close to us that one of his shell casings went through our wing."
T/Sgt Frank Apeterry, radio operator 95BG, *Blues in the Reich*

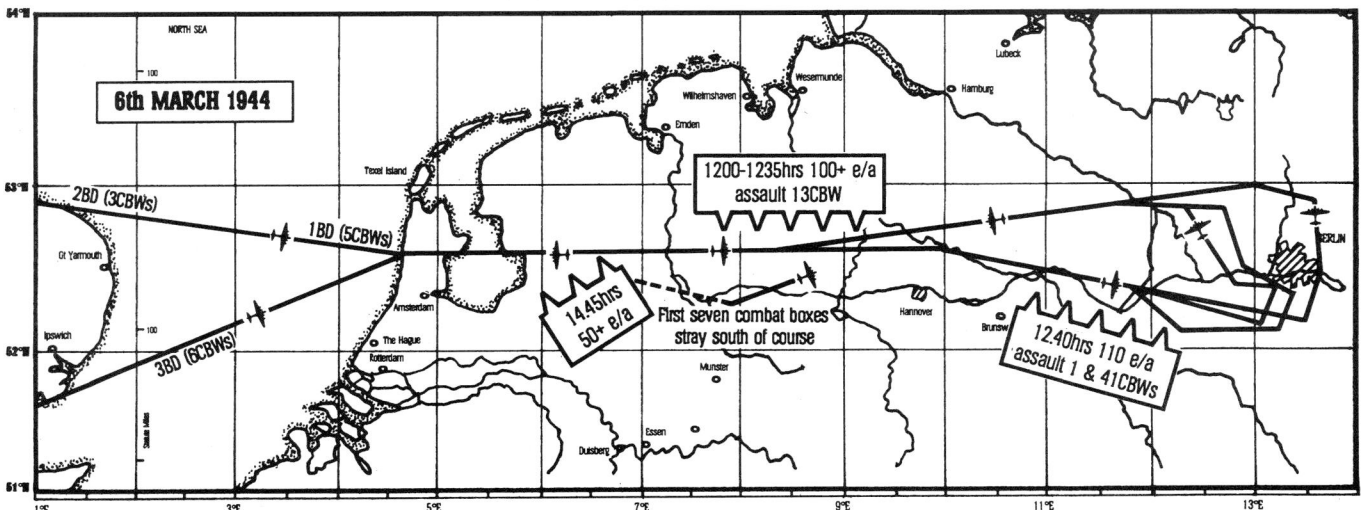

6th MARCH 1944

2BD (3CBWs)

1BD (5CBWs)

3BD (6CBWs)

1200-1235hrs 100+ e/a assault 13CBW

14.45hrs 50+ e/a

First seven combat boxes stray south of course

12.40hrs 110 e/a assault 1 & 41CBWs

High Noon – a long minute over Haseluenne

"The 13CBW was in excellent formation leaving the coast and was 3 minutes late. Fighter attacks began at the Zuider Zee and continued all the way to the target and to a point about halfway back.... The B Wing received very severe fighter attacks. These attacks reduced the wing to about a group which attached itself to the A Wing about 100 miles before the target...." So read the ten lines of the Mission Critique which summed up the day's action against the 13th combat wing.

The German 2nd Fighter Division had assembled more than 100 Me109s and Fw190s to the east of Dummer Lake. Fighters from JG11 and JG54 were joined by two Gruppen from JG 1. Directed due west they rapidly closed on the 13CBW, by then leading the second half of the bomber stream. The leading formations had drifted 20 miles south of the intended course and were thus spared the impending onslaught.

It took less than one minute for the huge formation of fighters to streak through the ranks of the 13CBW, leaving absolute carnage behind them. It was one minute to 12 noon. For many men in the wing, the 100th Bomb Group especially, it was their longest minute as the tight formations seem to dissolve around them.

Both pilots and the ball gunner died instantly in the first of the 100BG's bombers hit by fighters, David Miner's 42-38059. After the head on pass the plane lurched up on its tail, stalled and tumbled away. The aircraft's nose blew open and the navigator fell to his death without a parachute. The tail section of William Terry's ship, *Terry and the Pirates* (42-97482), broke away and tipped the plane into a deadly spiralling dive which ripped off its wings and carried seven men to their death. As it went down a hole suddenly burst open in the nose and the two officers there tumbled out, one was without his chute. The gunners became entangled in the writhing mass of broken control cables and the engineer lost his leg, blown off by a cannon shell. But he was bundled from the plane just seconds before it hit the ground near Quakenbreuck. The severed tail section came to earth some distance away.

Eight men leapt from another of the group's B17s, *Lucky Lee* (42-31735) piloted by George Brannen, which had two engines blazing furiously

"...the enemy controller, apparently having detected a gap in fighter escort in the center of the column, dispatched... two formations of fighters to harrass the front and the rear of the column and to occupy the attention of the escort fighters... then he slammed his remaining 100+ fighters against the momentarily unprotected center of the column..."
8AF Mission Summary, 6th March 1944

and a stream of fuel pouring from its right wing — it exploded seconds later. As the survivors floated down they came under machinegun fire from the ground. Lt John Lautenschlager's *Half and Half* (42-38197) was also blazing fiercely as the crew abandoned it. Robert Koper's *Goin' Jessies* (42-31051) disappeared in a fire ball — so intense that only three crew men escaped. The plane plunged into the ground at Jump near Oldenburg, almost into a Hitler Youth camp, where it exploded.

Three figures tumbled from Merrill Rish's *Spirit of '44* (42-38044) as it too was engulfed in flames. Bombardier 2Lt Kehm recorded later, "German fighters attacked in a group out of the sun at 12 o'clock high. Fire was visible around No.3 engine. The plane immediately went into a tight spin. Centrifugal force prevented me from releasing the escape hatch.... at about 3000ft the tail broke off of the aircraft and the ship began to climb. I could see all the objects coming

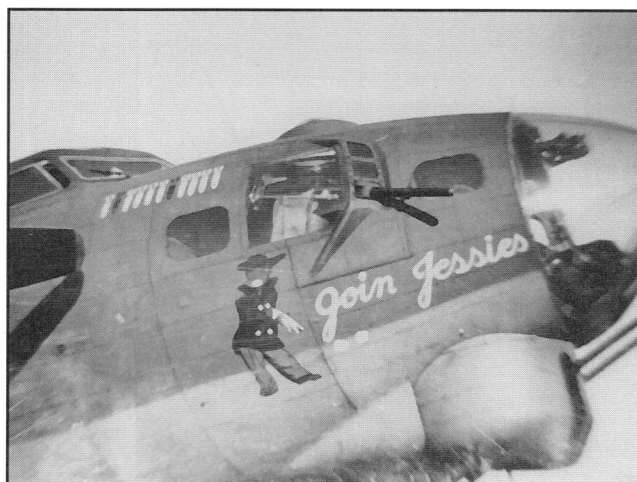

towards me. The plane must have exploded as next I awoke on the ground with two German soldiers approaching me."

Pride of the Century (42-30170) had previously survived two crash landings at Thorpe Abbotts and was the oldest ship listed on the 100th's complement. Now it also slid from the formation, rolled over and went straight down after pilot Lt Coy Montgomery was killed by fighter fire.

With two engines out, Dean Radtke's *Ronnie R* (42-97491) fell away to be picked off later by other fighters. The ball gunner was killed in his turret by 20mm fire and the bomb bay caught fire forcing the surviving crew to abandon the plane before it crashed near Twistrigen. The bomb load in Zeb Kendall's *Sly Fox* (42-30278) exploded without warning after the first fighter pass. The plane had earlier served briefly with the 385BG before transferring to the 100th but now not even a fragment of it remained, nor of the ten men on board flying only their first or second mission. On its right wing a fireball engulfed another stricken plane, 42-31800. Sherwin Barton's crew were more fortunate however and all survived the ordeal. In less than sixty seconds, nine B17s from 100BG had been knocked down, others would soon follow.

BigAss Bird II (42-30799) tumbled from the formation after the third fighter pass with its tail section blazing and the pilot, Lt William Murray, dead — decapitated by a 20mm shell. The tail gunner had also been

wounded and was in the radio room having his wound dressed. He and the radio man were still in the ship when it powered straight in to the ground and exploded. Albert Amiero's 42-31731 was last seen going into a slow spiral with engines smoking and four chutes blossoming below. All but one on board were killed.

Just as the sudden onslaught seemed to be over, a single FW 190 headed directly for the lead plane, Frank Lauro's *Nelson King*, (42-31306), and smashed away almost the entire fin and rudder. Severely damaged, the Fort continued on as a supreme example of the punishment a B17 could take and still bring its crew back home. Berlin would claim the Fortress another day.

Another Flying Fort knocked from the formation with its No.1 engine ablaze was Mark Cope's *Superstitious Aloysius* (42-37807). Two gunners were wounded as more fighters queued up for the kill. This time they would be frustrated by their victim. After jettisoning the bombs, Cope dived his battered plane into clouds below and began a long lonely journey home.

Sam Barrick, flying in his *Barricks Bag* (42-39994), had two engines knocked out and extensive damage throughout the ship. Rapidly losing altitude they also jettisoned the bomb load and at just 1500ft brought the plane back under control. With no hope of reaching England, Barrick headed for Sweden, flying directly over a German airfield en route. Fortunately they were ignored and made it

to safety — landing on a grassy area of Bultofta airfield. Interned for many months the crew eventually returned to England in November 1944.

After the tattered remnants of the group bombed what they thought was the Robert Bosch electrical works,the 100th turned for home. Edward Handorf's B17, *Kinda Ruff* 42-38011, had moved into the lead position and survived the initial fighter onslaught. On the way home, over Diepholz, it was hit by fighters coming in from 2 o'clock low. 20mm cannon shells penetrated the wing tanks and started a fire. Just as the crew began to bail out the stricken ship exploded killing most of them. There were only two survivors.

Damaged by flak over the target and lagging behind, Frank Granack's *Rubber Check* (42-39872) fell easy prey to marauding German fighters and it too went down with No.4 engine knocked out and two more badly damaged. This was the Fortress and crew that had claimed the first German fighter kill over Berlin just two days earlier. The Grim Reaper was balancing his books.

Half of the 100th's planes which had set off for Berlin that day failed to return. It was a devastating blow to the group but Berlin had not finished with the 'Bloody Hundredth' just yet and would reap another

terrible harvest from them a few weeks later.

Another member group of the 13CBW also caught the force of the second Luftwaffe attack a few minutes after noon. The 95BG had six aircraft shot out of their formation. James Conley's ship (42-97495), leading the high squadron, spiralled down with two engines on fire as the crew bailed out. In the low squadron, 2Lt A J Mailman's *Situation Normal* (42-29943) went down with only half the crew surviving. The right wing caught fire and there was fire in the bomb bay. All the enlisted men in the rear bailed out but the radio man was pinned by centrifugal force and was thrown clear only when the plane broke into two. Tom Barksdale's *Berlin First* (42-32002) fell away from the lead squadron. A few minutes later another head on assault set the No.1 engine ablaze on 1Lt Keasbey's 42-31251 over Diepholz and the crew abandoned the doomed plane. Two other 95BG Fortresses also went down as the battle continued periodically all the way to Berlin. Fighters caught them again over Magdeburg during the withdrawal and the group would lose two more.

The third member of the 13CBW, the 390BG, also lost two aircraft and the day would prove to be the most costly of the entire war for the wing.

"The enemy was very persistent in all of his attacks most of which came from head-on. Several rockets were seen and many crews reported the enemy using a 20mm incendiary shell.... our high losses, 24 in number, were undoubtedly due to inadequate fighter support."

13CBW Critique - Mission 6th March 1944

1st Division takes the second blow

Forty-five minutes after the first fighter attack swept through the 3rd Division's 13CBW, a second blow fell against the combat boxes of the 1st Bomb Division. Twenty miles short of Brandenburg to the west of the target a mixed force of Me109s and FW190s together with twin engined Me410s and Me110s launched themselves at their opponents in an attempt to disrupt the approach to Berlin.

At 12.42 the Luftwaffe swept in to attack in a tight formation just at the moment that escort fighters from 357FG arrived on the scene to assist those of 4FG and 354FG. A huge aerial collision occurred 20 miles north of Magdeburg as escorts, attackers and bombers wheeled through the sky. Twelve B17s were cut from the formations.

Three from the 91BG fell away blazing. Another, *My Darling Also* (42-31578) was severely damaged by fire from Fw190s. As it struggled to remain in formation, another Focke Wulf headed straight for it and rammed into the tail, knocked off the right stabilizer and cartwheeled away like a blazing catherine wheel. The searing wall of flame which resulted from the impact caught a second incoming fighter and it too burst into flames. Only two crew were able to claw their way out as the bomber began to spin. A fifth Fort was also caught by the fighters but struggled on over the target before fire forced the crew to abandon it.

A 401BG plane was also badly damaged by the fighter attacks but continued on until flak guns brought it down east of Berlin. Eugene Whelan's 457BG plane was blown apart by the impact of collision with an Me410 as it came through the formation in a second head on attack. His aircraft slammed into a second plane flying nearby and both went down with only one survivor. The 381BG lost three of their casualties during this air battle, although *Half Breed* (42-31448) survived for a further two hours before falling victim to an FW190 near Juelich as it limped towards home. *Linda Mary* (42-3215) was the last survivor of the group's original aircraft — now it too was gone. The group's 4th loss, Lt Cahill's Fort almost made it back to England but was forced to ditch into the sea just a few yards from the shoreline.

High Lady high tails it to Berlin

High above the bombers as they streamed back towards the North Sea, shepherded by the escort groups, a single American plane sped in the opposite direction — back towards Berlin. Major Walter Weitner (above) was flying a reconnaissance Spitfire XI, *High Lady*, assigned to the 7th Photo Group with orders to photograph the target strikes.

The Spitfire was specially modified and instead of carrying any armament it had two large aerial cameras installed together with extra capacity fuel tanks. Its only defence against attack was speed and altitude and both were required when Weitner spotted three contrails rising up towards him and closing to within 5000ft. Already cruising at 350mph and 39,000ft,

Weitner pushed his throttle to maximum and gradually pulled away, gaining a further 2500ft altitude. The German fighters were unable to match this impressive performance and fell away to search for easier victims.

Over Berlin a haze covered the ground and smudged the rising smoke columns still further. The lone Spitfire made several photo runs criss-crossing the city on different headings to capture on film as many of the obvious target areas as possible. Flak spotted the sky below him but only the massive 128mm guns on the flak towers had any chance of reaching him at his altitude — seven miles above them.

The task completed, *High Lady* high tailed it home to Mount Farm.

... and the final blow strikes the 3BD again

The 388BG had escaped the onslaught which struck the 3BD over Haseluenne, skirted round Berlin to bomb the Heinkel plant at Oranienburg and a factory area at Wittenberg and turned for home. As they withdrew over Dummer Lake at about 14.50hrs another Luftwaffe assault pressed in and the 388BG lost seven of their number. The attacks came in mainly from 12 o'clock high with two to six aircraft in line.

Blitzin Betsy (42-37886) had most of its tail shot away. It lurched upwards into Capt Brown's lead aircraft (42-40054), tearing away part of that plane's left wing and the ball turret as well as the cockpit roof of *Blitzin Betsy*. A mass of flame consumed the bomb bay of the lead plane and it exploded soon after. Four enlisted men from *Blitzin Betsy* died, as did the navigator and both pilots from the lead plane.

Shack Rabbits (42-38177) crashed near the Dutch-German border with five crew dead. So too did Grindley's 42-31194 with three more fatalities. One waist gunner had been killed instantly by a 20mm hit. The ball gunner lost most of his arm from another hit and the copilot sustained severe head injuries. Both got out as the plane went into a steep dive and exploded killing two other men still inside. 2Lt McLaughlin's B17 was abandoned south of Bremen but continued to fly on autopilot for a further 30 minutes to crash near Hamburg. Both right

engines of the irreverently named *Suzy Sagtitz* (42-31135) were set on fire forcing the crew to abandon it.

The group's last victim of the battle was Lt Wallace's B17 which left the formation over Wuskenbruck but made it to Sweden and landed at Rinkaby where the crew were interned. Further savagery of the 3BD was curtailed with the arrival of the 361FG and 355FG who succeeded in breaking up the attacks

"You didn't need a compass, just follow the line of burning aircraft to Berlin" Pilot, 357th Fighter Group

The burning 482BG PFF lead ship of the 3rd Bomb Division carrying Medal of Honor winner Capt John Morgan and Brig Gen Russ Wilson, hit by flak over the centre of Berlin. The fuel tanks exploded soon after and only three men survived, including Morgan who was able to clip on his chute as he fell through the debris towards the sprawling city below. (USAF)

Dottie Jane loses her man

"Nearly broken, torn, and holed in half and battered out of shape, trailing chewed cables, wires and flapping doors, a floundering hulk of a Flying Fortress came back from Berlin minus a crewman, vanished into thin air..." so read a report by the 447BG PRO after the 6th March raid on Berlin. 1Lt Arthur Socolofsky had taken his ship over the city in the face of the fighters and the flak and returned in a mass of twisted metal which they had called *Dottie Jane* (42-31227).

Just a split second after the bombardier had released the bombs an ear-splitting explosion shattered the air. The 30-ton bomber had heaved and shaken and reared up like a bucking bronco. The pilots fought with the shattered controls and hauled the plane back under control. Stunned crewmen viewed the inside of their ship with dismay. There was no floor left in the radio room, a jagged hole in the side and top was big enough to drive a jeep through! No-one saw him go but somewhere, through the floor that wasn't or the hole that was, the radio man had disappeared.

The main wing spar was also severed and the mid-section was dramatically weakened, the oxygen system was shattered in the rear, forcing all four gunners to use just one emergency bottle to hang on to consciousness and life itself. Under renewed fighter attack, Lt Socolofsky somehow managed to keep the plane together and flying, still in formation — for 600 miles!

Arrival over the base at Rattlesden was not the end of their troubles either. The main landing gear was damaged and had to be hand-cranked down into position. As they slowly lowered, it was then discovered that one tyre had been shredded by the flak. Socolofsky eased the big plane down to a perfect three-point landing, albeit with sparks streaming out behind it as the ball turret bounced and scraped along the runway. Finally brought to a standstill the crew surveyed the sorry sight that once was *Dottie Jane*. Cables and wires spilled from countless holes that punctured the plane's mid section, one bomb bay door was buckled to half its size, the trailing edge of one wing was ripped apart and long jagged tears stretched down both sides of the fuselage. Nine men stood on the tarmac and gazed upon the sight — and pondered the fate of the missing radio man.

"Berlin – heavy and accurate flak en route and over target. No fighters. Hit overcast east of Berlin. Target ball bearing plant covered - hit suburb of Hohenschoenhausen. B17 hit in tail on way out by flak – wing, with engines whirling, fell like a rock."
Arthur Mack, pilot 306BG's *Four Leaf Clover* (42-37942)

Staking a claim over Berlin

Victory claims during confused aerial battles were notoriously difficult to calculate with accuracy. Intelligence officers checked and cross-checked each claim to try to arrive at an accurate estimate so as to know how the enemy had suffered in the battle. With the benefit of hindsight and studying surviving German records it is possible to see how deceptive even these finalised claims were.

Luftwaffe records yield a total of 65 of their fighter aircraft destroyed on 6th March, with two more damaged beyond repair. A further twenty were damaged but considered repairable. This was the total loss to the Luftwaffe — a far cry from the 179 claimed destroyed by 8AF gunners and fighter pilots (97 by bomber crews plus 82 by fighters)! The loss of 25 skilled pilots killed in the action, and others wounded, was however still significant and the Luftwaffe would be hard pressed to replace them.

One of the sixteen B24s which failed to return on 6th March. 448BG's *Hello Natural* (41-29191) had accrued 19 consecutive missions without an abort but was hit by flak over Berlin which punctured fuel lines and put one engine out of operation. 2Lt Charles York took his crew to the safety of Sweden before bellying in. (USNARP)

Target planners considered that the VKF plant at Erkner was responsible for the production of half the annual requirements of ball bearings for the German Air Force. It was a high priority target and presented the opportunity to wield a double blow against the Luftwaffe. The fighters would have to rise to defend this vital target and thus present themselves for combat with the USAAF escorts. Destruction of the ball bearing facility would, it was thought, be bound to have a considerable effect on the subsequent production of replacement aircraft.

To this end, the 8th Air Force launched all three of its Bomb Divisions against the Erkner plant and despatched 623 heavy bombers in ten combat wings.

The escorts who would protect this force and, it was hoped, close with the Luftwaffe to sweep them from the sky was made up of 17 groups, some 890 fighter planes. These included units from 8th and 9th Air Forces and two squadrons of RAF Mustangs.

The attack was highly successful and reports indicated severe damage was inflicted on the plant cutting its production to just one third of that achieved for the same period one year earlier. The plan to lure the Luftwaffe into the air was also successful although most bomber formations of the 1st and 2nd Bomb Divisions reported only weak opposition. The 45CBW, however, suffered severely and lost 16 Fortresses to massed attacks.

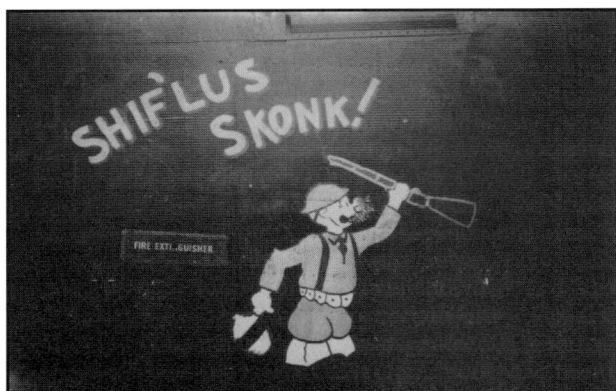

A *Shif'lus Skonk!* loses its tail

446BG's *Shif'lus Skonk!* (42-7595), flown by 1Lt Herbert Bohnet's crew, was caught by fighters at 14.10hrs, as it straggled behind the formation about 35 miles southwest of Berlin. The starboard wing was set on fire and it burned through sending the stricken Liberator into a spectacular wing over and then into a spin. Two crew were believed killed in the fighter attack and three others were trapped in the plane as it went down. The tail gunner's turret was severed from the fuselage but he was able to extricate himself as it plummeted down. The ball gunner was thrown completely clear of the wreck as it broke apart and observers flying nearby counted four chutes before the plane spun into wooded ground near Luckau. Two survivors were injured and two more captured but six men died.

Hi Mack – it's a long way home

It was a long way to Berlin and more than one heavy bomber only just made it back to land in England from the depths of Germany — by the skin of its teeth after surviving the fighters and the flak. Others were less fortunate. 447BG's *Hi Mack* dropped its bomb load over the target and turned for home with the pilots wondering if they had enough fuel left in their tanks to get them back to safety. A steady headwind over Germany added to their anxiety.

As they crossed over the English Channel it became clear that they would not have the fuel to get them back to Rattlesden safely. Pilot, 2Lt Don Fleming, took the decision to cut two of the engines in an effort to conserve their dwindling gas supply. Having successfully reached the English coastline, they headed for the first airfield they saw. The fuel gauges registered zero, but still the engines kept turning. Unable to land immediately, as a result of another plane taking off, the crew's desperation increased — and the engines finally quit!

By now they were barely flying and were passing back over the runway. With no power, the pilots were flying 'dead stick' and banked the plane to turn on to another approach. Running out of altitude and options *Hi Mack* had no alternative but to skid into a ploughed field close by, slicing through hedgerows before jolting to a abrupt stop. The crew had been given no time to get into crash positions but such was the skill of Lt Fleming that they and *Hi Mack* suffered very little damage in the wheels up landing. Dedicated repair crews would soon have the ship back in combat, back over Berlin.

".... we were all apprehensive on those first times we were briefed for Berlin, but once airborne it seemed almost like any other mission... The pre-dawn take-offs in fog and rain were about as scary as the flak.... It was particularly nerve wracking when you turned on the IP. With bomb bay doors open and the plane flying straight and level you felt like a sitting duck.... you could hear the 88's going 'whoomp' and shrapnel hitting the plane sounding like being in a tin roof barn during a hail storm."

Art Pickens, pilot 92BG's *Lil Brat* (42-31921)

On the previous Berlin mission, two days earlier, the escorts had become too intent on protecting the head and tail of the bomber column. This had left the centre under screened and German fighter controllers were quick to pin down the escorts and strike at the exposed 50 mile gap which developed in the centre. On this day, the escorts concentrated on covering the centre but the Luftwaffe were again able to exploit the situation and massed their force against the leading combat wing.

The bombing was made visually in clear weather and more than 70 direct hits were made on the Erkner plant. A nearby chemical plant and a plastics factory were also hit. Huge, towering columns of smoke soon obscured the target area however and caused difficulties to following combat wings. Thirty B24s were forced to head for the centre of city, unable to see their primary target. The bulk of their loads seems to have fallen into Kopenick, mainly across housing estates just west of the Muggelsee but

detailed German records could not be located.

Anti-aircraft fire over Erkner and Berlin city was intense and accurate and of barrage type but only one B24 is known to have been brought down by it. However, 230 bombers returned to England with battle damage, and at least twelve more were lost to unattributed cause.

> **"Only 15 crews were available and instead of the usual response at the briefing, cat calls and groans, there was absolute silence.... No one expected to survive as it was an identical mission to that flown two days earlier.... one of the worst ever for the group."**
>
> John Massol, pilot 100BG *Fever Beaver* (42-38047)

```
TARGET GZ 2714.
... TARGET INFORMATION:
    TARGET CONSISTS OF 3 VERY LARGE
AND 1 LARGE SHOP. IT OCCUPIES AN AREA
OF APPROX. 1400' X 800'./  IT IS
LOCATED AT THE E. EDGE OF A LARGE
WOODED AREA AND ADJACENT TO THE MAIN
BERLIN-FRANKFURT ON ODER RR./  THE
INLAND LAKES OF THE RIVER SPREE
SYSTEM FORM CONSPICUOUS LANDMARKS./
NOTE LAKES FORM A CHAIN RUNNING N-S
ABOUT 15 MILES LONG. / POINT OUT 2
LAKES TO THE S. RESEMBLING INVERTED
CPL'S STRIPES./  EASTERNMOST TIP OF
THE TOP STRIPE IS 2 MILES FROM THE
TARGET AND POINTS DIRECTLY AT IT./
LARGE OVAL-SHAPED LAKE (THE ONLY ONE
IN THE AREA) IS 2 MILES W. OF
TARGET./
    CAMOUFLAGE: DISRUPTIVE PAINTING
ON ROOFS OF 2 OF THE WORKSHOPS./
            MISSION BRIEFING, 8TH MARCH 1944
```

The fighter battle

Air opposition was rather less than had been experienced on the previous Berlin attack. However, powerful and aggressive forces were encountered near Hanover, and again over the target, and returning fighter pilots claimed 79 for the loss of only 18 American planes.

On the way in, near Steinhuder, 56'A'FG tangled with an estimated one hundred Germans as they escorted the 1st Air Task Force. 15 kills were claimed in combats which ranged from 18,000ft down to the deck. The 56FG had been lured by contrails of high flying aircraft but as they climbed to intercept, lower fighters commenced a vicious attack which sent three P47s down. Some 56FG victories came later as they caught the Luftwaffe returning to base at Wundstorf. The 9AF's 363FG also took up the challenge and downed another five fighters. One

of their P51s had its tail completely shot off, resulting in total disintegration of the plane.

Southwest of Brandenburg the 4FG beat off an attack on the bombers by 5-6 Me109s, destroying three of them. South of Berlin they encountered 65 fighters and claimed 15 shot down. Lt Col Edner, who had recently become the group executive officer, bounced four Me109s but was himself shot down.

352FG had a disastrous start to their mission and lost six Thunderbolts to mid-air collision in the overcast shortly after take-off, fortunately five of the pilots were recovered. Later, in combats near Meppen they .brought down two Me109s. Two more Me109s were claimed by 356FG , one without a shot being fired when it was chased until the pilot bailed out. Later, while strafing the airfield at

Hesepe, one of the group's Thunderbolts hit the ground, cartwheeled, then smashed into an enemy aircraft and hangar, and exploded.

Escorting the 2nd Air Task Force, 56'B'FG lost two of their number but claimed ten more kills in attacks on the bomber stream near Steinhuder and over Wagendorf airfield. Others were claimed in strafing runs at Wunstorf. Capt Gladych fooled two Me109s into escorting him over an airfield then fired a quick burst before high-tailing it out, leaving the enemy to be shot up by their own flak. The twin engine P38s of 364FG claimed nine victims in several combats with fighters attacking the bombers during withdrawal but lost two of their own. 355FG destroyed two FW190s in the air , but not before one of them had shot down one of their fellow pilots. They later

destroyed five Ju88s on the ground at Hesepe.

A 78FG flight leader lined up on an Fw190 and was about to open fire when he spotted roundels on the wings and broke off. The Focke Wulf turned away to reveal black crosses on the underside but was promptly shot down by a passing 361FG plane.

Five FW190s were claimed by pilots of the 353FG escorting the 3rd Task Force of bombers while the 357FG bagged another seven in a combat melee over the target which reached 25,000ft. 55FG lost one plane and pilot when they were bounced near Brunswick by two Me109s which promptly split-essed away into cloud cover. The 361FG, on its second sortie of the day, penetrated as far as Dummer Lake and added two more Me109s to the tally, their first sortie had been uneventful.

Top scoring fighter ace – for a week

The 56FG put up 74 Thunderbolts in two groups to cover the bombers' penetration. Sweeping ahead of the first bomber box, 56A group tangled with a hundred or so enemy fighters between Dummer and Steinhuder Lakes. A series of hard fought engagements followed in which fifteen Me109s were destroyed but with a loss of two pilots killed in the melee, and a third captured. The second group, led by Lt Col Gabreski, also encountered enemy aircraft near Dummer Lake and soon added a further nine kills to the tally.

While all this activity went on, Capt Walker Mahurin, flying his P47 *Spirit of Atlantic City NJ* (42-8487), remained with the bombers. His plane was one of those which had been named as a result of a fund raising drive in the States, $105,000 raised was the approximate cost of a P47 Thunderbolt. The majority of such planes were given the prefix of *Spirit of...* but were usually renamed on reaching the

> **"I noticed a Ju88 that had just taken off... this time I fired and hit the enemy quite hard from about 200 yards to pointblank... its right engine caught on fire – the ship then let down in a nearby field and exploded."**
> Combat Report, Walker Mahurin, 56FG

Capt Walker Mahurin is congratulated by Capt Robert Johnson while the crew chief paints on another victory symbol (USAF)

combat theatre, to something more relevant or personal to the aircrew assigned. Not so Mahurin's P47 and it was in this ship that he claimed most of his victories.

Approaching the end of his escort, 'Bud' Mahurin took his flight down after an Fw190 which was taking off from nearby Wesendorf airfield and shot it to pieces, causing it to crash into trees. He then caught and exploded a Ju88. Passing back over the airfield for the fourth time he chased another Fw190 until it rolled over and ploughed into a forest.

Shangri La for the dynamic duo

4FG's Don Gentile with his P51 *Shangri La* (M Samson)

The 4FG was the oldest group in the 8th Air Force, having originated from three RAF Eagle Squadrons. It was awarded the Distinguished Unit Citation for its action between 5th March and 24th April 1944 when a total of 189 German planes were shot from the air and another 134 destroyed on the ground.

One of those who helped achieve this remarkable score was Capt Don Gentile who had joined the RAF prior to the USA entering the war. With two victories in the RAF, he added another twenty more flying with the 4FG to become their top ace. Flying his P51 *Shangri La* (43-6913), Gentile added four kills to his tally on 8th March and his wing man, John Godfrey, added another two. Gentile later achieved a triple score on 29th March and doubles on five other occasions. *Shangri La*, sported a colourful nose art which had originated from the Disney-designed

RAF Eagle squadron insignia.

On 8th March, Gentile, with Godfrey on his wing, singled out two of five fighters attacking the lead bomber box over the outskirts of Berlin. Godfrey was the first to claim a victory as an Me109 rolled over and went straight down. As the pair of Mustangs continued the chase, Gentile went after another Me109 and caught it with a burst from 75 yards astern. Using his combat flaps to achieve an even tighter turn, Gentile

closed to within 100 yards of his second victim, saw the cockpit fill with smoke and watched the pilot leap from the cockpit of his doomed plane.

By this time the sky was filled with fifty or so German fighters, with Mustangs weaving in and out, intermingled with parachutes and desperate bombers firing green flares to signal for help.

Gentile and Godfrey then went after a pair of Me109s who seemed to take no evasive action at all before fire from the

pursuing duo smashed into them and sent one rolling away to port and the other to starboard. Climbing away from that success, they were suddenly confronted by another German fighter who came at them from head on. Breaking away they circled and waited for the German to come round for a second attempt. As it did so, Gentile broke sharply off to the left while Godfrey yanked his stick over and went right. Both men pulled back and climbed above the enemy

The day's victories made Walker Mahurin the 8AF's leading fighter ace with 19.5 kills accrued. But the title lasted only for one week before his 56FG colleague, Capt Robert Johnson reached 22 victories on 15th March flying his P47 *Lucky*.

On 27th March Mahurin was shot down while chasing a Do217 which subsequently crashed, bringing his victory score to 20.75. Forced to bail out at low altitude he was lucky to reach the ground uninjured after just four swings in his chute. Running into woods, Major Mahurin evaded successfully with the help of the Resistance and eventually returned to England on 7th May.

plane and turned onto his tail, spraying burst after burst into Me109 as it went into a steep dive for the cloud cover below. The chase continued as all three plunged three miles down through the sky, levelling out at just 500ft. As the German weaved his way across the landscape, at tree top height, a burst from *Shangri La* ripped through its belly tank. Pulling up to 1000ft, the pilot jettisoned his canopy and jumped. The pair of aces had scored their sixth victory in just a few minutes of combat.

By now, Godfrey was completely out of ammunition and Gentile had only a few tracer rounds left. It was time to go home but a straggling Fortress needed their protection so the pair stayed with it and began a long game of bluff with the Luftwaffe— it was a long way home and neither had the ammunition for a fight if confronted by any German fighters.

Tragedy strikes *Twin Tails*

448BG's Liberator *Twin Tails* (42-100122) was flying directly behind the lead PFF ship when it released its smoke bombs over the target. The oil from the smoke markers sprayed back over the wind shield, blinding both pilots until one was able to scrape away a small area to see through.

The radio man, James Nugent recorded "After dropping our bombs a few minutes past the target, we dropped out of formation and flew to the extreme left, until the enemy coast was reached. We were quite low on gas. We began to lose altitude in order to save what little we had left.... ran out of gas and ditched in the English Channel 25 miles east of Great Yarmouth at 1650hrs. Just prior to ditching we had thrown out everything possible in order to lighten the ship.

"When the ship hit the water it broke up, the tail section sinking immediately and the rest going down almost as soon. We crashed in a very rough sea... I was trapped in the radio compartment by the top turret that was torn loose by the crash. I didn't free myself until the ship was 8 or 10 feet below the surface, then I went up through the hatch. When I reached the surface, I saw Lt Daley, the pilot, struggling and tried to reach him and hold him by his harness.... the sea being rough made it very difficult. He turned to grab a piece of floating wreckage, missed and that was the last I saw of him. Next I saw the co-pilot ... on the half submerged body of the plane... trying to inflate his Mae West. It is my belief that the

sinking ship sucked him down. I tried to swim to a floating oxygen bottle.... When the RAF air sea rescue squad reached us in about 15 minutes they were not to be found."

The only other survivor from the tragedy was the engineer James Hood. He reported later "When the ship ditched, I was standing between the pilot and co-pilot out of the way of the top turret, in case it should fall. I was thrown out through the wind shield and was knocked out. That is that last I remember."

The two survivors, together with the body of the navigator, were the only ones picked up by High Speed launch 158 from Gorleston's No.24 Air Sea Rescue unit and taken back to the Royal Naval Sick Quarters at Great Yarmouth.

A *Heavenly Body* falls from the sky

At about 14.00hrs the 390BG passed Magdeburg and was about 5 minutes away from the turn onto the bomb run. At that moment, flak struck 1Lt Branum's B17 *Heavenly Body* (42-37812), ripped holes through the left wing, punctured the fuel tank and set the No.2 engine ablaze. Peeling away in a 180° turn, Branum hauled the damaged plane out of formation. Crews in the group observed flame pouring back from the damaged engine. What they could not see was the torch of flame which streamed back through the interior to cause the radio man severe burns. Observers in the 390BG formation reported that as the plane left the safety of the formation, fighters persistently attacked. They also noted that "aircraft 812

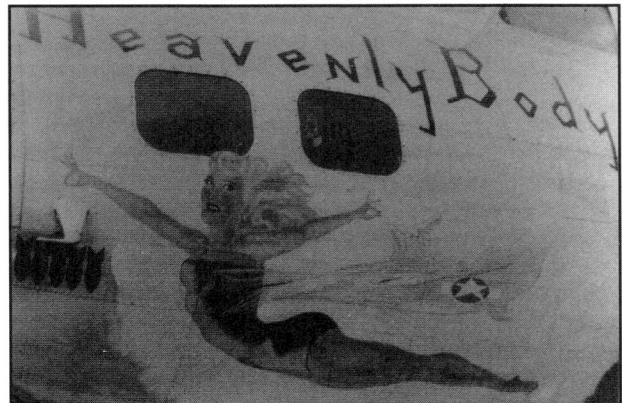

observed to shoot down several enemy aircraft" and two crews also recorded, "gas leaking from gas tank of a/c 812".

20mm shells from the attackers struck the plane and one hit a waist gunner, almost blowing away his leg. Apparently convinced that both pilots had been killed or badly wounded in these fighter attacks, the enlisted men in the rear bailed out. The badly wounded gunner, believed

to be on the final mission of his tour, was also able to exit the plane but he was to die later that day in a German hospital in Torgau.

As the German fighters kept up their relentless attacks Branum, together with the four remaining crew still on board, crash-landed *Heavenly Body* into woodland in Poucher Forest, 9 km southeast of Bittefeld.

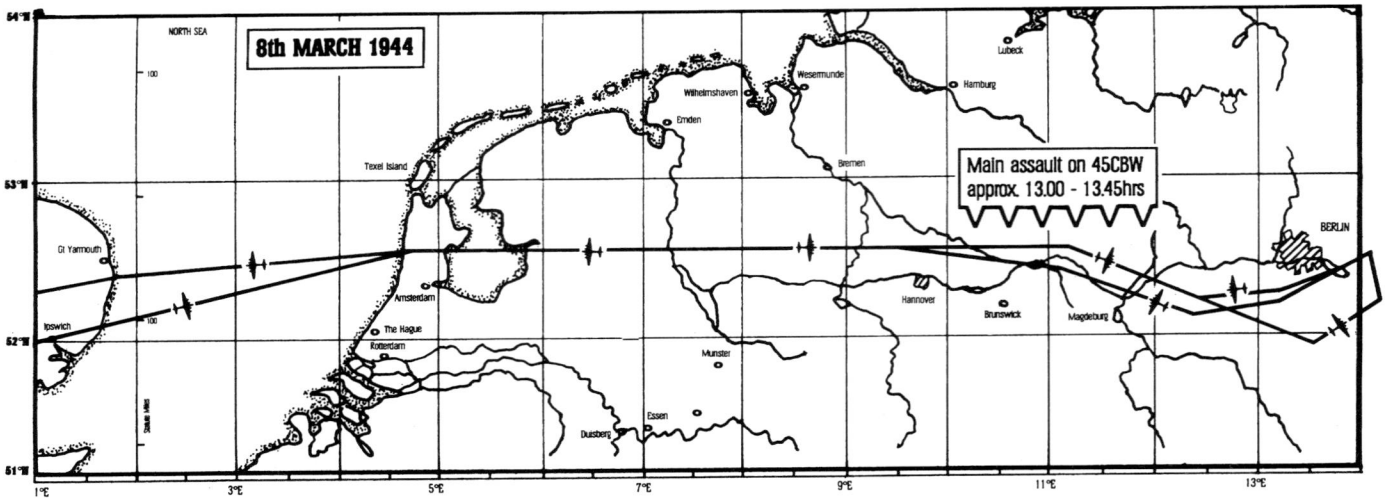

8th MARCH 1944

Main assault on 45CBW approx. 13.00 - 13.45hrs

45th Combat Wing pays a high price

Just after passing north of Hanover on the way in to the target, the Luftwaffe struck a devastating blow against the leading combat wing of the 3rd Air Division. 150 German fighters savaged the division soon after Neinburg, concentrating their assault on the 45CBW with attacks coming in from 10-2 o'clock. As many as twenty fighters at a time swept through the formation and caused grievous damage.

The 96BG was leading the division and its lead PFF Fortress was one of the first to be hit but did not immediately abort. In the subsequent confusion the wing lost its place in the bomber stream, turned short to avoid colliding with a following wing and missed the IP for the Erkner plant. Forced to head for an alternative they bombed the Berliner Machinbau factory at Wildlau which had, pre war, built locomotives but now turned out torpedo components.

The massed attack on the 96BG formation came soon after from FW190s, stacked diagonally in four rows of four. They swept through the bomber box then commenced a second attack hitting George Pond's *The Iron Ass* (42-39988) which had replaced the lead ship, setting three engines ablaze and smashing the controls.

Captain Thomas' Fortress was cut from the formation over Dummer Lake and was then escorted by several enemy fighters towards a nearby airfield before the crew bailed out and the plane plunged to earth, taking the ball turret gunner to his death.

In another attack Don Kasch, pilot of *Pegasus* (42-30847) was killed instantly, copilot Leroy Allen wounded and the plane set on fire. The crew bailed out of the burning aircraft only seconds before it exploded. A fourth 96BG bomber, Lemanski's 42-31576, was hit near Magdeburg and went down with no fatalities; a fifth B17 fell behind the formation as they

approached Berlin with one man dead, an engine burning and a large chunk missing from the tail fin. As the fighters closed in on the damaged Fort, Swendiman's 42-31716, a fire was started in the bomb bay forcing the survivors to abandon the

aircraft.

The sixth victim was the tail end Charlie, Clark Ross's 42-31403, hit by FW190 frontal passes which knocked out the oxygen system. As the pilots sought less rarified air, the plane plunged down from 24,000ft amidst further attacks which smashed the nose, killed the bombardier and wounded the ball gunner. The surviving crew men heaved the wounded man from the plane but his chute tangled on the tail and was shredded to ribbons before being torn away by the slipstream. One of the waist gunners prepared to jump but was caught in a hail of 20mm shells and killed in the hatchway before he could exit from the doomed

plane.

Flying as low group in the 45CBW, the 388BG was also hit hard by the massed assault. For forty-five minutes, 30-50 Fw190s pressed home their determined attack, mainly from dead ahead. The sudden approach of 10-12

enemy aircraft effectively split the defensive fire and proved a punishing experience for the group. The first ship, Lentz's 42-38138, was hit just inside the Dutch coast, rammed by a blazing fighter on its left elevator and rudder. It exploded over Celle and threw several crew clear. Also hit over Celle, 2Lt Moran's *Princess Pat* (42-30829) was lost when its left wing snapped off and the doomed plane flipped over on its back before tumbling down. Somehow, eight men escaped the spiralling tomb.

Near Magdeburg, *Screaming Red Ass* (42-30340) lost its No 3 engine to attack by an Me109 which also shot holes through its wings. Only one man, T/Sgt Quick, survived from 2Lt Amman's crew. Over Hanover it was 2Lt Pou's *Return Engagement* (42-31214) that took the hits and it too went down, with three men lost. The fifth and final 388BG loss (42-37819) fell out of formation after the fighter attacks and the crew bailed out over Helmstedt airfield just before it broke in two at the radio room. None of the officers in the front of the ship survived.

The third group making up the 45CBW and flying as the high group was the 452BG. They were hit by an estimated 35

"In successfully putting bombs on the enemy's capital and his vital plants, they (45CBW) furthered the war effort more than many of us can adequately evaluate.... they pushed the air attack into the heart of the enemy's territory and blasted Berlin."

Curtis LeMay, CO 3AD, 9th March 1944 Bulletin

---

single-engined and 15 twin-engined fighters between Neinburg and north of Magdeburg. They too lost five aircraft to head on attacks. The 452BG Operations Narrative filed on return reflected the obvious confusion they had suffered during the mission. "... hit repeatedly by fighters, the lead ship of the combat wing was crippled. Failure of the lead ship to abort caused the whole wing to be slowed to 135mph.... we (452BG) directed the deputy wing leader on the route to the secondary target. When the 96th and the remaining ships of the 388th which had attached themselves to the 96th turned onto the target they apparently did not recognise the target for they "S"ed across our path causing us to abandon the secondary target."

No one seems to have seen 42-31354, piloted by 452BG's 2Lt Sorenson, after a confused assembly over England. Some reported that it may have dropped down to join the 388BG for some unknown reason. The bombardier William Bader confirmed later that they were knocked out from the formation they had joined about 15 minutes prior to the target. A 20mm cannon shell had exploded in the tail hitting the unfortunate gunner in the left leg. The ball turret was also hit by cannon fire

from an FW190. Two shells exploded inside killing the occupant as he gasped over the interphone that he had got the Focke Wulf but that it had got him.

Bader later reported "The tail gunner was pinned in the tail, therefore we were going to try to make Sweden using cloud cover for concealment. Cloud cover was ineffective and we were followed down by an Me109 that continued to fire on us. Crew were given the choice to bail out or remain — all chose to remain." The radio man was still on his feet when the plane hit the ground. He was thrown out by the impact and killed as they crashed on the edge of the German airfield at Zerbst. 60 miles southwest of Berlin.

Glenn Butterworth's *Tangerine* (42-31331) was also hit 15 minutes prior to the target. The radio man Fred Thibedeau stated, "Our plane was hit by 20mm fire in the first attack, at which time the No.3 engine was completely knocked out and the supercharger on another was put out of action.... We jettisoned the bomb load... then we let down to the carpet and flew towards base at an altitude, I should judge, of one to two hundred feet.... We had flown about 10 minutes when four German fighters appeared. On their first pass they set

"Our fighter escort was very good except for one attack by about 60 enemy a/c which lasted about 15 minutes. The enemy a/c were FW190 and Me110 which came in from 1200 in a shallow dive about ten to fifteen abreast and in layers, completely saturating our formation..."
452BG Operations Narrative

us on fire, the shell exploding in the forward part of the ship."

The bombardier and navigator were both hit by fragments and the bomb bay was a mass of flames by the time Lt Butterworth gave the crash warning. The injured navigator tried to assist his fellow officer but got no response and only just had time to get himself into the well beneath the pilots compartment. Within a few seconds they hit the ground, at about 200mph, skidding across the surface until coming to an abrupt stop having smashed into the opposite bank of a small river. The impact hurled the dying bombardier through the plexiglass nose. They had come down about 15 miles north of Hannover and German troops were on the scene almost immediately.

The third 452BG ship caught by fighters was *Sleepy Time Gal* (42-38211) piloted by Theodore MacDonald. They swept in, line abreast, and two engines were knocked out, the radio room was reduced to a shambles and the tail gunner wounded in the first pass. A waist gunner claimed one of the attackers as they swept past but a second wave then hit the plane and started fires in the bomb bay and nose. The navigator's chute was shredded by a 20mm shell and Lt MacDonald ordered him to take his instead. Crew men pushed out the injured tail gunner who was suffering from shock and lack of oxygen, then bailed out themselves. The pilot succeeded in bellying in the ship, with a full

bomb load, about 12 miles northwest of Hannover. On his final approach, two Me109s took up flanking positions off each wing to ensure that the bomber made no attempt to escape. The copilot and bombardier were killed by ground fire during their descent and other crew members were lucky to escape the wrath of enraged civilians as they landed. Only the arrival and intervention of armed soldiers prevented lynchings by the mob.

An estimated eleven Me109s and five Me110s caught the fourth 452BG ship (42-37954). 20mm fire shot out the No.1 engine, smashed the nose and injured both officers stationed there. The pilot, Henry Wilson, chandelled the huge plane to the left very abruptly and dropped in behind the formation. Soon after, it made two complete 360° turns gradually losing altitude before straightening out on a reciprocal course. Five German fighters pounced on it again. Unable to open the bomb doors, the load was salvoed through them, followed by the crew, about 15 miles southeast of Magdeburg. The wounded bombardier and navigator did not survive.

The crew of the fifth 452BG loss, Stephens' 42-97525 *Invictus*, were more fortunate and all survived their ordeal to become prisoners of war. The 45CBW had lost 16 aircraft, with others damaged, but it continued on to bomb the torpedo works at Wildau. Scattered enemy fighter attacks continued to harass them throughout their withdrawal towards the coast.

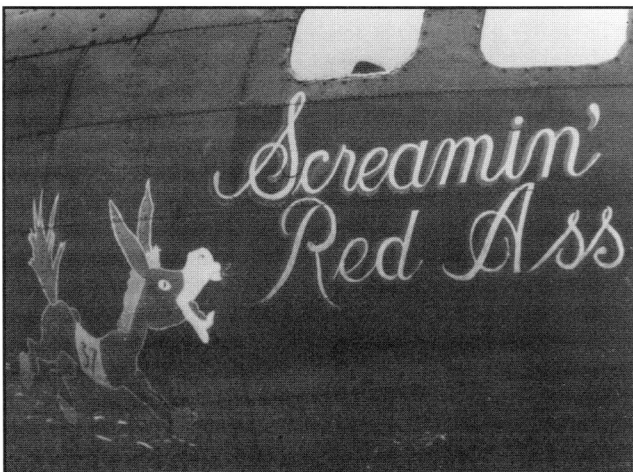

Phyllis Marie – what big swastikas you have!

Flying in the low squadron with 390BG was a veteran B17F on its 34th mission. 42-30713 had been named by its earlier pilot, Lt Perry Row, as *Phyllis Marie* after his wife. He had also added "Row's Rowdies" below the cockpit. The tail gunner, Sgt Louis Kiss knocked down three German fighters in the plane on the 8th October mission to Bremen and had decorated his tail gun position with the phrase: "A Kiss in the ass!"

Now, exactly five months later, *Phyllis Marie* was in the hands of another crew and seven small swastikas ranged along her nose to denote the tally of German fighters downed to date. Soon, she would sport somewhat larger German markings on her tail!

As *Phyllis Marie* approached the target, fighters hit her repeatedly and by 14.30hrs the plane was struggling to keep up with No.3 engine feathered. Then No. 4 engine was shot out but could not be feathered. As more fighters lined up to begin a final assault, the crew began to bail out while the pilot 2Lt Quakenbush held the plane steady until he too left his seat to jump. One wounded crew member however could not bail out and so Quakenbush returned to

25 mission markers and 7 swastikas adorned the side of *Phyllis Marie* on the day the plane was lost. (Bundesarchiv)

his seat to lower the main gear to denote it was all over. The incoming Focke Wulfs did not seem to be too familiar with this signal and continued to pump shells and bullets into the defenceless plane.

Quakenbush brought the ailing plane down into a field near Werben, about 11 km from Cottbus, with its undercarriage down and locked. As it careered across the make-shift landing ground it ran into a ditch and the port leg collapsed, bringing the plane to an abrupt halt. Quakenbush and the wounded crew man ran for the trees as the Fw190s strafed the area.

The entire crew were taken into captivity and soon the Luftwaffe salvage

Damage to the propellers was the only major obstacle the Luftwaffe faced before restoring *Phyllis Marie* to flying condition with their top secret unit, KG200. Note 'Row's Rowdies' below the cockpit window. (Bundesarchiv)

"Somehow I never thought it would happen to us...."
Max Quakenbush, pilot 390BG's *Phyllis Marie*

crews arrived to inspect the wreck. To their undoubted delight the plane was not seriously damaged and could be repaired. It was rapidly hauled away to a place of safety before marauding Allied fighters could find the prize and, as a matter of priority, strafe it into a useless junk heap. It was not the first B17 captured by the Luftwaffe — indeed, a 100BG B17G had landed in error just five days earlier during the previous strike at Berlin, that was the first G model the Luftwaffe would get. Now they had a second.

The Luftwaffe's highly secret unit, designated KG200, specialised in flying captured Allied aircraft. By 31st May 1944, KG200's I.Gruppe would list six B17s as part of its complement although none would be considered as operational at that time. Eventually *Phyllis Marie* was fitted with a new No.3 engine of German origin and a complete set of smaller diameter propellers — the only ones available. Almost all captured aircraft had damaged propeller blades and it proved to be a very

difficult component for the Germans to replace.

Full details of what the Luftwaffe did with their prize have never been established. However, many USAAF aircrew reported the appearance of "strange unidentifiable" B17s and B24s shadowing their formation and then turning away just prior to fighter assault or an intense flak barrage. The first reported incident was on 21st April 1943. It was generally assumed that such planes were radioing details of altitude and course to the German controllers before making their escape. Interrogators of Luftwaffe personnel after the war were unable to confirm any such events. In fact Adolf Galland, Luftwaffe General of Fighters, stated unequivocally that captured aircraft had never been used to shadow enemy formations. They would have had no value in such a role which existing fighters could more easily accomplish, he stated, adding that they would have been shot down just like any other B17. 8AF Intelligence, however, were deeply concerned about the possibility but still urged great restraint among the bomber crews who were eager to shoot down these suspect aircraft. "Positive identification that a B17 is an enemy plane has not proved as easy as one might expect" they warned in one report during the summer of 1943.

In April 1945, as the US 1st Army slogged their way through Germany, *Phyllis Marie* was discovered at Altenburg airfield, south of Leipzig by the 6th Armored Division. Two huge swastikas had been painted onto the tail fin. *Stars & Stripes* reported the finding in the 26th April 1945 issue. "They had taken out the ball turret and the bomb sight is gone," stated the text. "Wooden 2x4s are stretched across the bomb bay floor.... Luftwaffe identification marks, have

A huge German swastika adorns the tail of *Phyllis Marie* rediscovered at Altenburg in April 1945 (S Markz)

been painted on both sides of the tail fin, one on each side of the fuselage by the waist windows and one on the top and bottom of each wing." Some believed the plane had been held in readiness for Hitler, with the intention of flying the Fuhrer to Spain and ultimate safety in South America. Hitler, however, had a better idea and committed suicide in his underground bunker in centre of Berlin.

Shade Ruff for one 401BG crew

The 401BG took delivery of 42-31488 barely two months before the mission to Erkner on 8th March and the crew of 2Lt Dale Peterson were on their very first raid that day. The name of *Shade Ruff* probably indicated the regular crew's opinion of their combat tour or that the plane suffered from mechanical problems during its short career. Whatever the cause, as the 401st formation began its long flight home from Berlin, *Shade Ruff* was seen to be lagging further and further behind.

Near Stendal, as the plane dropped further back and began to loose altitude, 15 red flares were fired from the left waist window. The crew's desperate call for fighter cover was answered by four P38s which swooped down to escort the bomber.

For almost half an hour they patrolled back and forth between the straggler and the main formation but they could do nothing to help as *Shade Ruff* continued to drop away further and further behind.

About ten miles short of the Dutch border the crew abandoned the plane. German reports indicate that the aircraft was on fire when it came down, hit by flak near Meppin which caught the left inner engine ablaze. All the crew exited safely and most were captured in the vicinity of Teglingen, 5km southeast of Meppin. Pilot Dale Peterson received a gun shot wound in his arm, presumably after landing, but otherwise all were uninjured. Three men managed to evade captivity for two days but they too were rounded up to become POWs.

A dense pall of smoke hangs over the VKF Erkner ball-bearing plant as the 2nd Bomb Division's B24s come off the target (USAF)

9th MARCH 1944

The primary targets for this mission were the Ernst Heinkel aircraft component factory located north of Berlin at Oranienberg and the Arado plant at Brandenburg to the west. In the event of cloud cover, PFF bombing was called for on the city itself. Thus, with 10/10 cloud blanketing the continent and rising up to 12,000ft, the 8th Air Force struck at Berlin for the fourth time in just six days.

Pathfinders leading the 2BD's three combat wings experienced radar equipment problems. As a result, B24 formations milled around areas of Germany seeking targets of opportunity. Most bombed on a flak concentration, believed to be Hanover, thirty B24s dropped on Nauen and some

units were forced to jettison their loads when fuel became critical.

The 331 Forts of the other two Bomb Divisions, seven combat wings, dropped a total of 775 tons of general purpose and incendiary bombs centred on the southwestern part of the Berlin's Tiergarten. In addition, more than two million leaflets were spilled out over the city.

Unlike the previous missions to Berlin, on this day fighter opposition was practically non-existent and only five Luftwaffe planes were reported sighted by bomber crews — resulting in just a single combat. One Me109 fighter attacked a B24 pathfinder ship from 12 o'clock level and closed to within 500 yards

Where is the Luftwaffe?

Thunderbolts from the 8AF Fighter Command comprised the bulk of the escort on 9th March, 530 of them. They were supported by 42 Mustangs and 88 Lightnings. 9th Fighter Command furnished a further 111 Mustangs and 42 Thunderbolts. The RAF contributed a small force of two dozen Mustangs to bring the total assigned escort up to 837 fighters. Aborts and mishaps reduced this to just over eight hundred effective fighter sorties.

This impressive force of 23 groups later reported seeing only twenty or so enemy aircraft during the entire operation in what was one of the smallest reactions experienced to date against a major daylight raid. The 352FG, who rendezvoused with

the bomber force in mid-Channel, reported later sighting ten enemy aircraft attacking bombers with rockets but curiously no similar report was made by any of the returning bomber crews. Other penetration escorts rendezvoused with the bombers more or less as per their schedule and made no reports of enemy aircraft activity.

The same was true of those escorts assigned to accompany the bombers over the target area. Generally, the bomber forces were reported to be 35 minutes later than scheduled. 354FG and 55FG took the 1st Task Force over Berlin, the 4FG

orbited and waited for the 2nd Task Force and 20FG picked up the 3BD. 357FG rendezvoused one hour early with B24s who were experiencing PFF equipment problems and eventually dropped most of their load over Hanover.

One P38 from 364FG was lost near Osnabruck when it was caught in intense flak and went down out of control. It was the only fighter lost in action for the day. 55FG did lose two of their P38s however, when one crashed on take-off and another returned early and was abandoned near Tuddenham. A P51 from 355FG also crashed soon after take-off, killing its

pilot. The RAF, supporting the withdrawal, also had two of their Mustangs, from 19 Sqn and 65 Sqn, fail to return.

During withdrawal the bombers drifted 50 miles north of their course and although they had caught up some lost time were still reported about 15-30 minutes late. This resulted in some escort groups missing their rendezvous or joining other formations they happened upon. Since only a handful of German aircraft were spotted, the mild disruption to plans was not a problem. It was a situation which could so easily have been exploited to deadly effect by the Luftwaffe if they had been active but on this day they remained firmly on the ground — in the words of General Doolittle, "Broken but not utterly crushed".

"I'll be a Sad Sack – not a Jerry the whole damn way! Not even over Berlin."
Col Don Blakeslee, 4FG

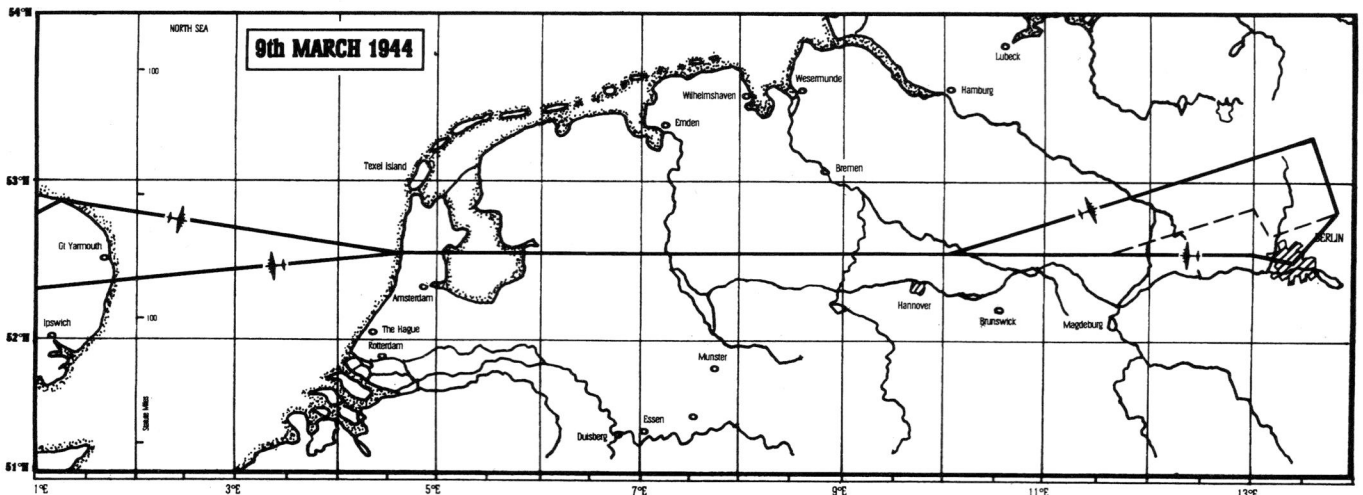

9th MARCH 1944

— it was promptly shot down and became the only victory claim of the day. A 100% success rate! The groups of escorting fighters returned frustrated by the lack of opportunity to close with the enemy and continue the success they had achieved on previous missions to the German capital.

Flak, however, was intense over the city and ripped through the formations as they passed overhead. Ground rockets were also reported and by the day's end six bombers and one P-38 were lost over enemy territory, another two bombers were down in the sea and 221 returned with damage.

The air raid alert lasted almost two full hours in the city until the all clear was sounded at 14.34hrs. The majority of the bombs fell into the Lichtenberg district, mostly north of the Frankfurter Allee, cutting the subway track, totally destroying fifty buildings and leaving 1600 persons missing. Zehlendorf district also received two concentrations which fell across residential areas and severely disrupted electricity and water utilities. Horst Wesel and Steglitz took their share of incendiaries and high explosive and the AEG plant at Treptow reported "numerous dead and injured". German records for the raid are sparse.

Silver Dollar brought bad luck

The 384BG faired well during the first month of American raids on Berlin, losing only four of its aircraft on those missions, three of them on the diverted raid of 4th March when they bombed Cologne. 384BG crews survived the slaughter of 6th and 8th March when flak and fighters claimed more than 100 heavy bombers. Then, on the day that the Luftwaffe stayed away and the 8AF lost only six of its Fortresses, the 384BG recorded its only loss over Berlin itself during March — under tragic circumstances.

Lt Merlin Reed and his crew were flying in *Silver Dollar* (42-37781) when a stray bomb chopped off its tail section completely. The 384BG had drifted on the bomb run and was directly below the 379BG at their point of release. Eye witnesses reported that the stricken plane broke up into three sections, with the nose heading straight down and the tail catapulting outward. So swift was the disaster that overtook them, that there was no chance for any of the crew to bail out and there were no survivors from the ten men on board.

Little Willie – home alone

388th Bomb Group's Fortress *Little Willie* (42-37839) was no stranger to Berlin, nor its flak. Three days earlier, on 6th March, it had been forced to leave the formation over the city after flak hits. Always quick to exploit the situation, two German fighters plunged after the straggler. With one engine useless and one prop windmilling, threatening to vibrate the plane apart, the pilot F/O Bernard Dopko dived away to shake off the fighters.

Little Willie headed for home — alone — crossing Germany and Holland at barely one hundred feet and following the roads back to the coast, weaving between church spires and trees. Back at Knettishall other crews had reported *Little Willie* as shot down but over the sea, when all seemed lost, an engine suddenly roared back to life and lifted the plane to 5000ft, enough altitude to make it back to safety.

But the respite was short-lived, now *Little Willie* was back over Berlin, with F/O Dopko and his crew. They had tacked onto a 96BG formation to fill in as a spare. Flak struck yet again, tore through an oil line in No.2 engine and sent flames licking back from it. This time, Dopko couldn't feather the prop and as the fire began to spread he rang the bail out bell and the crew abandoned their ship. This time, *Little Willie* wasn't going home.

All on board survived but it would be many months before they got back home after being held as prisoners of war. Two men did escape, however, and eventually reached a British tank unit sometime after D-Day.

"This Berlin haul is sure a long tiresome ride. I never thought I'd get so tired of sitting down.... The flak was so thick we could hardly see through it... the sky, again, was black with Forts over the city."
Diary extract – LOUIS LAHOOD, Pilot of *Queenie* (42-31353) 91BG

"...the turning point of the war in the air."

"On 9th March for example the German fighters elected to remain on the ground, citing solid overcast as an excuse for their failure to operate. There are indications however that in spite of inclement weather, German controllers could have sent up on that day considerable numbers of fighters, for some, which did not engage, were able to come up through the overcast. From this it must be assumed that the German fighter units are broken but not utterly crushed, and that the enemy has made a decision to temporarily conserve aircraft and pilots........ The admission by the German fighter controllers that they preferred to keep their aircraft on the ground even when Berlin was under attack, marks the turning point of the war in the air."
J. H. Doolittle, Major General
Extract from Commendation Report, 11th March 1944

9th MARCH 1944

Dry tanks – wet night

1Lt Joseph Jurnecka's 447BG crew, like many others on the long trip to Berlin and back, ran short of fuel and were forced to take desperate action to try to get home. In a press release issued on their return the engineer recorded, "We were about half way there when I checked on the gas.... consumption was higher than usual... it was a ticklish spot for a decision.... but we had never aborted, and we were almost through our tour." After bombing the target, the pilots and engineer kept a watchful eye on the gauges unaware that they were giving an incorrect reading. They soon discovered that although the gauges read 50 gallons they were practically empty. The engineer frantically transferred fuel from one tank to another, then

feathered a prop to reduce consumption. Lt Jurnecka ordered all loose equipment to be jettisoned to lighten the ship as it began the final stage of the journey back across the North Sea.

Engineer, T/Sgt Jerome Wodin continued, "Just as we left the coast another engine quit.... I moved my top turret toward the front so the pilot and co-pilot could grasp it and help themselves out of the cockpit when we ditched. I took the flare gun, flares and first aid kit to the radio room where we all assembled for ditching.... At this time another engine quit and we lost sight of our formation. The radio man got the SOS out and we went into crash positions. The first shock was slight as the tail hit and then came a loud crash. I was thrown backwards.... everyone else

was in a mess too.

"Water came rushing in from all directions but we all kept calm and went out in good fashion... We never thought the ship would stay afloat as long as it did, about half an hour.... it was a sight seeing such a large plane just lying on that sea and suddenly the tail went up and down she went.... Soon after, an RAF Hudson came overhead and dropped us an airborne lifeboat, which overturned as it hit the water. We thought that it would be only a matter of an hour or so before a boat picked us up. That's what we thought....

"The plane dropped some flares to identify our

position and then left. We had ditched about 4pm and this was about two hours later.... we all huddled together and tried slapping each other's bare feet to keep warm and prevent frostbite... it was getting dark." Although the crew had scrambled into the lifeboat they could not start the engine, which was drenched. It was a long, cold, wet night for them as they were tossed about on the North Sea but they remained confident that rescue would soon come with daylight.

It was three o'clock in the afternoon before two air sea rescue launches finally reached them and the hauled the exhausted crew men aboard.

> "...the flak over Berlin was the blackest and the most intense ever encountered.... huge fires and black smoke was seen coming up through the clouds. Daylight was turned into nightfall by the flak bursts and smoke."
>
> Extract from 94BG Mission Summary

"I can recall how we used to 'suit up' for Berlin. Go sit in our planes awaiting the Start Engine flare .... and then see the red 'scrub' flare and go back to our bunks. The idea of going to Big B was something which sent shudders up and down our spines. I actually believe the High Command purposely scheduled those first several missions, knowing they would scrub them, so that by the time we DID go, we would consider it just another damn mission! It worked for me, because by the time we finally went, I was actually *relieved* that we were going!"

Bill Heller, pilot 303BG's *Miss Liberty* (42-31340)

452BG's *Four Winds* begins the bomb run on Berlin with its load of ten 500lb GP high explosive bombs (M Samson)

Lil Brat pestered by Me210

Art Pickens was on his 21st mission, his fifth take-off for Berlin, on 9th March. Poor weather had frustrated the first two attempts before the successful raids on 6th and 8th. Each of these missions was flown in *Lil Brat* (42-31921), a camouflaged B17G assigned to the 92BG. It was his second ship to carry the title *Lil Brat*, which the Pickens' crew had named after his wife-to-be. Art recalled: "Our old B17F was shot up on

our 6th mission to Halberstadt on 11th January. When we returned to base we counted 150 flak and bullet holes in our plane. It flew one more mission on 29th January and then was grounded to use for spares. Then, on 30th January we received a brand new B17G for our 8th combat mission.

"On the 9th March we lost our No.1 engine just 40 minutes short of Berlin and then No.2 started to run

away when we tried to keep up with the group. We dropped our bombs and headed back towards England alone and looked for some fighter protection. The only one who showed up was a German Me210. Thankfully, there was a stratus layer of cloud about 500ft thick and we dived into it. As we came out of the bottom, so did the Me210. We pulled back up but the layer was getting thinner and we popped back out of the top side. So

did the Me210. Neither he nor our gunners were able to get off shots and I wasn't about to hold position to give them a chance!

"This up and down dance continued for at least four trips through the clouds. As we entered France, the cloud began to disappear altogether but our tailgunner reported that the 210 was disappearing too — heading east. I guess he was low on fuel."

Jezebel tempts fate and returns to Berlin – again and again and again

One Fort which was among those to make the greatest number of return trips to Berlin was 91BG's *Jezebel* (42-38144). Seven times it succeeded in getting its bombs onto targets in the city, another attempt involved the recall of the entire 8AF, and it would have been credited a ninth time but for a mechanical problem which caused an early return.

Jezebel was assigned to the 91BG at Bassingbourn on the last day of February 1944 and flew with the group for a full year. Assigned to John Davis' crew, its first mission came on 2nd March to Frankfurt. The following day it was scheduled for the 8AF's first strike at Berlin but was not despatched. On the 4th March the Davis crew did join the armada heading for the German capital but was recalled, along with most of the 8th Air Force, and narrowly missed destruction as the group careered headlong through formations in the huge aerial traffic jam over the North Sea.

Finally, on the 6th March, and then again on the 8th and 9th, *Jezebel* reached her target and bombed Berlin. Routine maintenance kept the plane out of the formations heading for the city on the

The crew of Captain Marshall McKew who took *Jezebel* to Berlin three times in May (M. McKew)

next four attacks in late March, through April and early May. Three more Berlin missions were added on 8th, 19th and 24th May, with Capt Marshall McKew's lead crew, and on 21st June yet another bringing the total to seven plus one recalled.

Having tempted fate and survived so much flak and fighter combat over Berlin and other major targets, *Jezebel* almost ended her days over England. On a flying exercise with five other

B17s on 24th October, fire broke out in the top turret electrical system. Unable to extinguish the fire, pilot Lt Flanders bailed out, together with the engineer and bombardier. The co-pilot, Eldon Gaston, and radio man however succeeded in reducing the blaze and brought the plane back to base.

Jezebel was repaired and put back in the air for the mission to Merseburg on 2nd November. It survived the slaughter which would claim no less

than 13 Fortresses from the 91BG alone. By 5th December the plane had completed 57 missions and headed out towards Berlin for the ninth time. But the stresses and strains of nine months of hard combat were beginning to tell and the pilots were forced to abort with mechanical problems and return early.

Soldiering on into 1945, *Jezebel* would have been in line for the maximum effort of 3rd February to 'Big B'. But on 1st February, it accompanied the 398BG to Mannheim and tempted fate once too often. Badly damaged by flak it was forced to land on the continent at an emergency field. Languishing there, it was salvaged two weeks later.

> "When you walked into the briefing room and the curtain was raised to reveal the red ribbon stretched out to Berlin, a certain amount of fear rose up in your mind. But the fact remained, we had a job to do and 'Lady Luck' played an important role." Marshall McKew, pilot 91BG's *Jezebel* (42-38144)

Fortresses and Liberators of all three Air Divisions set out for aviation industry targets with Oranienburg and Basdorf as their primary objectives. Heavy cloud cover diverted them to the secondary target, designated as the centre of Berlin with the aiming point of the Friedrichstrasse railway station.

Luftwaffe interference was minimal and only a few groups reported sighting any enemy fighters, no more than 15 in total, and these did not carry through any attack. One Fortress struggling home on its own did receive the attention of two Me109s and four FW190s near the Frisian Islands but even these proved unaggressive before being driven of by Mustangs. Some gunners amongst the bomber crews

were beginning to believe the stories of a broken Luftwaffe alluded to in Doolittle's Commendation Report — but it would not be for long.

Flak was ever present and over Berlin was described as intense and accurate, cutting at least three heavy bombers from the formations overhead. One flak-hit B24 lurched into another aircraft in its formation and both went down. Only twelve heavy bombers were lost on this day but almost 350 would return with the scars of flak damage.

Poor weather conditions forced several groups to make a second run over the target. In all, more than 18,000 incendiaries were dropped together with 2000 high explosive 500lb bombs. Although unobserved,

"When the Group Commander pulled back the curtain to reveal the red string running from our base to Berlin, what happened, in reality, was unbelievable. There wasn't the expected gasp, no muffled expletives, not a sound prevailed, just deep silence. The CO said "This is it!", paused and then, "Berlin!" At that moment the surprising cheer that emanated from the assembled crews was ear-shattering, bouncing off the curved Nissen hut and booming back in a deafening sound..."

Ernest Aita, 100BG

Third time lucky for *Lazy Daisy* ?

The 384th Bomb Group's *Lazy Daisy* (42-31222) had arrived at Grafton Underwood back in November 1943. The plane had set out for Berlin on the recalled mission of 3rd March and again five days later with rather more success on the 8th.

On the 22nd March, *Lazy Daisy* lifted off and headed for the flak filled skies over Berlin for the third time. All went well until the ship was hit over the target area and one prop, unable to be feathered, began to windmill and create a violent vibration which left the pilot, James Miller, struggling to control the plane. Plunging to low level, *Lazy Daisy* shuddered its way home alone, without fighter escort, but with the constant fear that the errant propeller might suddenly shear off at any moment and slice into the cockpit with devastating consequences.

The crew prepared to bail out as they watched the whirling propeller shaft turn cherry red from the intense heat, only

inches from fuel lines and wing tanks. Approaching the coast and roaring at low level over the Zuider Zee, flak once again peppered the sky around them to add to their woes. This time, however, the accuracy of the German gunners below would prove to be *Lazy Daisy*'s saviour.

A flak splinter smashed into the propeller and sheared it clean away. In moments the vibration ceased and the engine began to cool. Had that splinter struck but a few inches either way then a fuel line might have been cut and the red hot prop shaft would surely have ignited the vapour into a fire ball. It was probably the only time the crew thanked the German gunners for their shooting accuracy! *Lazy Daisy* had been lucky on her third trip to Berlin. With the damaged prop cut away and the risk of fire drastically reduced, the pilots were able to bring the ship safely back home to fight another day.

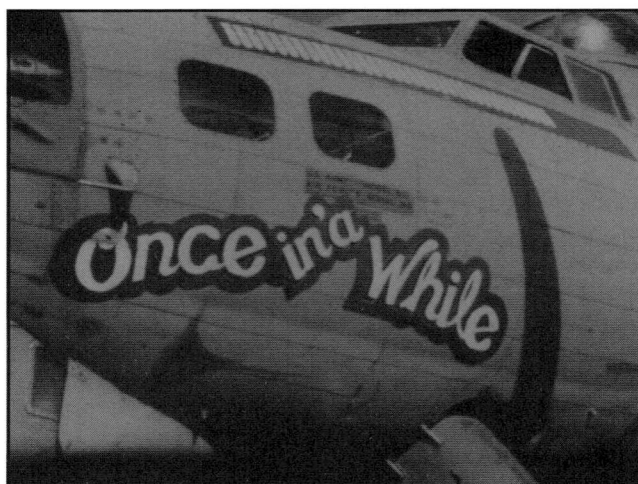

Lucky *Once in a While*

Three hundred and forty-seven bombers returned from Berlin with flak damage. The 100BG's *Once in a While* (42-31986) was typical and received a peppering of flak splinters. Closer inspection revealed just how lucky it, and the crew, had been to survive the experience.

An 88mm flak shell had scored a direct hit and ripped through the fuselage below the right waist window, cut stringers, an oxygen line and severed electrical lines as it exited without exploding. The right outer wing was

badly shredded by splinters from flak which did explode and it would have to be changed before the plane could fly again.

Splinters had also narrowly missed the pilot and cut through the oxygen bottle just aft of him. Other stringers and ribs were severed near the tail wheel and the leading edge of the left wing was also torn and battered. Of less severity were the innumerable skin punctures throughout the wings and fuselage requiring hours of laborious patching by the ground crew.

bombs from all formations were deemed to have fallen within the bounds of the city.

A heavy concentration struck a residential area 3000yds north of the Tiergarten, at Wedding, where it caused many fires and destroyed a tram repair depot. In the administrative district south of Friedrichstrasse station, the Reich Chancellory was hit, together with the Air Ministry building, Interior Ministry, main post office and the Reichsbank headquarters. In the Horst Wesel district to the northeast, a hospital and town hall received considerable damage, as did the fire station and the Strausberger subway station. At Weissensee, the gas works narrowly escaped a concentration of high explosive which fell just east and north. Other concentrations fell across the city from Spandau to Tempelhof.

22nd March marked the end of US involvement in the so-called "Battle for Berlin" which RAF Bomber Command had begun on 23rd November 1943. The 688 bombers despatched brought the total number of effective sorties flown by the USAAF to Berlin to 2600, dropping more than 5000 tons of ordnance. By nightfall on this day, the Allies had lost more than 550 heavy bombers in the battle, 148 of them American plus their escorts. And still the Berliners' resolve had not cracked. Some of the German High Command, however, were beginning to wonder how long Berlin could endure the ordeal.

The fighter battle that never came

Not a single fighter combat was reported on 22nd March but the day still proved to be a costly one for the 18 groups of escorts assigned to the mission, due to flak and the weather. More than 600 single-engined fighters and over one hundred twin-engined Lightnings were despatched with the task of escorting the bomber stream. It would prove to be a frustrating day's flying for the pilots who were keen to close with the enemy. Even Berlin was failing to force the battered

"Berlin – Oh hell, the milk run again!"

Maj Pierce McKennon, pilot of *Ridge Runner*, 4FG

Luftwaffe into the air.

The 4FG, escorting the 1st Air Task Force, did spot six Fw190s as they approached the city but these were distant and made no attempt on the bomber boxes. The 364FG reported four Me109s in the vicinity of Wittenberg but they too quickly disappeared into the clouds, as did four others spotted by 55FG east of Bremen.

In all, twelve fighters failed to return. The 56FG lost four of its P47s, three of them disappeared into cloud over England shortly after taking off. They are presumed to have collided or become disorientated in the dense cloud and spun in to the sea. Another of their Thunderbolts pulled up sharply after strafing a locomotive near Meppen, hit by small arms fire, and plunged into the ground. 361FG also lost one of their Thunderbolts when it crashed into the sea 35 miles off Southwold. It had been hit by flak while strafing the airfield at Leeuwarden and had almost made it back to England.

Another Thunderbolt, from 78FG, was lost shortly after takeoff when it was caught in prop wash at just 100ft altitude. Cartwheeling into the ground, the plane was totally destroyed — the pilot, however, miraculously walked away. The group also lost two more fighters on the mission. The 55FG and 357FG also lost one each to unknown causes.

The 9AF's 354FG lost two of their Mustangs after one turned back with his wingman, reporting his high blower had cut out. Neither were ever heard from again. A third P51 from the same group was hit by flak over Diepholz and the pilot was seen to bail out.

The 355FG, escorting the second bomber force over Basdorf, was surprised and 'bounced' by a force of Lightning P38s but the error was soon realised and no damage was done to either force. As a small consolation for the frustration of the day's flying, two 355FGs Mustangs strafed and destroyed a couple of trains during their return flight.

A flight from 352FG caught a four-engined He177 bomber on the ground at Hespe and four of its pilots shared the victory claim. Even ground targets proved hard to find on this day.

A broken Luftwaffe ?

Allied intelligence staff estimated that the German Air Force defending the skies over the Reich homeland may have lost more than 20 per cent of its pilot strength during the air battles of March. More than 220 pilots killed and another one hundred wounded — these were losses they would find hard to replace. Although its production of single engine fighters actually increased during 1944, the Luftwaffe's ability to train fresh pilots could not keep pace with the losses being incurred. Many of those killed had been the best Germany had — aces who had learned their trade over Poland, France, Britain and Russia. Their replacements would be untried novices who might not live long enough to acquire those same skills.

Never again would the Luftwaffe be able to call the shots and attack the bombers almost at will , as they had in the early days, without taking significant losses. Increasing numbers of American long-range fighters would see to that.

Battered they may have been — but broken they were not! There would be many more occasions in the following months when skilful exploitation of tactical situations by Luftwaffe fighter controllers would prove painful and costly to the 8th Air Force. And as each day went by, the Luftwaffe's secret jet propelled fighters were being readied for operational deployment over Germany.

(The Luftwaffe could) "...still hit, and hit hard; but it was no longer capable of that sustained counterattack which had at one time so nearly frustrated the entire Combined Bomber Offensive."

Intelligence Summary, March 1944, US 8th Air Force

22nd MARCH 1944

Jamaica? No, Berlin first!

When Larry Booth's crew picked up their brand new Douglas-built B24 (41-28746) it had only recently been delivered from the production line in Tulsa. Soon after being assigned to their new bomber the crew received orders to transfer to England, by the southern ferry route via South America and Africa. The bombardier on the crew was Ralph Beggs and he recalled, "I started painting the right side in Fortaleza, Brazil, added finish in Marrakesh, Morroco. Having had so much fun, I then painted the left side using Gillette Elvgren's pin-up — little knowing that it was widely used for nose art. I took it from the back of a playing card. By our first mission both sides were painted. Later at Attlebridge, our crew chief Sgt Bailey, an expert sign man, painted the name *Jamaica?* and also the names of the crew at each station on the bomber.

"Our navigator, Paul Bishop, was an addict of the pun, always coming up with a play on words. I remember when he came up with this one. Our pilot said it would be a good name for our ship. And so it was." Ralph continued, "I brought my oil tubes and brushes with me to England. I didn't varnish the paintings which in hindsight I should have done. The Group Engineer Officer wanted me to do his A-2 jacket but I was too busy flying missions by then."

On 22nd March, Ralph and the rest of the Booth crew climbed aboard their painted, but at that time un-named, bomber for their first mission. Not just *their* first mission but the entire 466th Bomb Group's first mission — 300 men who had expected a 'milk run' for their initiation and had been given Berlin as

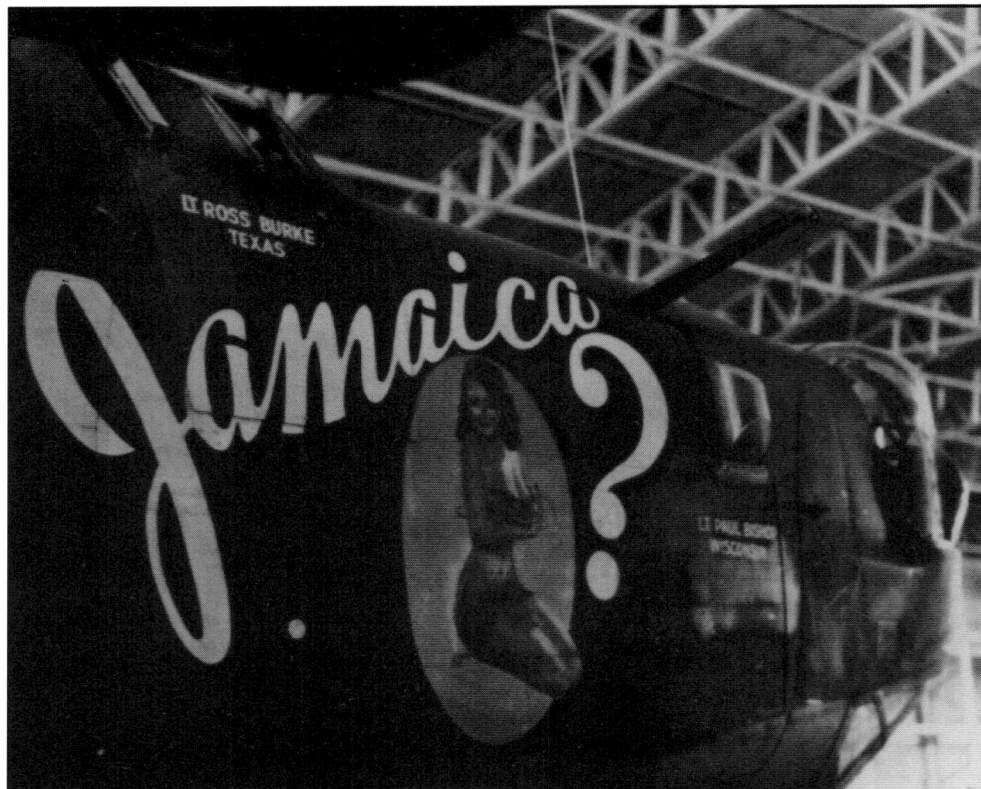

Ralph Begg completed this nose art painting in Marrakesh during the plane's deployment overseas (R Beggs)

the target instead.

As Berlin missions go it could have been tougher but for green crews on their first combat sortie it was plenty tough enough! The primary target for the group was the Brandenburgisch Motor Works at Basdorf, where 300 aero-engines a month were produced. Dense cloud cover, would force them on to the secondary target, the Friedrichstrasse rail station in the centre of Berlin.

As the bombers moved along their run over the target, Ralph Beggs watched the lead plane. A curious black shroud seem to hang over the city precisely where they were due to unload their bombs. Closing on the target, the shroud became hundreds of exploding flak shells. "Suddenly I saw a bomber directly ahead and below — with its tail missing! It was desperately trying to stay upright but finally slid

off to the left and turned belly up. Its bomb bay doors were open and all the bombs were still laying in their racks. Then it fell away into a spin. I was stunned. I realised for the first time that a heavy bomber could spin as easily as a small plane. My eyes came back to the lead ship and almost immediately we dropped our first bombs on Germany."

The 466BG received a commendation from General James Doolittle for undertaking the longest first mission ever flown by any group in the ETO.

Ralph Beggs flew a further ten missions in *Jamaica?* over the following month. Then the crew was transferred out to the 389BG at Hethel for radar training, leaving their plane behind. But that was not the last Ralph saw of his plane. On 15th June, *Jamaica?* force landed on an British emergency field near Cabourg in France

with two engines knocked out by flak. It had earned itself the dubious distinction of being only the second heavy bomber to land in liberated France since the invasion. Fighting was still going on three miles away. Two replacement engines were despatched and the plane brought back. Ralph went over to see it, "It looked tired and beat, and there was French writing all over the fuselage. Then on 25th September 1944, *Jamaica?* was lost. By then we had done our 30 missions and were at Prestwick waiting to be flown home."

Jamaica? was lost on a trucking mission hauling fuel to the front lines near St Dizier in France during August. It took off and was never seen again. It was hit by ground fire and somewhere over the continent six men died and a tired B24 ceased to exist — turned into scrap in an instant.

"....we dropped our bombs near the river and they really hit something. There was one big burst of red flame that shot thousands of feet into the air..."

".... one tremendous explosion. I saw one big puff of red smoke and flame come clear up through the clouds at 8000ft"

Lead crew, 303BG's *Miss Liberty* (42-31340)

One of those fortunate to return without serious damage on 22nd March 1944 was 94BG's *Idiot's Delight* (42-30301). It was the plane's 50th combat mission, the first to reach that score in the 94BG. Pilot 1Lt Austin Francis and his crew had taken it over Berlin to return without so much as a scratch. With no battle damage to repair the ground crew could take some time to proudly add an extra, larger, bomb to the aircraft's leering nose art and higgledy-piggledy mission symbols (USNARP)

Junior throws 'spaghetti' over Berlin

Bob Fickley was engineer top turret gunner on 385BG's *Junior* (42-31762) and made five visits to Berlin in that plane with Rice Sherril's crew. He remembered the heavy flak thrown up over the target each time they crossed the city. "Flak was the hardest part once we had started the bomb run. If you were further back in line you got the worst of it", he recalled. "Bursts looked like miniature mushroom clouds — predicted, following or concentrated barrage. We used chaff which gave a double image on their radar predictors. It was 12" long aluminum foil, $1/4$" wide — we called it 'spaghetti'. The radio man was responsible for throwing it out of the plane. Sometimes you could see the flak exploding well below."

The chaff, or 'spaghetti' was indeed a saviour to many crews but it was not always the case. Another veteran of Berlin, 91BG's Phil Mack, recalled turning off the bomb run over Berlin and seeing the chaff they had just tossed out. It tumbled like a silvery, shimmering cloud — straight into the path of a B24 Wing, three thousand feet below. The resulting flak immediately began to burst amongst them and "they caught hell", he recalled.

"Only a few enemy aircraft were sighted coming thru undercast over Denmark and they did not attack... Flak encountered along route in and back.... a large amount of continuously pointed fire... Ground rockets were seen over Berlin and after bursts small parachutes were observed to come down with balls of fire..."

452BG Intelligence Narrative

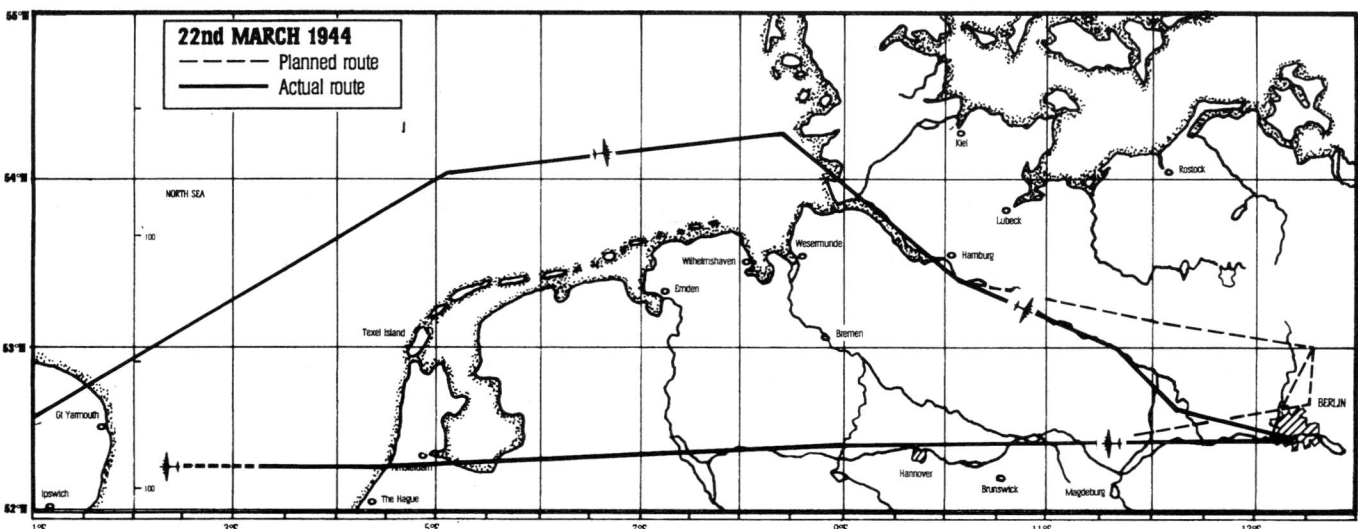

22nd MARCH 1944
- - - - Planned route
───── Actual route

The last of being first for 482BG

The 482nd Bomb Group's primary role in early 1944 was to provide the PFF radar pathfinder ships and the trained crews to lead each combat wing over the target. The group had provided the first B17 to fly over Berlin on 4th March. The last major mission to be led by their PFF aircraft, with the exception of the important D-Day missions in June, was on 22nd March 1944. With the arrival of improved H2X airborne radar equipped aircraft each Bomb Division established its own pathfinder squadron.

These newly trained squadrons continued the practice of dispersing their aircraft prior to each mission to act as combat wing leads.

A programme of expansion was planned which would ultimately provide pathfinder aircraft in each combat wing and, eventually, in each group. The 482BG meanwhile, would concentrate on special operations as well as training the radar operators and operational testing of new equipment as it became available.

Winnie C, seen in better times before being lost over Berlin

Winnie C lost to friendly bombing

On a second bomb run over Berlin due to poor weather, 96BG's Winnie C (42-6099) fell victim to three bombs dropped from a Fort flying above. Pilot, Lt Nathan Young, and all on board were killed.

Winnie C crashed into the Demag military vehicle factory between Falkensee and Henningsdorf. Investigators suspected that overloading of bomb racks may have been the cause of the misfortune.

Able Mabel gets disabled

Debriefing of a 355FG pilot returning from the frustrating escort mission yielded the following report: "B17 with triangle 231524 picked up at 14,000ft with left outboard engine burning and losing altitude, with bomb bay doors open. Followed down to 9000ft where it was hit by flak. 4 chutes seen near Cloppenburg. Bomber continued on losing altitude." Low on fuel the fighter pilot was forced to leave and headed back to base, assuming that the B17 would soon become another statistic, another loss to the German flak gunners.

The Fort he had seen was Able Mabel from 306BG. It had joined the group towards the end of January and, assigned to Lt Ragnar Carlson, had already made at least two previous attempts on Berlin, on the 3rd and 4th of March. They had been hit by flak which shot away half of the No3 engine and set it, and No4, on fire. The hydraulics were also damaged and oxygen exploded in the cockpit, stunning the pilots and destroying most of the instruments. Plummeting several thousand feet, the pilots managed to regain control as burning hydraulic fluid flooded the cockpit floor. But at just 115mph they were barely flying.

When flak struck again over Osnabruck, five crew in the rear bailed out. The pilots, however, would not give up their plane and, with a lone P51 as escort, nursed it across the North Sea a few feet above the waves. The No.2 engine finally gave up the struggle and quit but even so Able Mabel made landfall and slithered into a ploughed field. She would never fly again but she had, like so many Fortresses, brought her surviving crew home.

First and last for Terry & the Pirates

One of the 466BG's brand new Liberators, flying the group's first mission, had been given the title of Terry and the Pirates. It had been named after its pilot Lt Terry and the popular newspaper cartoon strip of the same name created by Milton Caniff. For this crew and their plane, the first mission would be a tough baptism of fire.

Dense cloud obscured the primary target at Basdorf and the radio man heard the code words "Black out" — the signal to abort the attack on the primary and head for the centre of Berlin. As Terry and the Pirates went in over the city, flak sheared away two propellers and sent them sailing on ahead, one engine exploded and the huge lumbering aircraft rolled over to briefly fly upturned before crashing down onto another B24 close by, carrying away one of its tail fins. That aircraft also struggled to stay upright but it too rolled over to expose its open belly, still packed with high explosive bombs, before plunging down into a deathly spin.

Somehow, almost miraculously, Lt Terry and his co-pilot regained control of their battered aircraft and turned it away to limp towards the safety of neutral Sweden and internment. The other crew involved were not so fortunate — all died. One of their gunners had only arrived on the base at Attlebridge on the previous night, his gear would never even need to be unpacked.

A rough trip for the *Merry Widow*

91BG's Philip Mack was making his second raid on Berlin, his 25th mission — just one more would complete his combat tour. He was flying in *Merry Widow* (42-31580) chaperoning a replacement crew. Turning the controls over as they crossed the Channel, Phil Mack noted the erratic flying of his copilot and his inability to hold formation. There was a real risk of mid-air collision. On querying him, it was discovered that he was unwell, had a fever and had not seen the Flight Surgeon to get grounded because as it was his first mission and it might have looked bad to the crew.

Phil took up the story, "I took over the controls, and proceeded to lecture the other pilot. This was a two-man job. Flying a wing position at altitude was especially hard work. It was normal that each pilot was relieved every ten minutes or so by the other pilot. Any crew member going on a mission unable to perform his duties put himself and the entire crew in jeopardy. Pride and vanity had no place on a combat mission."

"Frankly I did not know how I was going to be able to fly all the way to Berlin without a break. But there was no choice. The mission took 9.0hrs.... I remember it as the hardest work I have ever performed in my entire life."

"As we turned down the bombing run from the IP, the flak was intense. We were at high altitude but the 105mm cannons were reaching us. Half way down the run, the left wing man of the second element of the lead flight — the ship closest to us — was severely hit. My top turret gunner called out 'He's coming into us'. He was out of control.

Phil Mack pulled *Merry Widow* out of position to avoid a collision but then found he was above his flight with bomb doors open. Drifting further back to avoid bombing the planes below he was then straggling the formation. Fighters appeared in the distance and then the flak started again....

"I woke the other pilot and told him to put on his flak helmet. He had barely put it on when a shell passed in front of the nose of the ship and exploded above the cockpit... shrapnel burst the plexiglass above my head. One piece struck him on the flak helmet, and another piece struck me on my right thigh."

"The piece of shrapnel stung. I was flying the airplane and though I wanted to look down to see how bad I was hit, I couldn't take my eyes off the other aircraft. I took my right hand off the throttles momentarily, rubbed it over my thigh, and passed it in front of my face so I could take a quick look to see if I was bleeding. The glove was clean. I repeated the act, and again the glove was clean. Still disbelieving, I looked directly at my thigh. There was no blood, no torn flying suit, nothing. The particle had spent its energy. There would be no Purple Heart for me that day."

"We dropped our bombs and after turning off the bomb run, the other pilot was by then able to give me the break I badly needed. I was so tired that I really didn't care if the other pilot didn't fly a good position. What's more, the other aircraft that had been close to us wasn't there any more. What was sad, though, was that one of my closest friends, Joe Wellman....., had been on that aircraft."

"On reaching Bassingbourn and preparing to land, the tail wheel would not extend fully.... I attempted a wheel-landing to keep the tail wheel off the ground as long as possible. Unaccustomed to making anything but a three-point landing, my wheel-landing was not smooth. I bounced several times but managed all the while to keep the tail wheel from touching until I could lower it gently. At first it held up, but as I made the first brake application near the far end of the runway, the tail raised up slightly and then went down completely. I had to shut down the engines and leave the aircraft on the runway." The next day Phil Mack completed his tour. It would be a while before *Merry Widow* took to the air again but it did return to Berlin on 7th May — caught by the city's flak, it struggled to the coast before being abandoned.

Extracts © by Philip G Mack, 'Twenty-five Missions'. Reprinted by consent of author

... but the *Lassie* came home again

Another of Bassingbourn's Forts *Lassie Come Home* (42-31673) went to Berlin eight times in all. The first trip was on the 8th March followed by another, flown by pilot Louis LaHood, on 22nd to Oranienburg. The poor weather over the primary sent the bombers towards the centre of Berlin. It was a rough trip even without the hangover Louis was taking with him.

"I was afraid this was going to happen. We had a dance and party here at the base last night and everyone was loaded, including myself. I got into bed at 2.00am and the alert officer came around and woke me at 3.15am. I knew it was going to be a long one because they got us up so early.... boy, did I feel bad... damned near fell flat on my face when I saw the target was Berlin...

"This trip is always a back-breaker. It seems like it takes all day to get there, and twice as long to get home. We drove and drove and finally reached the city about 14.30. It was hardly worthwhile for me as I was carrying the propaganda today... 3000 pounds of leaflets instead of TNT... We drove smack over the centre of Berlin. They were sending flak in barrages — the sky was covered with flak bursts and we ploughed right through it.... some of the planes carried incendiaries and when we left the city there were a thousand fires started. Black smoke was rising high into the sky.

"It's always a long drive back home. It's a great feeling to cross the French coast and head across the Channel."

Diary extract, Louis LaHood, 91BG pilot Lassie Come Home (42-31673)

Although not directed at the city itself, the Eighth Air Force set out for targets in the Berlin area and planners selected a previously unused route for the day's mission. The bomber force proceeded out over the North Sea to a point north of Wilhelmshaven and then turned directly southeast towards the German capital. Withdrawal was planned along a parallel route.

501 B17s and 275 B24s were dispatched to attack important aero-engine and electrical plants just outside Berlin at Genshagen, Oranienburg, and Rathenow. West of the city, a towering mass of cloud rose up to 30,000ft and the 3BD became disrupted by its solid front and were prevented from attacking their primary target.

The Luftwaffe's response was varied and the 1st and 2nd Bomb Divisions reported negligible interference from fighters. The 3rd Division however encountered stiff resistance, north of Brandenburg and lost fourteen aircraft. The flak defences around Berlin once again cut a share from the attackers and five Fortresses were brought down, a further four bombers were lost to unknown causes. Five escorting fighters were also shot down by flak. Their loss was, however, appeased by claims of 33 German aircraft destroyed, although 16 of these were as a result of ground strafing attacks.

The brunt of the air opposition was borne by the

The end for *Miss Dallas*

Dallas-born Captain Victor France had been assigned to the 4th Fighter Group in October 1942. Naturally enough, his choice of name for his P-51B was *Miss Dallas* (43-6832). The crew chief to his plane was a highly skilled mechanic and acclaimed artist of nose art in the 4th Fighter Group, Sgt Don Allen. Allen embellished the fighter with one of the superb pieces of artwork for which he had become renowned. By 18th April 1944, he had already painted two earlier P47s with similar artwork and now the plane also had eight German crosses adorning it, just forward of the cockpit, denoting France's victories.

Led by Col. Blakeslee, on 18th April, the 4FG took up their escort role above the 3rd Bomb. Division

near Stendal. Twenty-five German fighters were engaged over the Rhine but most of the enemy aircraft were chased into clouds and contact was lost. Two of those downed were claimed by Major George Carpenter, before he himself was shot down near Rathenow. Two more of the enemy were caught near Stendal.

Captain France flying in *Miss Dallas* shot down an Me109 harassing a straggling Fortress. As he chased another Me109 it split-S'd and dived away for the ground. Following it down in a screaming dive, France continued to fire at his opponent until it slammed into the ground. Unable to pull out from the high speed dive, *Miss Dallas* followed its victim into a second searing fireball.

Captain Victor France and one of the *Miss Dallas* Thunderbolts (M Samson)

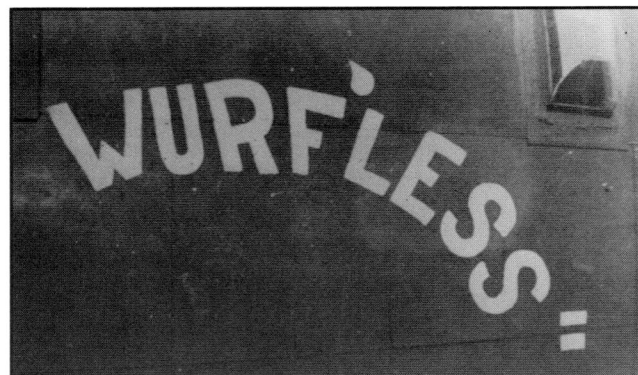

Wurf'less strafed worthless

When the B24s of 2BD neared Berlin they were confronted by a cloud bank which rose to 40,000ft. Navigator Saylor Zimmerman in 458BG's *Wurf'less* (42-52382) recorded, "The mission leader incorrectly judged that we could drop our bombs before we entered the cloud bank." *Wurf'less* headed straight into the cloud and was caught in prop wash from another group. "We went into a spin at about 25,000ft and I thought we would never come out of it," continued Zimmerman. "Lt Schuman's expertise as a pilot brought us out of the spin at about 15,000ft... we immediately started to look for another group we could join for protection."

"We could find none, so we went down on the deck after Newell (WG) had kicked the bombs out ...after about two hours we were 30km from the North Sea at Oldenburg when two FW190s picked us up.

The first pass they made at us they sized us up... on the 2nd pass they knocked out our No.1 engine... on the 3rd pass they evidently put a shell into the cockpit which hit Lt Schuman, flash-blinded Lt Jordan and knocked me out..."

Wurf'less was flying just 50-100ft off the ground and crashed immediately at about 200mph with no one at the controls. Lt Zimmerman was thrown through the side of the ship. The copilot climbed out through the hole he had made in the side and dragged him into a ditch as ammunition began to explode. Climbing out the ditch a few minutes later, they quickly dived back in again as a P47 roared over and strafed the crashed B24 into a worthless junk heap. A menacing crowd of civilians gathered but Luftwaffe soldiers were soon on the scene. Only four survivors were found and one, pilot Lt Schuman, died soon after.

lead group of the 4A Combat Wing. Just north of Brandenburg, about one hundred fighters pressed home three separate passes from out of the sun in attacks which lasted 15 minutes. Ten bombers went down — all from the 94th Bomb Group.

Other 3BD groups also received well co-ordinated attacks from FW190s and Me109s, each directing its assault against a specific target. Sneak attacks from out of the cloud were also pressed home vigorously and effectively.

The largest force of attackers struck at Oranienburg, just north of Berlin city outskirts, with 229 Fortresses. Here, at the Ernst Heinkel Flugzeugwerke, wings for Ju88 night fighters were produced as well as twin-engined He177 assembly. These were the Luftwaffe's heavy bombers which carried a crew of six, nine machine guns and cannons, and a payload which could include two Hs293 guided missiles and 13,000lbs of bombs. Although mostly deployed against the Russian front, a few had been used to bomb Britain. Known to be under top secret development was a long range four-engined version, the He277, it was to be the Luftwaffe's 'Flying Fortress' with projected targets in mind as far afield as New York.

The main concentration fell west of Heinkel's Annahof factory airfield and only eight He177s of the 39 seen dispersed on the ground were destroyed. No hits were achieved on the factory itself. Sub-assembly buildings, testing ranges and the main assembly hangar did take hits and near misses. A larger force struck the nearby Heinkel Germandorf components plant but although the main concentration of high explosives fell right across the target they failed to start significant fires. Three workshops were severely damaged from direct hits, as were stores buildings and offices.

A small, mixed force of about 80 bombers also struck another Heinkel plant at Brandenburg with unobserved results due to cloud cover.

The Arado Flugzeugwerke components factory at Rathenow, 45 miles west of Berlin, was the recipient

of 390 tons of high explosive and incendiary bombs dropped by 2BD Liberators and one group of B17s. Incendiaries carpeted the whole target area hitting at least six workshops, starting fires in stores, offices and barracks buildings, and gutting the power plant. An optical plant and I G Farben chemical plant also received some damage. One concentration fell into the northeast sector of the town itself. Others fell into open fields.

The 3BD did not reach its primary target of Genshagen, 45 miles west of Berlin, because of the weather front which broke up its formations. There was considerable confusion as wings and groups wheeled about and zig-zagged in an attempt to get clear of the massive cloud barrier confronting them. Instead, its groups dropped on targets of opportunity. One, Luneburg airfield, took numerous hits on hangars, refuelling points and other installations from fifty-two B17s. At least six aircraft were caught on the ground during the raid and destroyed.

Many of the returning crews were highly critical of their leadership on this day. Especially the events surrounding their penetration of the massive cloud front encountered near Berlin.

"..lead ship gave away time for IP and target."

"Leaders poor, all Wings zig-zagging at same altitude and getting in each others way."

"..ignored requests not to enter cloud banks over Berlin... then made 360 turn at 30 degrees bank to go back over the target at 16,000ft. The turn scattered the formation and low altitude might have made a field day for Berlin AA fire."

AFTER ACTION REPORTS - 3rd Bomb Div.

Little action for the 'little friends'

Eighteen fighters groups from 8th and 9th Air Forces, with an additional 17 RAF Mustangs, provided an escort to the three bomber forces.

The 4FG lost three P-51s but claimed a total of 18 kills. Only four of them, however, were in air combat after successfully breaking up a fighter attack on the last group of bombers. North of Genthin, they also caught four Me109s in a landing pattern, destroyed one in the air and two on the ground. Most of the escorting groups, however, saw little or nothing of their enemy in the air. 20FG, escorting the 1BD, failed to be lured away from their charges. Twenty German fighters flew parallel to their force for the duration of their escort, diving and climbing in an effort to entice them away. 364FG spotted a force of two dozen Fw190s near Stendal but they dived away to avoid combat.

Those tasked with strafing operations had a better day and reaped a rich horde of ground targets. One 4FG squadron destroyed eight Ju-52 transports on the ground

at Juterbog. At Fassberg, three He177 heavy bombers were also caught by 4FG and left as scrap. 361FG lost one of their pilots after strafing Zwischenhahn airfield and destroying a Ju88 and Arado 196 on the ground.

Lt Lou Yank on 381BG's *Princess Pat* (42-97503) witnessed the end of one Luftwaffe transport. "It was a six-engine job" he reported, "and a big baby. The P51s spotted it, immediately swooped and caught it before it was 500ft off the ground... I saw it crash less than 300 yards from the take-off field and it blew up with a great explosion when it hit the ground."

A flight from 355FG strafed a train pulling a long line of Army trucks on flatbed wagons and left many burning furiously. Other groups, from 66th Fighter Wing, also strafed several trains and airfields. The 67th Fighter Wing had little luck on this day and sighted no enemy aircraft in spite of examining a number of airfields around the vicinity of Neumunster, Rendsburg, Wohrden and Scharhorn. Their pilots returned home empty handed and frustrated .

A deadly ambush through the flak catches the 94BG

As the 94BG formation dropped down due to bad weather around the target area and turned onto the secondary target, the lead PFF ship was damaged by a flak hit which knocked out its two outboard engines. With no time to transfer the lead to the deputy PFF, a target of opportunity was selected, the village of Barnewitz. At that point the Luftwaffe struck with a fighter force believed to be from JG3 and took the group totally by surprise.

"They came right in on the light touch of flak that met us first," recorded S/Sgt Southard, tail gunner on *Mission Mistress* (42-97082). "We started to look at the flak and all of a sudden fighters were diving through our formation in over-whelming numbers." That first attack was a shock but did not cause severe damage to the formation. Immediately after bombing, however, another attack swept in from head-on, in waves of twenty at a time, going straight through the formation with devastating results. The lead and low squadrons took the brunt of the assault and both PFF ships went down together with six other aircraft. Two more peeled away from the high squadron.

Impatient Virgin (42-31650) was leading the low squadron and had just salvoed the bombs when an Me109 came at them from 12 o'clock. The radio operator, Gene Martin recalled, "It hit us! Severed the right wing completely between the engines and knocked us into a flat spin.... I was pinned in my compartment by the centrifugal force but within seconds was thrown out into space. I was wearing my back pack and don't know if the ship just broke in two or blew

up. The navigator and I were the only two survivors."

20mm shells tore into the cockpit of the un-named 42-107019 killing the pilot Lt Schommer instantly, shattering the instrument panel and sending the plane into a steep dive. Also on board as command pilot was the 333BS Operations Officer Capt. Alex Hogan. Lt Erwin Pomerantz's ship, known to its crew as *Lonesome Polecat*, (42-38139) also caught 20mm shells in the cockpit which set the oxygen system ablaze. Another shell smashed the bomb bay doors before they could be closed. As the crew bailed out of the stricken plane the pilot's harness caught on the extended crank handle and he was held dangling below the plane in the searing flames until he could release himself. All survived but three men were hospitalised in Berlin after capture.

Bill Brinkmier, piloting 42-37797, was also caught by the attack and recalled, "The previous crew had named the ship *Gin Mill Special* but had not painted the name on the nose.... it had been known as *Wolverine*. The plane had poor superchargers and could barely reach 35,000ft and was miserable to hold in any kind of formation.

"60 to 100 FW190s and Me109s in each of three successive attacks.... from 11 to 12 o'clock, high to level, right through the formation, coming through in waves of 20 at a time.... e/a were hiding in high cirrus clouds waiting to come down below..."

Extract 94BG Intelligence Report

The first pass did little damage, however, the second pass knocked off our No.2 engine and cut the control cables. Most of us had minor injuries but the navigator and co-pilot were fatally hit. We spun out of control and were finished off by a flak barrage. Everyone bailed out and the survivors became guests of the German government for the next 13 months."

The PFF ship (42-97569), already damaged by flak, took 20mm hits in the cockpit which decapitated the pilot and also struck the No2 engine. The shocked co-pilot held the ship steady just long

enough for the crew to bail out successfully. *Chief Chilletacaux* (42-31407), *Old Hickory* (42-31401), and *The Payoff* (42-37852) also fell away from the formation with fatal damage as did another un-named Fort and the deputy lead PFF aircraft.

Then as suddenly as they had appeared — the enemy were gone leaving the shattered 94th formation to head for home. At debriefing, the returning combat crews likened the attack to an ambush in the style of the old Wild West, by Indians on a wagon train of Forts — sudden, vicious and deadly.

Wolverine was repaired and put back into combat as *Gin Mill Special* but was finally lost on 18th April 1944

Lorelei: "If you can read this you're too damn close!"

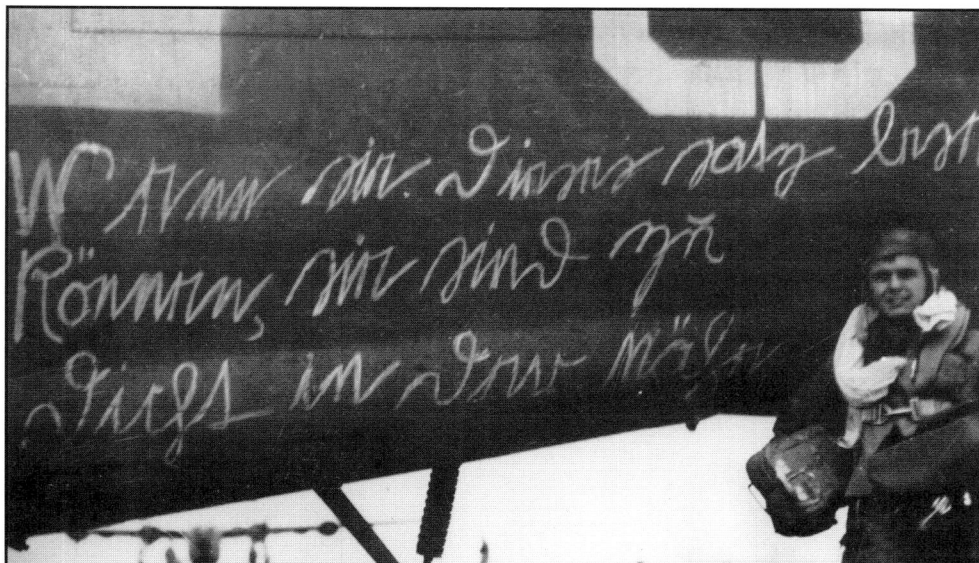

The fuselage of B24 *Lorelei*, which headed towards Berlin on 18th April, had that message chalked on it written in German by gunner Sgt Ed Kobs. Photographed on his safe return, it was Kobs second raid on the city from which his grand parents had emigrated many years before.

Lorelei (41-29300) took its name from a legendary Teutonic maiden who lured men to their deaths by drowning in the Rhine. It proved to be a prophetic title as the plane was ditched into the North Sea returning from Munich on 11th July with the 458BG.

The Road Back led to Stalag Luft

Turning off the target, 303BG's *The Road Back* (42-97552) was hit by flak. Two engines were mangled and their props windmilled as the ship continued along a straight course, away from the formation. Losing altitude the crew desperately jettisoned all the loose equipment they could prise away to lighten the plane. For an hour and a half they struggled on — approached at one stage by an Me109 who flew alongside. To their surprise, on seeing they could offer no resistance the German pilot saluted and flew away.

65km north of Hannover, *The Road Back* came to an end and the battered B17 slid, wheels up, into a field. After attempting to evade as civilians closed in on them, the crew began a long imprisonment at a Stalag Luft POW camp.

Lucky to survive the crashlanding, they were unlucky in that they had been on the final mission of their tour.

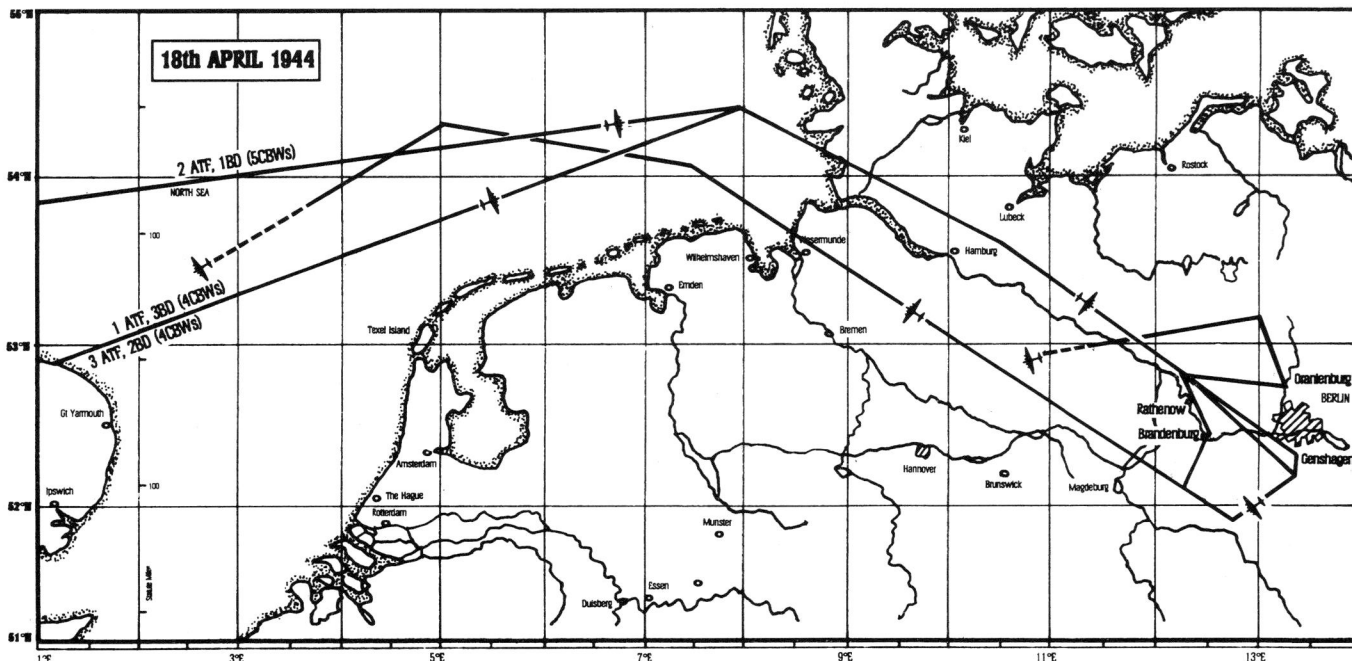

29th April saw twelve combat wings from all three Bomb Divisions launched at the centre of Berlin. The Fortresses of the 3BD led the way over the target and reported no air opposition at all. "Unbelievably, an unopposed raid on Big B", recorded one airman from the formation. The 1BD followed and reported just one minor attack. But one combat wing from the "unopposed" 3BD would suffer a different fate entirely. For in spite of these reports, 27 of the 63 bombers lost were downed by the Luftwaffe's fighters. Other bombers were caught by the intense flak thrown up by the city's defences.

Generally, the German fighters evaded the friendly escorts successfully, refused to engage, and waited for a favourable situation to strike at the bombers. The brunt of the fighter assault fell against the 2nd Division's Liberators who were scheduled as last in the bomber stream.

The heaviest aerial attacks began over Celle on the way in, right up to the IP, and then continued again on the route out. The 2BD, flying behind schedule, reported that up to one hundred German fighters hit them in groups of 10-15, with Fw190s and Me109s roller-coastering through the formations from the rear, then picking off damaged victims who began to lag behind. After bombing, and without escort cover, the Liberators were again subjected to a concentrated attack from another 75-125 fighters between Hanover

Playboy – down and out!

The assigned target for the 466th Bomb Group and the rest of the 2BD was the Friedrichstrasse rail station in the middle of Berlin, the centre of the main rail and underground system networks. One of the group's planes airborne that day was an ageing camouflaged B24H named *Playboy* (41-29399) by its crew. The left nose of the ship was painted with a rendering of Donald Duck in top hat and tails.

The enlisted men on the crew that day had not expected to be flying. They had notched up their 10th mission two days previously and anticipated a respite, freely indulging in the local brew the previous night confident that they could sleep it off in the morning. Their dreams were shattered, however, just three hours after getting to bed when they were woken and told to prepare for day's mission — to Berlin!

Missing both breakfast and the briefing, they arrived at the hardstand to find their pilot, Lt Cotner, ready and waiting to start engines. All went well, as *Playboy* flew the course along with the group, until at the IP a direct hit from 88mm flak smashed the No.3 engine. Lt Cotner feathered the prop and managed to keep his place within the formation. After

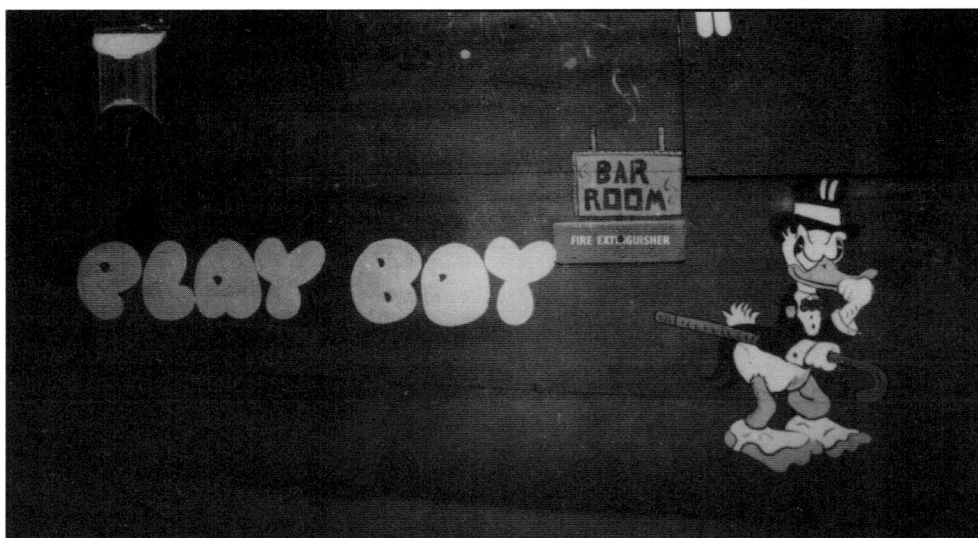

bombing *Playboy* headed for home.

Without their heavy bomb load the other B24s were able to pick up speed but *Playboy* fell further and further behind. Just as the plane filled into a vacant slot in a following B17 group, twenty Fw190s launched an attack. Singling out their victim, five fighters streaked in from the rear to be met by a hail of tracers and armour-piercing bullets from the tail and top turret. In the ensuing seconds, fighters broke away left and right, some streaming flames, others leaving a trail of black greasy smoke. The tail turret on *Playboy* took several direct hits from incoming 20mm shells, plexiglass shattered and

the turret caught fire. The tail gunner sustained injuries and burns, a waist gunner died instantly — shot through the head. The No.2 engine shuddered and seized up as more 20mm walked across the left wing piercing the fuel cells and sending chunks of metal flying back from the cowling. The onslaught was halted only when a flight of Thunderbolts arrived to drive the attackers away.

As fuel drained from holes in the tanks and pipelines, the engineer estimated just 30-40 minutes flying time left. Lt Cotner decided to continue flying towards the coast for as long as possible.

The B24 Liberator was notoriously difficult to ditch into a pitching sea. If

the plane did not break up on impact its high wing format meant that the bulk of the fuselage would quickly submerge making it difficult for any crew to evacuate without loss. It was therefore decided to abandon *Playboy* over land and not ditch into the sea.

At 9000ft the fuel finally ran dry and the crew began to abandon the aircraft. In spite of his injuries the tail gunner managed to bail out, as did all the surviving members of the crew. *Playboy* continued on in a shallow dive, disappeared into cloud and eventually made a soft landing at Daarleveen, narrowly missing a house. There would be no more nights at the pub for the crew for a very long time.

and the Zuider Zee with especially vicious encounters developing over Dummer Lake. Several fighters were reported to have dropped aerial bombs in attempts to break up the bombers' defensive formations. The missiles burst immediately above the bomber boxes and brought down at least two B24s.

While all this went on the 3rd Division was also suffering badly. One of its Combat Wings was 15 minutes early, another more than 20 minutes late, making effective escort cover impossible. 4A CBW's PFF radar equipment failed and the wing lost visual contact with the other formations and also their escorts when they deviated 40 miles south of their planned course, repeating the same error as had occurred on the previous Berlin raid. It was not left unnoticed by the Luftwaffe fighter controllers. Over Magdeburg, several Gruppen launched attacks in waves from nose and tail positions. They vigorously pressed home their assault and the wing lost eighteen bombers cut from two of its groups. Survivors bombed Magdeburg and withdrew.

It proved to be another tough day for the 8th Air Force. In all, 38 B17s and 25 B24s were lost, almost half of them to fighters and eleven to flak, described as intense and accurate at several points along the route. More than 400 of the 8AF's heavy bombers sustained battle damage and two were destroyed in crashes back in England.

"The Luftwaffe will be up to knock the Americans and English out of the sky"
Radio interception by 355FG at 11.30hrs

Over 1400 tons of ordnance fell into the centre of Berlin, mainly in three large concentrations. More than fifty high explosive bombs burst in the immediate vicinity of the Air Ministry building, with at least five direct hits and many near misses which severely damaged almost half of the structure. The Anhalter rail station received a direct hit and Potsdamer station took six strikes on the platforms with a concentration of incendiaries extending west and south into the rail yards. Another concentration spread across the Tempelhof marshalling yards, its main rail lines and warehouses. The third cluster struck Tempelhof airfield facilities as well as the heavily built up areas just west of the field. Gross Beeren marshalling yard 8 miles southwest of Tempelhof was also hit. Other bombs fell into the residential districts of Steglitz, Zehlendorf, Grunewald, Schoneberg and Mariendorf cutting rail tracks, causing considerable damage and starting numerous large fires.

German damage details and casualty statistics could not be located in the Berlin Landesarchiv records.

"... but the enemy refused to engage..."

Sixteen fighter groups from the 8th and four from the 9th Air Force furnished a continuous escort of over 800 Mustangs. Lightnings and Thunderbolts for the bombers, some flying two sorties. In addition, the RAF provided 24 Mustangs for area support. In spite of the considerable numbers of enemy aircraft encountered, especially by those groups guarding the trailing 2BD, only thirteen fighter kills were claimed by escorts from the 8AF, for the loss of six of their own aircraft. Escorting groups from the Ninth Air Force added a further eight to this score but for a loss of seven.

Although escorting the Fortresses of the 1BD, Lightnings from 364FG became embroiled in the combat over Steinhuder Lake when two groups of Fw190s and Me109s savaged the right hand box of B24s from the 2BD.

Twenty-five enemy aircraft swept in from the north while at the same time another fifty attacked from head on into the bomber boxes. After the first attack the German fighters broke off into small groups of 3-4 aircraft, seeking out stragglers. Fuel shortage forced the 364FG to break off contact but not before one of their P38s had spiralled down. Later, two others collided in mid-air north of Brunswick. The 364th claimed two victory kills as a compensation for their losses.

354FG (9AF) was also engaged in a running battle to protect the B24s over Gardelegen and they too lost three of their number but claimed six enemy destroyed. Both 55FG and 361FG were unable to locate the Liberators they were assigned to protect. However, two squadrons of the latter group did

encounter two Me109s and destroyed them both before turning back at the limit of their endurance. The majority of the 55FG suffered mechanical problems and were forced to turn back for England.

Escorting the 3BD to the target, 352FG engaged three formations of German fighters and destroyed two for no loss. 355FG was engaged in several encounters, first just prior to the target with a small group of Focke Wulfs, then scattering 75+ fighters which roller-coastered towards the bombers. After the target, 25 Me109s were driven off near Brunswick as the group continued along the bomber path even after the escort had been broken. The result of this long running melee was one Mustang lost for a claim of one Me109 destroyed.

20FG also escorting the 1st Task Force, observed

three groups of enemy fighters, totalling some 150 aircraft, west of Berlin, but the enemy refused to engage and remained at 30,000ft. Except for eight fighters which made a single diving pass at the group.

Ground strafing runs by 4FG aircraft left five German planes burning as well as a number of damaged locomotives spewing steam and smoke into the sky. P47s from 359FG also enjoyed a field day when they strafed the rail yards at Hannover, claiming 13 locomotives destroyed and another six damaged. One FW190 was also claimed by them over Gehrden after it made a pass at the bombers. 362FG destroyed two Me410s on the ground at an airfield east of Gardelegen but saw no airborne enemy at all.

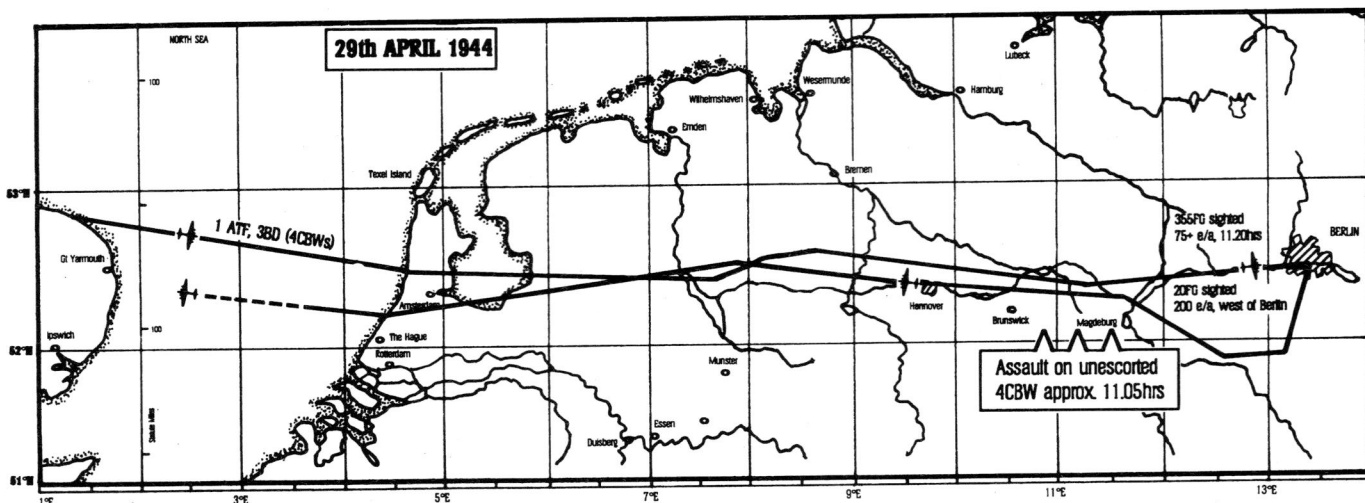

29th APRIL 1944

1 ATF, 3BD (4CBWs)

355FG sighted 75+ e/a, 11.20hrs

20FG sighted 200 e/a, west of Berlin

Assault on unescorted 4CBW approx. 11.05hrs

Suicidal onslaught takes out eleven 447BG Forts

The 447BG was also caught in the aggressive attacks made on the isolated 4CBW. Its A Group lost five planes to fighters, flak claimed a sixth; B Group lost four more and another ditched into the North Sea. The group lead navigator's report gave a graphic account of the disaster that overtook them.

".... the Group Commander decided on a 360° turn to pick up the Wing. At the conclusion of the turn we were south of course and about one minute behind the wing leader. During the climb toward the enemy coast, the 447th formation became rather ragged.... Intermittently, flak was encountered throughout the penetration. The Wing PFF made a false start at the IP about 10.50hrs..... at about 11.00hrs, the formation was subjected to heavy fighter attacks. A force of about 100 to 120 single engined fighters, mostly 109's attacked with ferocity and persistence. They came head on through the formation taking three bombers in their first pass. The attack continued for 35 to 40 minutes. The attackers, however, relented after the first two major attacks; attacking four or eight at a time. During the fighter attack, and with intense flak at the same time, the

formation became scattered. At about 11.20hrs a left turn.... took us out of the battle area. At 11.30hrs, the remaining bombs of the 447BG 'A' were dropped after a 20 second run on an unidentified village.... Somewhat confusing information from PFF caused more difficulty."

A PR report issued later quoted the more personal viewpoints of

An unidentified 447BG Fortress caught by the camera gun of an attacking FW190 from IV/JG3 on 29th April. (S Markz)

"He caught on fire almost immediately but still kept coming on, intent on ramming us... he hit our transmitter cable as he went by."
Extract from press release, T/Sgt John Urdia, 447BG

gunners on one of the 447BG Forts. "The flak was pretty rough but nothing compared to the fighters that were to come. There were about sixty of them in the first wave," recorded engineer T/Sgt John Urdia. "They were mostly Me109s but there were a few Fw190s to add to the fun. They flew, for about ten minutes, parallel to our formation before they pressed home their attack. About ten of them lined up on our right wing, and started to peel off. I put my sights on one and started to blast away with all I had. He caught on fire almost immediately but he still kept coming on, intent on ramming us.... he hit our transmitter cable as he

went by. The ball gunner also shot down one plane"

The two Fortresses on either side of their lead plane were shot down in this first pass. With barely time to catch their breath, a second, even larger force struck the formation. "Our right waist gunner accounted for the third fighter of the day for our crew," continued Sgt Urdia. Then an attacker came in at 2 o'clock high after having sent another B17 tumbling downward, was caught by fire from the tail guns and exploded. Sgt Minton commented, "...he peeled off in front of me, 75 yards away, I started shooting.... First his tail flew off, half a second later the entire

plane blew up and went down in a stream of fire."

But the crew had not finished there. As a third attack swept through, the navigator and bombardier each added another fighter and raised the total to six. In the same attack, Urdia put a burst into the belly of another Me109 and sent it too down in flames. By this time the Fort was the only survivor of the high squadron and pilot 1Lt Gibbons joined the lead squadron for a little extra security. Still the enemy fighters came on, diving through their own flak in near-suicidal attempts to further break up the shattered formation.

In a fourth and final attack, the plane's right waist gunner claimed his second victory of the day bringing the crew's total to eight. Riddled with holes from flak and gunfire, the Fort hauled them safely back to Rattlesden.

One of the first to be hit when the fighters raced through the formation was Hayden Hughes crew in the un-named 42-31144 flying in the high squadron's #4 position. It was knocked out of the formation by the onslaught and subjected to continued attacks until last seen diving into cloud with No.2 engine smoking. There was only one survivor after the airplane crashed at Destedt, 8km from Konigslutter.

Also flying in the high squadron, as #7, was Edgar Farrell's 42-102479. Hit by flak just as they turned onto the bomb run and then by the fighters, it went down almost immediately trailing flames from the left wing. Only a single chute was observed but six men on their third mission safely exited the stricken plane before it exploded in mid-air at 11.35hrs showering wreckage over a wide area. The German salvage report at the crash site near Grasleben, 4km from the perimeter of the airbase at Helmstedt, noted "aircraft exploded in mid air... 100% destruction. Unknown writing on the pilot's turret: *Mississippi Lady*."

Crashing nearby was another B17 shot out of the high squadron, Charles Dowler's 42-102421. 20mm fire from the fighters had slammed into the cockpit, started a fire and almost certainly killed both pilots instantly. Other cannon shells shredded the tail section of the plane as it went out of control. The right waist gunner, Kenneth Shrimp, was the only man fortunate enough to survive and he later recorded, "About 10 minutes from the target our plane was attacked by enemy fighters. The left waist gunner was hit in the forehead by a 20mm shell and fell to the floor. Then I was hit by flak and I think the plane was hit in the right wing at the same

time. When I came to, I was sitting on the floor of the plane putting on my parachute. Then I passed out.... when I came to again, I was in a German car riding down a road with four German guards around me."

About 14km north of Helmstedt, at Eickendorf, another 447BG victim plunged to the ground. William Davidson's 42-31124 had also been caught in the attack about 10 minutes prior to the target. The top turret gunner was hit and the crew bailed out. According to German records, all survived except for the injured man whose chute did not open. Survivors were greeted by a hostile crowd and suffered beatings and abuse before being taken into military custody.

So many aircraft crashed into the vicinity of Helmstedt and Magdeburg that the German authorities had great difficulty in establishing accurate records for individual crews. The report for aircraft 42-31217 reads "26km west of Magdeburg. 1130 hrs.... 25 captured from different crashes." Another report, on 42-37866, recorded "43 recovered alive..."

Harold Paris's ship, 217, had been flying as #4 in the lead squadron but the fighter attack had started a fire in the left wing and forced him to peel away from the formation. 45 seconds later the plane was thought to have exploded before any anyone exited from it. However, all the crew did succeed in bailing out, although several were injured, and all were rounded up by the Germany military when they came down near Eggenstedt. "We were all out of the ship when it blew up, south of Berlin," recorded one of the crew later. "Hanley (tail gunner) was wounded very badly in the throat, stomach and

legs and damaged his throat with his chute. But the Gestapo Police threw him in a truck and knocked me out. Took me to a flak battery. I saw Lt Marcy's crew of ship *Hey Mable!*, they were all OK but some wounded... seen crew of B17 *Dear Mom* from 709th... can't remember the pilot's name."

Flying off Paris's wing was 1Lt Warren Donahue in 42-37866, in the #5 slot. It too caught fire at once and fell out of the formation to explode soon after. The ball turret was hit and the gunner caught by cannon shells before he could escape. "I don't think he had time to get out ... I had just cleared the plane when it exploded," recorded one survivor. The vertical stabiliser and tail section was also severely damaged by the fighter attack and the tail gunner was the other fatality on the crew. Waist gunner Norbert Arvin later reported, "We were several miles off course. About 4 or 5 minutes from the target. It (the plane) was in a million pieces all around where I landed..." The million pieces had showered down around Abbenrode, 10km west of Koenigslutter.

More fortunate was the crew of Arthur Peper, also brought down in the vicinity of Magdeburg. All survived when their ship came down northeast of Zerbst. They were rounded up by civilian police within an hour or two.

Hey Mabel! (42-97135) had its radio room and tail wheel blown out by Focke Wulf cannon fire. The No.1 engine burst into flame and shells exploded through the nose section. Charles Marcy slid the plane out of the formation and went into an almost vertical dive with a column of flame and smoke streaming back from two engines and the left wing, close to the fuselage. At

about 15,000ft he levelled off and chutes began to pop out from below the plane. Marcy had been hit in the right hand and lost two fingers shot away, suffered burns to the face and a splinter wound in the leg. Copilot, Jesse Kendler later recorded, "Because of the fire in the nose and flight deck the radio man, ball gunner, tail and both waist gunners bailed out just after the ship was hit. This was in the Magdeburg/Halle area. We managed to extinguish the fire and attempted to reach Sweden. However, we broke out of the clouds over Berlin at 7000ft and were caught in an intense flak barrage."

Another of those shot out of the lead squadron was the #5 ship, 42-97501. The No.3 engine was completely blasted away from its mounting and an uncontrollable fire created a blow torch through the flight deck and consumed parachutes, leaving many with no hope of escape. Only one man, engineer Joseph Kotulak survived the attack which came from below the ship. "I believe the aircraft blew up immediately after I left..." German reports confirm that the explosion occurred in mid air and the wreckage came down 3km northwest of Weferlingen, near Helmstedt.

Not all of those caught in the devastating fighter attack went down. Other planes, battered and shattered, struggled on to complete the mission. One final victim was 42-31519 which made it as far as the Channel before being forced to ditch into the sea. Fortunately for the crew of ten they were picked up safely by a launch from No.24 Air Sea Rescue Unit based at Gorleston and subsequently returned to Rattlesden. One hundred 447BG air crew would not return that day, 33 men would never return at all.

29th APRIL 1944

A rough ride in for Wendling's Libs....

As the combat wings from the trailing 2BD passed over Celle on the route in to the target they were subjected to considerable flak before receiving a vicious attack from the Luftwaffe fighters assembled in the area. One of the first to be hit was 392BG's *Double Trouble* (42-100100), named after the airplane serial number. Flak splinters ripped into the ship and it swung left out of the formation and turned for home. It had been lucky to survive a fighter assault less than three weeks earlier when cannon shells set it ablaze and also set off the alarm bell, causing the two men in the nose to bail out. The fire was extinguished on that occasion and *Double Trouble* made it home. Now it was caught in another deadly attack as the fighters came in, double line-abreast, to make a level pass through the group.

An instant after the bombardier called "60 enemy planes at 12 o'clock!" he was struck by a 20mm shell which completely demolished the nose turret. Other hits slammed home and the crew immediately began

tumbling from the doomed Liberator. The pilot, Gerald Rogers, was seen making his way towards the bomb bay to bail out but he never made it. A few minutes after 11 o'clock, *Double Trouble* crashed into a deer enclosure 17km south west of Celle.

As the fighters screamed through the formation at 11.02hrs another 392BG plane (42-110062) took hits and veered sharply to the right — slamming directly into the wing man and losing its tail assembly as a result. "The bail out bell rang at almost the same instant the ship jinked into a spin..." recorded one survivor. "Just before I bailed out I took a last look at my pilot and copilot. They were at their positions struggling with the control columns," stated another. The remnants of the B24 went into a steep dive, out of control and on fire until it crashed near Marklendorf. Incredibly half of the crew clawed their way out of the plane as it powered down, and some of them evaded capture for three days. Five bodies were found in or near the wreckage.

The other unfortunate plane caught in the mid air

collision over Enschede was 42-100371 with William Kamenitsy's crew. Part of its left wing was torn away by the impact and it started down, still under control. 23km north of Hannover, near Meitze, Kamenitsy succeeded in bellying the damaged plane in.

The crew of a fourth 392BG Liberator shot out of the formation by the first attack was not so lucky. It fell away from the group with the right elevator badly shot up and also crashed not far from Meitze with the loss of the entire crew.

Many other ships in the B24 formation also suffered damage but stayed in the air and struggled on to the target. Believed to have been caught by flak over Berlin, 41-28759 peeled away soon

after. Lt Fred Shere and his copilot held the plane steady while the crew bailed out. But before they themselves could clear the ship, the tail assembly broke away and it plunged into the ground near Nortrupp close to the Dutch border.

Bert Wyatt managed to get *El Lobo* (42-7510) as far as the North Sea but was forced to ditch before reaching England. Air Sea Rescue succeeded in plucking all of the crew from the inhospitable waters.

The 392BG had despatched 18 planes from Wendling on the mission, one third of that number failed to return. But their misery was not over and they would lose two more before the day was through. 2Lt J Reed's plane had also been caught in that first fighter attack and badly damaged. Although successful in getting the ship back over England it could not be landed and the crew were ordered to abandon it. All did so safely except Reed who was thought to have struck the aircraft as he left and was killed. Then, just when everyone thought the slaughter was finally ended for the day, another 392BG plane exploded while in the landing pattern. Eight B24s from the group were struck off the inventory, six more returned badly damaged. More importantly, 61 men were dead, missing or destined to be prisoners.

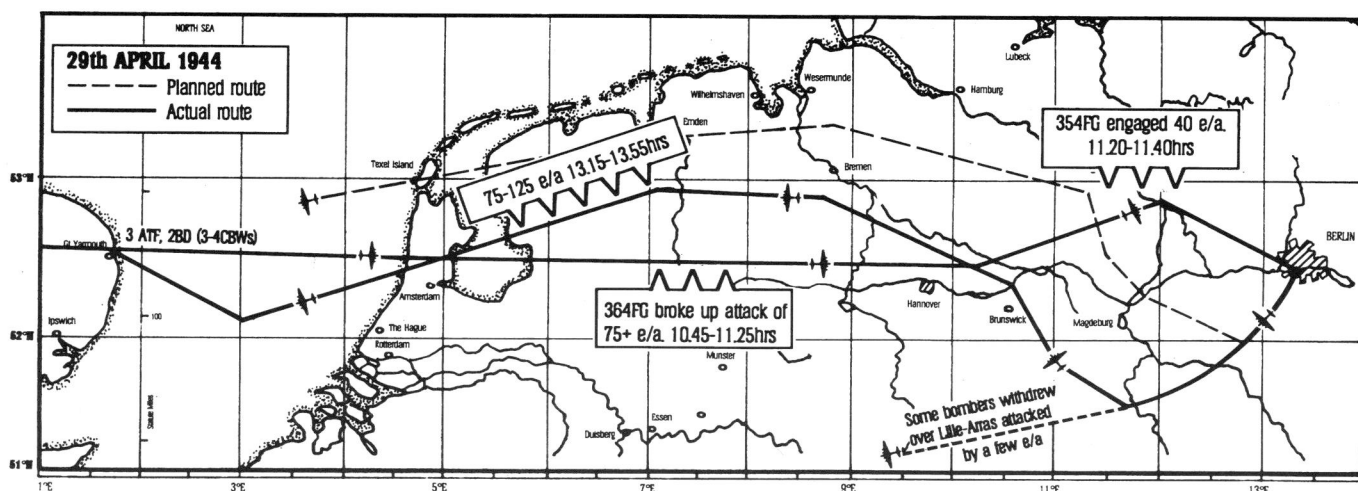

29th APRIL 1944
- - - - Planned route
———— Actual route

75-125 e/a 13.15-13.55hrs

3 ATF, 2BD (3-4CBWs)

364FG broke up attack of
75+ e/a. 10.45-11.25hrs

354FG engaged 40 e/a.
11.20-11.40hrs

Some bombers withdrew
over Lille-Arras attacked
by a few e/a

... and a rough ride home for Seething's 448BG

When the Luftwaffe fighters struck near Dummer Lake and roller-coastered through the returning combat boxes of the 2BD, the 448BG lost several of their Liberators.

Sweet Sioux (42-7683) was about 45 miles east of Dummer Lake when it was hit by fighters. The plane had been one of the 448BG's original complement but it was seen to go into a near vertical dive before disappearing into clouds at 15,000ft. Ralph Meiga, waist gunner, later wrote "We were returning from the mission over Berlin. Near Vechta we were under attack from several FW190s and the fight continued for 10-20 minutes... A 20mm shell hit our plane about one foot from me, I was wounded and knocked unconscious. When I came to, the aircraft was going down." All the crew were captured except for the pilot William Rogers who may have been murdered by civilians.

Also caught by the fighters east of Dummer Lake, near Neinburg, was *The Sad Sack* (42-99988). 20mm cannon fire set one engine ablaze and a direct hit below the cockpit started a fire on the flight deck. The pilot, William Pouge, is thought to have been killed in the attack along with two others in the nose. Two more crew members in the rear of the ship were also wounded. Henry Maynard was in the waist and, as the ship tumbled out of control, was forced to adopt an unorthodox means of exit. He later recorded, "The first time anyone knew that something was wrong with the aircraft was when it peeled away from the formation... looked out of side window and saw front end of the ship on fire... grabbed my chute, opened it, pushed it out the side window and was dragged out of the aircraft." The top turret gunner was less fortunate. Standing in the bomb bay ready to jump, he became entangled in the interior and was dragged to his death. The nose gunner had no chance to escape. As a result of a faulty door catch, he had been sealed into his tiny compartment with a twist of wire before the plane had even taken off. Only three of the crew survived.

An un-named B24 (42-52435) also went into a steep dive after the waist gunner had been killed by fire from fighters. The navigator, Lt Joseph Kwederis, stated later that "the bombardier, F/O Carlson, bailed out in excellent condition, he was not wounded at the time of jumping. He was however found by us about half an hour later in the company of Wehrmacht soldiers. At this time we discovered he had been shot at close range... and was nearly unconscious, losing much blood. In talking to the co-pilot, Carlson told him that he had been shot by a German soldier for no apparent reason. However, it is believed that he was trying to evade the enemy." The German report of the incident simply states "4km west of Elbergen, Lingen-Ems, Carlson — dead, shot while trying to escape."

Miss Happ (41-29523) was also caught by head on attacks which pumped 20mm cannon fire into the plane killing the nose turret gunner. The survivors abandoned the plane near Minden.

Another of those hit was *Chubby Champ* (42-7655). Fighters attacked from the rear and, on the first pass, hit two men in Jim Clark's crew. Further attacks sent the battered Liberator into a spin which trapped five men in a tumbling tomb. The remainder struggled through the nose wheel door to escape. Top turret gunner Manuel Cabellero later recorded, "We bailed out at 4000ft. I watched the ship go down in a spin.... When I hit the ground.... I started off towards where the ship had crashed thinking some of the crew might get thrown out by the explosion... but the Germans had me in no time and wouldn't let me go to where the plane was burning." He, and four survivors, had come down at Weldeschousen-Estorup near Oldenburg.

A sixth 448BG ship, whose crew had never had time to paint on their selected title of *Big Bad Wolf*, was also brought down — not by the fighters but by flak. Orland Howard, the pilot, recorded later, "We had three engines shot out by flak, the nose turret was badly damaged... pieces of flak went through the flight deck and tail turret.... right stabiliser damaged." The hydraulic system was also shot out and the plane fell at a rate of 600ft per minute until stabilised by the pilots. Over Poulsker island off Denmark, the crew tumbled out through the bomb bay and waist escape hatch. Six men were successfully spirited away to Sweden by the underground.

"... grabbed my chute, opened it, pushed it out the side window and was dragged out of the aircraft."

29th APRIL 1944

> "Rows of ten and twelve Me109's weaved through our formation in head on, do-or-die attacks in a seemingly endless stream. And a lot of them died.... but they took a lot of Forts with them too. I've never seen the sky filled with so much confusion – exploding planes, flying debris, white and brown parachutes, bursting flak, exploding shells – it was fantastic but horribly real to us up there." Extract from Press Release: 1Lt Richard A Spencer, 385BG pilot

A 100th-mission nightmare en route for Berlin

The 385BG, flying its one hundredth mission, led the 4CBW away from their briefed course on the route in, reportedly attempting to avoid the prop wash of a preceding Wing. PFF equipment also failed and the lead crew, on loan to the 385BG, became disorientated and missed the IP — disaster ensued.

Jim McDonald, the 385BG's leader, recalled the circumstances which led to the catastrophe. "The first mickey squadron was activated in the 1BD area and we were instructed to send our best crews because these would be our leaders. We did. But many others sent crews with no lead crew training or experience.... Two crews arrived at 04.30hrs to lead us. It didn't take long for me to evaluate them but what could we do?"

"My mickey (radar) equipment went out nearing the coast," continued Jim McDonald. "I took the No.2 position and relinquished the lead... I became an observer and also became increasingly uneasy. We made a turn about 10 minutes too early (with sixty other planes depending on us). I called

the lead and asked why — no explanation. I asked our navigator — he couldn't reply... he didn't know where we were. We had, by mistake, left the bomber stream and our protective fighters."

Isolated from other formations, the Wing soon experienced intense fighter attacks. Unable to hit the primary target they headed for Magdeburg. At about 11.05hrs the Wing was struck by 150-200 enemy fighters, described by many surviving crews as "looking brand new." Rockets and 20mm fire was used in an aggressive assault which lasted about twenty minutes.

The fighters followed the formation, high and to the right, pulled in front, peeled off and attacked from dead ahead in waves of 15-20 aircraft using the position of the sun to great advantage. The initial onslaught opened up the defensive boxes, coming in so close that Forts were forced to take avoiding action. Between the mass attacks, two Me109s slow rolled through the formation but were cut to pieces and went down. Several crews later

reported that the enemy's formations resembled a B-17 formation. Luftwaffe fighters came in as three or five ship elements which cut through the 385th, coming out and under the following group.

The 385BG lost seven of their planes and seventy men, their compatriots from the 447BG suffered even greater losses totalling eleven aircraft.

The first two 385BG ships left the formation with engines burning about 16 miles west of Magdeburg. Soon after, another left with one

engine burning and a second feathered, making a series of 'S' turns before bursting into flame. Another pulled out into a slow spiral with No.4 engine windmilling; one minute later a fifth victim dived away with a badly damaged tail. Two other Forts went down over the city of Magdeburg, one with 20mm hits in the wings and another exploding in mid air.

The losses had not been all one sided, the 385BG alone claimed nineteen fighters destroyed. Richard Spencer's crew from the 385th were lucky to survive the slaughter and they spoke about their traumatic experience when they returned to Great Ashfield. In a press release issued later, Spencer commented, "The Luftwaffe's fighters were so thick and so close to us

today that I feel sure that if I had a .45 calibre automatic up there with me I could have picked off a Jerry myself!" When the attack began Spencer, and his co-pilot Don McNeeley, threw their Fort into evasive action making the task of the gunners on board even more difficult. In spite of the bucking and rolling which ensued as the pilots desperately tried to avoid the incoming fire, the plane's gunners still lodged claims for six aircraft destroyed. Don McNeeley added, "The first sign that we had of fighters was when the whole attacking force hit us at once. Sixty Me109s and FW190s suddenly loomed up dead in front of us, and for a moment I sat there amazed as they seemed to come from nowhere. I thought for a moment that I was seeing

> "The 100th Mission Party that evening was a very low-key affair – the group had lost 70 men that day going to Berlin!" Jerry Ramaker, ball gunner *Wells Cargo* (42-31778), 385BG

things, but when they started to blaze away at us I knew that it was no nightmare."

As the first wave of fighters roared in the bombardier opened fire, "I just singled him out, pressed the triggers long and hard and watched one wing fly off and the rest of the ship explode immediately. For a while it looked as though he was going to hit us, but fortunately he blew up in time." Another Me109 fighter came up underneath the main wings of the Fortress but the right waist gunner tracked it and watched it explode into a brilliant flash of crimson flame.

The ball turret gunner, Marvin Baird, claimed two more in quick succession. "I saw an Me109 coming from the nose and not more than 10ft below my

385BG Fortresses stream dense vapour trails through the rarified atmosphere over Germany (J Ramaker)

turret. I cut one wing off close to the fuselage. He fell like a rock. The second plane came the same way, only not quite so close — his wing came off and he spun crazily towards the ground."

As the Fort bucked and weaved through the incoming waves of fighters, trying to remain in formation, the top turret gunner T/Sgt Kushner was almost caught off-guard. "Just as the ship suddenly put its nose down a Nazi fighter came into my sights. I was a little surprised momentarily but let him have a rather long burst with both guns and the next thing I knew the entire plane was enveloped in flame and going straight down." The left waist gunner caught a sixth fighter as it flew along parallel to the Fortress about 1500 yards out to one side.

When the attack subsided, Lt Spencer's Fort was in a sorry state. 20mm shells and machine gun bullets had riddled the plane and shot out both rudder cables, the right wing was like a sieve and No.3 engine was damaged. In spite of the damage, they were able to keep up with the formation and its vital protection. Other damaged and straggling Forts were being picked off by the ever watchful Luftwaffe.

Back over Great Ashfield, the Fort circled the field while the gunners desperately spliced together the severed rudder cables using wires stripped from gun charging handles. Their efforts were rewarded and the pilots brought the battered ship down for a perfect landing.

(Right)
A 452BG Fortress passes over central Berlin on 29th April 1944. Several parked German aircraft, stationed at Tempelhof airfield, can be seen on the ground just off the starboard wing. (Mark Samson)

55

29th APRIL 1944

The Germans took a different view – monitored by the BBC

KM 37. : BERLIN RAID   = BOMBERS TOOK THE DANGEROUS STRAIGHT ROAD =
GERMAN TELEGRAPH SERVICE (DNB HOME) 13.47 30.4.44   (EXTRACTS)
BERLIN : WHEN AT NOON ON SATURDAY THE SIRENS WAILED OVER BERLIN, AND A LITTLE LATER SINGLE GROUPS OF US GANGSTERS
AIRCRAFT APPEARED OVER THE CAPITAL TO DROP THEIR TERROR BOMBS AIMLESSLY ON A WIDE-SPREAD RESIDENTIAL AREA OF THE
CITY, THE OPERATIONS ROOM OF THE GERMAN AIR DEFENCES HAD BEEN WORKING AT A HIGH PITCH FOR A LONG TIME.
        = NO FEINT ATTACKS POSSIBLE OWING TO LENGTH OF TIME FOR ASSEMBLY =
IT WAS QUITE CLEAR THAT THE AMERICANS ORIGINALLY HAD NO INTENTION OF APPEARING OVER THE TARGET AREA IN SUCH SMALL
AND DISPERSED FORMATIONS, BECAUSE AT THE BEGINNING OF THE OPERATION IT TOOK THEM ALMOST TWO HOURS OF VALUABLE TIME
– VALUABLE IN VIEW OF THE EXPENDITURE OF FUEL – TO ASSEMBLE THEIR FORMATIONS OVER BRITAIN AFTER THEIR START FROM
THE VARIOUS AIRFIELDS. THIS ASSEMBLING COST THE ENEMY GESCHWADERS SO MUCH OF THE TACTICAL SCOPE OF THEIR OPERATION
THAT, CONTRARY TO THEIR HABITS ON EARLIER OCCASIONS, THEY HAD TO DO WITHOUT DECEPTIVE MANOEUVRES AND FEINT ATTACKS
ON OTHER TARGETS, SETTING OUT ON THE DANGEROUS ROAD TO BERLIN ON A STRAIGHT AND RIGID EASTERLY COURSE.
        = MURDEROUS MAGIC OF BERLIN'S A.A. FIRE =
AS THEY REACHED THE BERLIN BARRAGE, THE BOMBERS WERE RECEIVED BY HIGHLY CONCENTRATED A.A. FIRE. IN THE WORDS OF
RETURNING U.S. CREWS.... THE GERMANS MUST HAVE PUT "AN A.A. GUN ON BERLIN'S EVERY ROAD AND HOUSE" – SO MURDEROUS
WAS BERLIN'S MAGIC OF FIRE.
        = FRESH FIGHTERS TO ESCORT RETURNING BOMBERS =
NOR WAS THERE A PAUSE IN THE SAVAGE AIR BATTLE WHEN THE ENEMY FLEW HOME.... BADLY MAULED, THE RETURN FLIGHT OF THE
U.S. FORMATIONS TURNED INTO A ROUT OF A SMASHED AIR ARMADA. FRESH LONG DISTANCE FIGHTERS, IT IS TRUE, HAD MEANWHILE
APPEARED ON THE SCENE TO ESCORT BACK THE BOMBERS. BUT ONCE AGAIN THE MUSTANGS, THUNDERBOLTS AND LIGHTNINGS WERE
SEPARATED FROM THE BOMBERS AND THE CREWS OF THE HEAVIES FACED MORE ATTACKS FROM FOCKE-WULFS AND MESSERSCHMIDTS.
        (BBC MONITORING)   +++++   = 17.31   +++++   30.4.GEH.R +

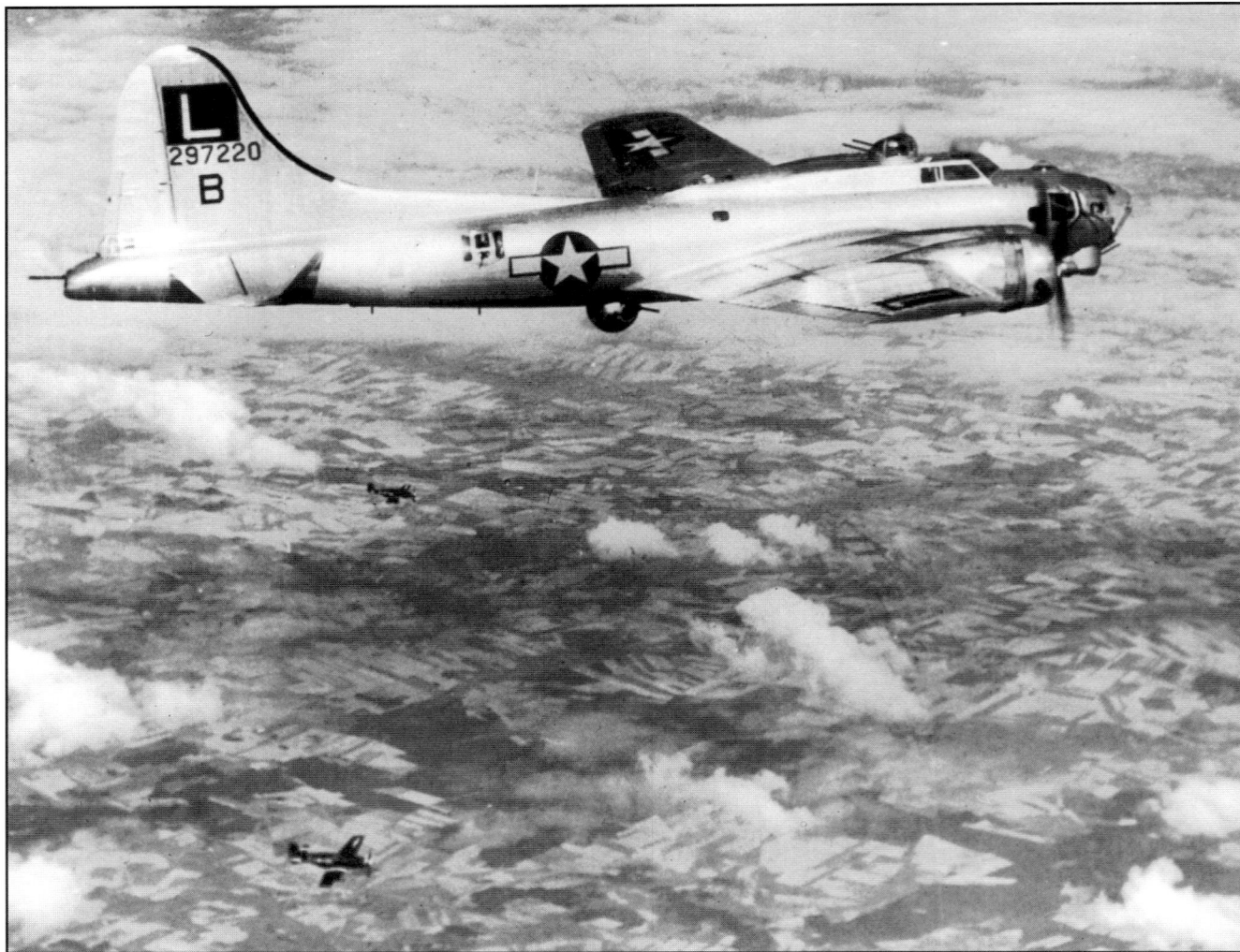

452BG's *Kickapoo Joy Juice* (42-97220) takes comfort from two escorting Mustangs as it struggles back towards Deopham Green on 29th April 1944. A few days later, on 8th May, it was back over Berlin but this time it would not return. Hit by 20mm shells from FW190s, the left wing caught fire and blazed towards the No.2 engine. Lt Morehouse peeled away and went into a vertical dive. All ten men on board survived the ordeal and parachuted to safety south of Braunschweig. (USAF)

GERMAN TELEGRAPH SERVICE (DNB EUROPEAN)   10.03   30.4.44

BERLIN : THE I.I.B. LUFTWAFFE CORRESPONDENT, SURVEYING YESTERDAY'S OPERATIONS BY U.S. BOMBER FORMATIONS OVER REICH TERRITORY EXPLAINS WHY THE ENEMY HAD SUCH HIGH LOSSES IN FOUR-ENGINE BOMBERS.

EXTRACTS..... THE TACTICS USED BY THE AMERICANS SHOWED NO NEW ELEMENTS, AND RELIED ON A VERY STRONG FIGHTER ESCORT. THE U.S. COMBAT-BOX FORMATIONS PENETRATED ON AN EASTERLY COURSE TOWARDS THE CENTRAL ELBE, COMING IN FROM NORTHWEST IN SEVERAL WAVES. BEFORE THEM CAME SWARMS OF LONG-DISTANCE FIGHTERS WHOSE ASSIGNMENT WAS OBVIOUSLY TO OPEN THE WAY FOR THE FOUR-ENGINE BOMBERS.

= GERMAN FIGHTERS' PINCER ATTACK AS BOMBERS REDUCE SPEED TO CLOSE UP =

ON THEIR WAY IN THE U.S. BOMBER WAVE WERE ATTACKED WEST OF THE ELBE BY A LARGE NUMBER OF GERMAN FIGHTERS WHICH ENGAGED THEM ALMOST SIMULTANEOUSLY FROM VARIOUS SIDES. THE GERMANS SENT UP ONE OR TWO ENGINED FIGHTERS IN FORMATIONS OF VARYING STRENGTH WHICH ATTACKED THE BOMBER WAVES IN A BIG PINCER MOVEMENT WHEN THE FOREMOST ENEMY COMBAT-BOX FORMATIONS HAD REDUCED THEIR SPEED TO CLOSE UP AND THUS INCREASE THEIR DEFENSIVE POWER.

= ONE OF THE BIGGEST AIR BATTLES EVER FOUGHT =

THE BATTLE WAS TURNED WHEN THE GERMAN FIGHTER FORMATIONS BROKE THROUGH THE U.S. FIGHTER SCREEN FROM SEVERAL SIDES, MAKING DIRECT ATTACKS ON THE FOUR-ENGINE BOMBERS. THE BOEINGS AND LIBERATORS ATTEMPTED TO PUT UP A WALL OF FIRE AROUND THEM BY THEIR MANY HUNDREDS OF GUNS, BUT WERE UNABLE TO STOP THE FURIOUS ONSLAUGHT OF THE GERMAN FIGHTERS. A GREAT MANY U.S.FOUR-ENGINE BOMBERS PERISHED IN ONE OF THE BIGGEST AIR BATTLES EVER TO BE FOUGHT OVER CENTRAL GERMANY.

= U.S. FIGHTERS INFERIOR TO MESSERSCHMIDTS AND FOCKE-WULFS =

THE BATTLE WAS ALL THE MORE DISASTROUS TO THE ENEMY, AS THE U.S. LONG-DISTANCE FIGHTERS DID NOT SUCCEED IN WRESTING BACK AIR SUPERIORITY WHICH THEY LOST TO THE VERY FIRST GERMAN FIGHTER ATTACK. DESPITE THEIR LARGE NUMBERS, MUSTANGS, THUNDERBOLTS AND LIGHTNINGS SHOWED THEMSELVES INFERIOR TO THE MESSERSCHMIDTS AND FOCKE-WULFS.

= BOMBER FORMATIONS FORCED TO REGROUP OWING TO HEAVY LOSSES =

SEVERAL COMBAT-BOX FORMATIONS LOST SO MANY AIRCRAFT IN THIS BATTLE OVER THE ELBE THAT THE SURVIVORS HAD TO DRAW CLOSER TOGETHER TO FORM A NEW FORMATION CAPABLE OF OFFERING RESISTANCE. SOME DAMAGED BOEINGS LEFT THEIR FORMATIONS TO FLY AWAY ON A NORTHERLY COURSE. IN MOST CASES THEY WERE TOO BADLY DAMAGED TO REACH SWEDISH TERRITORY.

= GERMANS MAKE FLANK ATTACKS ON RETURNING BOMBERS =

ON THEIR RETURN FLIGHT THE ENEMY WAS STILL SET UPON BY THE GERMAN FIGHTER GESCHWADERS, WHICH ATTACKED THEM IN VIGOROUS AND SUDDEN FLANK THRUSTS. THERE WAS NOT A MOMENT OF RESPITE FOR THE CREWS OF THE FOUR-ENGINE AIRCRAFT. BEING IN DIRE DAMAGE THEMSELVES THEY HAD TO WITNESS AIRCRAFT AFTER AIRCRAFT BEING SHOT DOWN FROM AMONG THEIR OWN FORMATIONS. AND HOW THE CREWS OF THE CRASHING AIRCRAFT TRIED TO SAVE THEMSELVES AT THE LAST MINUTE WITH THEIR PARACHUTES. BUT IT IS ALREADY CERTAIN THAT ONLY A FEW DID, IN FACT, SAVE THEMSELVES WHILE IN MOST CASES THEIR FATE OVERTOOK THEM.

= EACH FORMATION HAS TO FEND FOR ITSELF DUE TO FIGHTER PROTECTION FAILURE =

ANY ORDER AMONG THE BOMBER FORMATIONS WAS VISIBLY SHAKEN FROM THE MOMENT WHEN THE BIG AIR BATTLE OVER THE ELBE BEGAN, AND WAS INCREASINGLY DISSOLVED AS THEY FLEW ON. THEIR FLIGHT BACK GAVE THE IMPRESSION THAT EACH U.S. COMBAT-BOX FORMATION WAS TRYING TO RUN THE GAUNTLET OF THE GERMAN DEFENCES ON ITS OWN, AS THE LONG-RANGE FIGHTERS HAD PROVED SUCH FAILURES.

= NUMEROUS BOMBERS FORCED TO ABANDON COURSE =

A NUMBER OF THE ATTACKING WAVES HAD TO ABANDON THE COURSE TO BERLIN AT AN EARLY STAGE, AND HAD JETTISONED THEIR BOMBS, HARD PRESSED AS THEY WERE BY THE GERMAN FIGHTERS AND A.A. FIRE.

=500 BOMBERS PENETRATED TO BERLIN — 25% DESTROYED =

ACCORDING TO SUPPLEMENTARY REPORTS NOW AVAILABLE SCARCELY MORE THAN 500 U.S. BOMBERS PENETRATED TO BERLIN. AT LEAST 25% OF THEM HAVE BEEN DESTROYED. IT MAY BE ASSUMED THAT MANY OF THE DAMAGED BOMBERS, WHICH AT FIRST REMAINED IN THE FORMATIONS ON THE WAY BACK, CRASHED LATER.   (BBC MONITORING) +++ 12.55 ++++ 39.4 ++++ MS (O)

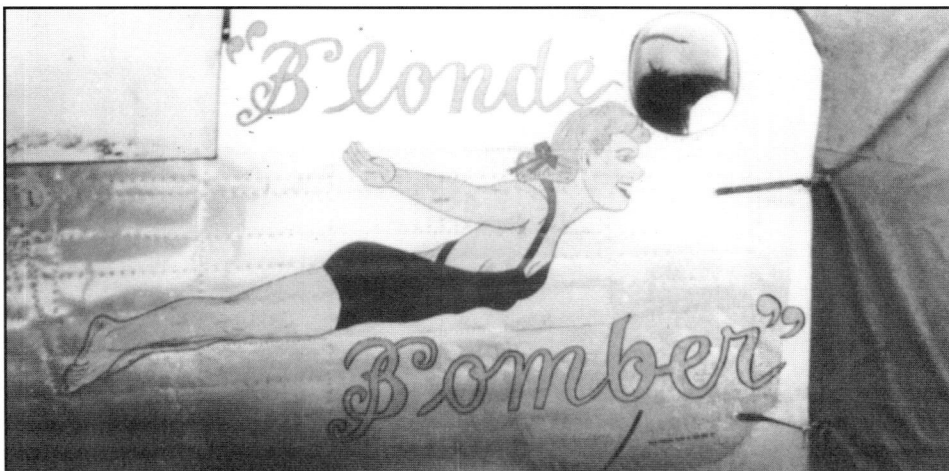

Blonde Bomber (41-28730) was one of three B24 Liberators from Rackheath's 467BG that were lost on 29th April. Four of the crew were unable to get out of the plane before it crashed into the ground near Essel, 30km from Hannover. Five survivors were caught almost immediately but the tail gunner John Angus managed to evade for five days before being cornered by a farmer near Rotenburg.

The mission to strike the German capital on the 4th May was recalled less than one hour from Berlin when formations encountered clouds towering up to 23,000ft. However, on 7th May forces comprising of 17 combat wings, escorted by 20 groups of fighters and four squadrons of RAF Mustangs were dispatched to attack Berlin, Munster, Osnabruck, and rail yards at Liege.

Berlin was the primary target for twelve combat wings of Fortresses of the 1st and 3rd Bomb Division, escorted by twelve fighter groups while an additional three groups carried out area sweeps. One escort group failed to rendezvous with the bombers but German air opposition was remarkably weak anyway and only a handful of fighters were seen, in the vicinity of Berlin. There were no fighter claims logged for the day's activities.

Intense and accurate flak proved to be the primary defence for Berlin, cutting four bombers from the formations and damaging 265 other B17s. Four more were lost to unknown causes.

Almost complete cloud cover obscured Berlin at 10.34 in the morning when it was attacked but it had been anticipated and PFF radar aircraft placed markers to guide the attacking force of 600 Fortresses.

Six combat wings from the 1st Bomb Division unloaded almost 700 tons of ordnance through the cloud with unobserved results. A second force of six

A flying Dutchman hedge-hops home in *Cabin in the Sky*

It was not their regular ship, it was more usually flown by the crew of Capt Robert Brown, but the necessity of war and the need to get every available crew in every available plane saw Melvin Van Houten's crew climbing aboard 390BG's *Cabin in the Sky* (42-30338) on 7th May. The plane was a true veteran and had been named by Brown during its trans-Atlantic crossing, no doubt his crew had watched the MGM movie of that title before leaving for England. In addition to the nose art, his crew had also added "She'll fight the fighters, storm and flak — thru it all Lord, bring her back." Van Houten would have good reason to be grateful for that prayer.

As *Cabin in the Sky* turned onto the IP, accurate flak sent splinters slicing through the oil lines to No.2 engine. At the same time the No.3 supercharger failed, forcing the pilots to pull their plane out of the protection of the tight defensive box. Although the No.3 engine still had good oil pressure the damaged supercharger meant it offered no power. The No.2 engine, on the other hand, had drastically reduced oil pressure but with careful handling could be induced to provide some of the desperately needed power

to keep the plane flying. The bomb load was jettisoned and the pilots kept a constant eye on the pressure gauges, wary that a sudden loss of pressure would force feathering of the prop and leave them with just the two outboard engines to get home.

The oxygen system also began to fail and Van Houten found himself with little choice but to 'hit the deck' and go it alone. Plummeting from 25,000ft to just fifteen hundred in a matter of minutes caused the cockpit windows to frost over completely leaving the pilots to rely solely on their instruments. As they approached ground zero the side windows were forced open, so as to give a better appreciation of where they were. After an immense

struggle both pilots pulled the plane out of its dive, levelled off and called for a heading for home. The windows cleared and suddenly the faulty supercharger roared into life again.

Alone and highly vulnerable, *Cabin in the Sky* dropped to even lower altitude, skimming the tree tops. The ball turret gunner scrambled from his position in case the plane should unexpectedly strike the ground. Skimming over open fields and pulling up to clear tree lines proved to be highly exhilarating for the crew, like a long distance buzz job so frowned upon when performed back in England.

For three and a half hours they roared across the landscape scaring the

hell out of all who had the misfortune to cross their path. Trains, flak positions and airfields received a peppering of machine gun fire in the few moments available as the aircraft raced past. Rarely did the enemy have a chance to return the fire, they were gone in a flash. Crossing a canal and sighting flak barges, the gunners opened up but his time they did take incoming fire and 20mm shells ripped through oxygen lines, control cables and shattered the radio. The ball turret gunner, who had left his position for safety, was hit with a massive wound. Medics would later remove splinters, rivets, radio parts and pieces of wood from his back.

A sudden loss of trim

combat wings followed and added another 545 tons onto unobserved targets in city areas.

Air crews and cameras above the cloud cover could not see where the bombs had fallen across the city. In the Mitte district, heavy casualties and extensive damage had been inflicted by high explosive bombs, especially south of the river Spree. The Reich Chancellery, Air Ministry and Interior Ministry buildings had taken hits. Rail stations of Friedrichstrasse and Stettiner were damaged as were buildings of the Propaganda Ministry, the University, State Library and a police headquarters. But so too were a number of hospital buildings.

The rail station, town hall and fire station were all

damaged in Prenzlauerberg to the northeast. The district of Horst Wesel sustained heavy casualties and damage to the town hall, fire station and Strausberger subway station as well as a hospital. Police and fire headquarters in Kreuzberg were hit. Weissensee and Pankow also received concentrations of high explosive bombs which took a heavy loss of life, falling across residential areas.

> "It was completely uneventful except for flak over the city. We didn't even see one enemy aircraft and had no opposition when we dropped our bombs."
> PRO Extract, Major Richard Cole, 303BG low group leader

Uneventful escort

caused the plane to plummet towards the ground and into a tree line. The force of the impact slowed it and gave the pilots the few moments they needed to recover from the plunge. As they steadied the plane, crew men became aware of foliage sprouting from the engine cowling but *Cabin in the Sky* just kept on flying. As they skimmed low over the Zuider Zee a wave of water followed them. Approaching the last barrier to freedom, more German flak opened up and churned up the water all around. Two fighters appeared and the crew felt sure that now they were doomed. The aircraft, however, were American and escorted them back safely to England.

Firing red flares to ensure medics would be available to tend their wounded man, the pilots finally lowered the plane down, fearful that their hair-raising ride would have damaged the undercarriage or burst the tyres. It had not and they were home!

Ground crew later removed broken plexiglass and water from the ball turret, replaced the plexinose and battered cowlings, refitted leading edges on the wings, patched the holes and put the plane back in service.

Five fighter groups escorted the first bomber force of Fortresses from the 1BD. Two groups, 56A and 56B, also carried out supporting fighter sweeps in search of the enemy. The escort was uneventful and no enemy aircraft were observed. 364FG had 21 of their Lightnings abort in the terrible weather for various reasons and one failed to return. 339FG also lost one of their Mustang pilots, to flak over Sulinger, and another plane had to be salvaged after returning early with engine trouble. It spun in near the base and the pilot bailed out.

Fighter groups accompanying the second force from 3BD faired no better, although 20FG did report sighting five Me109s near Bremen. These were in the process of attacking a lone P38, aborting from escorting the first force. It was a 364FG plane and the pilot Lt Stepman later bailed out over the sea and was lost. Two groups, 55FG and 356FG, failed to rendezvous with the bombers and saw neither friend nor foe. Both, however, lost a plane. The 55FG Lightning caught fire and ditched into the sea where the pilot was rescued; the 356FG Thunderbolt was hit by flak from Bremen, the pilot bailed out near Lingen.

357FG also failed to

Boeing Belle – home and dry

"Arose 0200 and in a clear sky the group dispatched 36 planes to Berlin. Got a little flak in ship — ran low on oxygen.... Lost one of the engines, pulled out of formation ... When enemy aircraft was sighted, we pulled close to the group for protection. Using a lot of gasoline with three engines, we were concerned about our gas supply. Returned to our base downwind, firing red flares for right of way. The other planes that were circling for landing

had to circle around again. When we landed, a second engine ran out of gasoline. Colonel Jeffrey came to our plane and asked about the wounded because of firing red flares. We said we were running short of fuel. He called for a gasoline truck to fill the tanks to check how much we had left. Twenty-eight gallons and most of it in the tanks to the dead engine!"
Diary extract, Bob Stachel, tail gunner, 100BG's *Boeing Belle* (42-39867)

rendezvous with the bomber formations and the entire group had to make do with escorting a single 305BG Fortress as it straggled home. Pilots from 361FG also spotted a lone Fort and reported "B17, 1BD, triangle J — heavy flak damage to tail, two engines feathered, going down jettisoning equipment. 13.01, Rheine, 12000ft." This was the sole loss from 351BG flown by

Robert Presley's crew and nicknamed as "Ronchi" (42-37714). They had been hit by flak approaching the target and in spite of their valiant efforts to save their plane, were forced to abandon it. The plane was a combat veteran, having joined the group in November 1943, but the crew were on their first mission. They survived their ordeal and became prisoners of war.

> "I would hate to have to bail out over Berlin during one of our bombing attacks.
> I fear the survival rate for these unfortunates must be slim indeed.
> I have noted that the navigators and tail gunners are usually the first to leave the stricken bomber. Our Chaplains are always at combat briefings."
>
> Diary extract, Abel Dolim, navigator 94BG's *Frenesi* (42-39775)

Ragged but Right – battered but lucky !

Lil Abner's Daisy Mae sheds a tear on the nose art of 385BG's *Ragged but Right* (42-97790) but she had a lucky escape over Berlin on 7th May when hit by a 500lb bomb dropped from another Fortress flying above. Battered and bent, the plane made it safely back to Great Ashfield. (R. Dennis)

Flak! The Devil's cauldron – unavoidable, ever present

May 7th proved to be the least costly raid made upon Berlin by the 8th Air Force during 1944. Eight Fortresses were lost from the force which totalled 600 aircraft despatched. Four of these losses were known to be as a direct result of flak and a further 265 returned to England requiring various degrees of repair as a result of the ever-present German anti-aircraft defences.

Every effort was made during the planning stages of each mission to route the bomber stream away from areas known to be heavily defended by flak. But there was no way across northwest Europe which could avoid it completely and every major target was ringed by increasing numbers of radar guided 88mm, 105mm and 128mm gun batteries. In an attempt to continually keep track of this defensive network, Intelligence officers were keen to extract every bit of information from the returning crews with regard to the location, intensity and accuracy of flak they had encountered, en route and over their targets.

The following is an extract taken from the 100BG's Form 4 addressed to the A-2 Section of 4th Bomb Wing describing flak conditions encountered on 7th May:

"About 50 bursts of unseen controlled flak to right from Ijmuiden was seen on route in. From there to Dummer Lake area no flak was seen. In Dummer Lake area meagre flak was put up from several places on both sides of the route, of which one place at 0946 probably near Dummer Lake was accurate and used shells described as large bursts which burst with a brilliant yellow instead of the usual red flash. At the same time as the Dummer Lake area flak, heavy distant barrages were noted to right and left probably over Osnabruck and Bremen. Flak meagre unseen was reported at Neinburg. From there to target no flak was seen. At the target the cloud cover had a very few small holes in it, and it is possible that some seen flak was used. Continuous pointed fire, probably unseen, together with predicted concentrations of from 20 to 50 shells, a predicted barrage and ordinary

barrage methods were all seen at the target. The flak was mostly inaccurate with only an occasional accurate salvo. Most of the bursts were low. Some ground rockets were also used. On the route back heavy accurate fire using continuous pointed methods through the undercast was encountered at Brandenburg and again over the Dummer Lake area....."

The result of all this anti-aircraft fire on the 100BG was serious damage to three Fortresses and lesser damage to another two. The three seriously damaged planes included *Shining Hour* (42-107011) which took a jagged chunk of flak through the left side.

Stringers were chopped out and the radio room door braces and tab cables were badly damaged before the splinter exited through the right side. There were other holes and skin damage elsewhere but the ground crew had the plane back in the air two days later for its next raid.

Another of those badly damaged was *Rosie's Riviters* (42-31504) which took splinters through its #1 oil tank requiring it to be changed. Five days later that plane would be lost to a direct flak hit which took out two engines. The group's third serious flak victim was an un-named ship (42-31903) which received a large hole through its left horizontal stabilizer and several others in the fuselage.

```
INTELLIGENCE ANNEX TO FIELD ORDER NO. 220
   BOTH THE PRIMARY AND SECONDARY TARGETS ARE A
PART OF THE CURRENT PROGRAM TO DISRUPT THE GERMAN
TRANSPORTATION FACILITIES SERVING THE WESTERN
FRONT. THE PRINCIPAL OBJECTIVE IS TO DAMAGE OR
DESTROY AS MANY OF THE ENEMY'S LOCOMOTIVES AND AS
MUCH OF HIS LOCOMOTIVE SERVICING FACILITIES AS
POSSIBLE, THE MPIS HAVE BEEN SELECTED WITH THAT IN
VIEW. THE ENEMY'S CURRENT SUPPLY OF OPERATIONAL
LOCOMOTIVES IS CRITICALLY LOW AND FURTHER DAMAGE
NOW WILL ADD TO HIS TRANSPORTATION HEADACHES WHEN
THE CRITICAL PERIOD ARRIVES.....
       - - - LE MAY - - -
```

Blues in the Night ends with a blinding flash

Thomas Morrison was the bombardier on 2Lt Smith's fledgling 379BG crew. For their first combat mission the crew had been unlucky and had drawn Berlin. Climbing aboard *Blues in the Night*, a veteran plane of some 35 missions, Morrison noted that the plane "seemed to be in fair condition". About two hours out, however, No.1 engine developed trouble.

Smith did not alert the crew but pressed on. Some time later, they ran into flak which knocked out No.2 engine causing the ship to lag behind the formation. Having struggled to regain a position in the formation, Lt Smith deemed it better

to press on with the group and benefit from their protection rather than abort and return alone. Unable to keep up when the group climbed to bombing altitude, the bombs were jettisoned short of the target but *Blues in the Night* continued to lose altitude.

Morrison was ordered to the waist to prepare the crew for a crash landing or quick bail out. His later report continued, "I stationed the men around the main escape hatch and pulled the emergency release on the door. We never saw the ground during this time as we had entered the overcast which was very thick. We flew

through the overcast for some time, losing altitude. The plane then went out of control.. Just before this, I noticed that No.3 engine was shooting heavy flames. From this time on I don't remember just what happened except that there was a blinding flash... I woke on the ground with two men dragging me away from a fire which I later learned was our

plane. The two men were German soldiers..."

The German report stated ".... (4 engine) type Boeing, crashed 11.00hrs... about half way between Ziggelmark and Wittenberg near Hagenau.... crashed with nose into the ground, exploded and burned completely." Morrison was the only survivor from the crew of nine.

".... over Dummer Lake I saw a number of contrails coming in at us, but they broke off and jumped a bunch of B24s behind us in the next CBW. One I know exploded, because I can recall the main tanks burning as they fell to the ground. Sorry! But better them than me."
Diary extract, Earl Dahlgren, waist gunner 92BG

A formation of B17s steers straight for the Devil's cauldron. Up ahead the concentrated flak barrage has already caught one victim (USNARP)

The 8AF's operational order for 8th May assigned 500 Fortresses to attack Berlin, flying as nine combat wings. The B24s from 2nd Bomb Division were aimed at Brunswick and massed more than 300 aircraft in four combat wings for that attack.

Heavy cloud obscured Berlin city as the bombers passed over and bombardiers had to rely on smoke markers placed by the accompanying PFF radar ships.

Escorts reported that the capital itself was not strongly defended in the air but some 200 German fighters massed in the Hanover area. More aggressive than of late, they savaged the Forts.

Equipment failures and losses reduced the number of B17s over the target to 386 aircraft but they managed to drop 852 tons of general purpose and incendiary bombs and toss out a quarter of a million leaflets into the dense cloud cover below. Most of the guiding PFF equipment worked well but 45CBW experienced serious problems and did not reach Berlin at all.

In fact, for the 45CBW the mission was to prove to be a disaster. The combat wing had been scheduled to fly in the centre of the 3rd bomb Division but arrived over Germany some 12 minutes ahead of the rest of the formation. The consequence was a huge aerial traffic jam as the 45CBW became disrupted by the B24 formations over Dummer Lake. As had

Little Boy Blue cheats Fate at 50+

One of the combat veterans that set out for Berlin on 8th May was the 388th's second oldest plane, *Little Boy Blue* (42-30851). It had flown its 50th sortie the previous day, also to Berlin. On board flying their twelfth mission was the crew of Lt Arthur Pohl.

Waist gunner, Byron Cook, noted in his diary: "There was a heavy undercast all the way over the continent. As we approached Brunswick, the PFF on our wing lead ship went out so it was decided that we would drop on the smoke markers of the Liberators which had preceded us, instead of continuing on to Berlin. Just before reaching the markers, we were bounced by a band of fifty or sixty FW190s and Me109s. They were very aggressive in their tactics, attacking through heavy bursts of their own flak.

"All the attacks on the 388BG were from the nose. The skirmish lasted 40 minutes during which 18 bombers were shot out of our Division. One was a plane that we had been originally scheduled to fly. However, Pohl traded planes with Lt Pittman, so that we could fly in our *Little Boy Blue* — Pittman's assigned ship for the mission. As a consequence it was assumed that we had gone down in the other Fort.

"*Little Boy Blue* fought back like a dandy, however, and Babicky, Hay, Bleem and myself all put in claims for FW190s destroyed! Eventually our P51s showed up and chased the rest of the fighters away.... Upon landing, everyone greeted

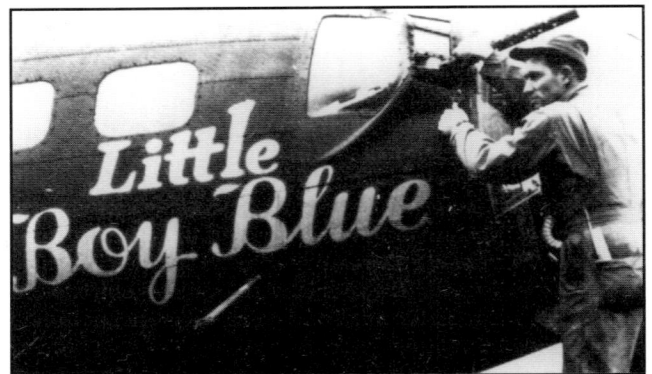

us with amazement, for we were presumed lost! In fact, for a week afterwards, I kept running into my old buddies who thought they were seeing a ghost!"

"... after the IP, two planes in the high group touched wings, shearing off some from each plane. One fell off to our right, the other to our left... I was watching the copilot in the plane flying off our left, I could see him squeezing his oxygen mask to crack the ice out of it... a B17 inverted and struck the plane's #3 and #4 engines. The inverted plane broke in half at the ball turret, like breaking a cracker in two, both started down. No fighters or flak in the area at the time, just mid-air..." Earl Dahlgren, gunner, 92BG

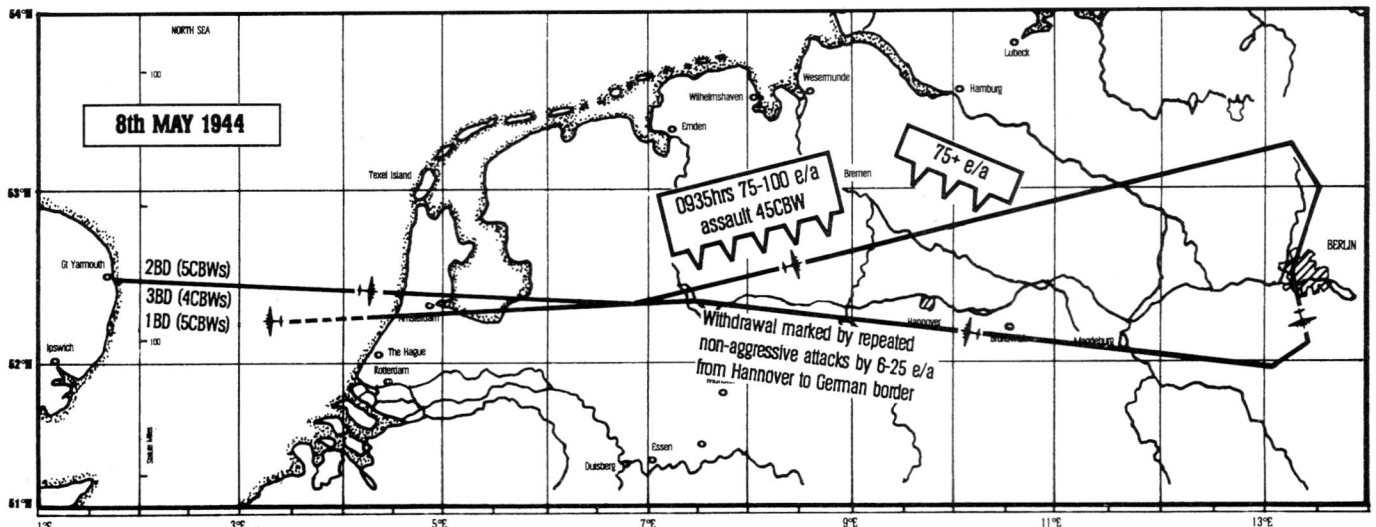

happened two months earlier, the exposed wing was savaged when the 96BG became detached from the main force — a situation the Luftwaffe fully exploited! 45CBW bombed Brunswick and withdrew.

The Berlin force lost 15 bombers to fighter attacks and only one was brought down by flak even though it was described as moderate to intense and accurate. Nine more were lost to accident or unknown causes.

German records reveal damage over a wide area with the Wedding, Tiergarten, Mitte, Lichtenberg and Horst Wesel districts particularly severely damaged. The Stettiner, Guter and Tiergarten rail stations were all hit. In Treptow a direct hit on an air raid shelter killed 60 people and the tram depot was completely devastated by three direct hits. Subway stations and a military school were also struck. Lichtenberg gas works was 80% destroyed.

> "... at a distance of about 20 miles, a huge explosion was seen at 20,000ft. Upon closer observation, a B17 formation was picked up in the vicinity of Steinhuder Lake with Me109s and Fw190s making head-on attacks."
> Encounter Report, Col Gabreski, 56FG

Wells Cargo hit by the 'Little men'

"8th May — It was a long haul," recalled Jerry Ramaker, ball turret gunner on 385BG's *Wells Cargo* (42-31778). "For the first time ol' #778 needed the full runway... we kept eating it up. Big fuel load, big bomb load that day and the ammo boxes were full to the brim. We pulled up 50ft off the ground and sucked up the main gear right away, opened up the cowl flaps and just hung there clawing for altitude. We formed up in the dark and it was a scary time, all you could see was exhaust flames all around.

"We got a lot of flak once we had crossed the enemy coast and were into Germany. A dazzling display of those 'little men' — that's what we called the 88mm and 105mm flak bursts on account of the way it looked when it exploded — like a head and shoulders with its arms and body just hanging below. We lost a crew that day... saw seven chutes before the aircraft fell into a cloud bank below. It was always a sickening feeling to see a '17 lose an engine

and dive straight down into the ground.

"After bombing, we turned away and left the flak behind us but were hit by fighters. We beat them off but they hit B24s flying behind and they slaughtered them! Lots of explosions in the sky. When we got back we were all dog-tired and just lay on our bunks listening to Axis Sally on the radio — it was all propaganda but they played great American music"

Jerry Ramaker would return to Berlin twice more, on 24th May and again on 21st June, both times flying in *Wells Cargo*. His crew had been assigned to the plane after their first mission, to Hamm, on 22nd April and named it after their pilot, Lt Charles Wells and the famous Wild West stage coach company of Wells Fargo. The B17G had originally been delivered to the USAAF back on 18th December 1943 after rolling off the line at Boeing, Seattle. "The crew had an idea of painting a stage coach with wings instead of horses," recalled

The fighter battle

Three hundred and twenty Mustangs, 268 Thunderbolts and 190 Lightning fighters escorted the bomber force, drawn from seventeen 8th Fighter Command groups and three 9th Air Force groups. Strong opposition was encountered more than 125 Luftwaffe fighters marshalled in the Hanover-Brunswick area. A further force of 60 enemy fighters was encountered during the withdrawal stages of the operation. Over Berlin itself, however, little aerial opposition was found.

The 357FG escorted the 3BD through the target area and encountered twenty German planes near Ulzen, downing two but losing two of their own. The 354FG claimed four fighter kills in combat south of Dummer and Steinhuder Lakes for the loss of a single Mustang. They also successfully dispersed another group as it prepared to attack the bomber stream, but without further losses to either side.

Escorting the 1BD , the

56FG overwhelmed a large force of the enemy and shot down six with the loss of just one of their Thunderbolts. The 361st intervened to assist bombers of the 3BD under attack, shot down three but not before three Forts had gone down.

Lightnings from the 364FG also swept to the rescue of three B17s under attack from ten fighters. Two bombers went down but in a running battle which stretched from 26,000ft right down to the deck, the P38s claimed six of the enemy for the loss of three of their own.

The remaining escort groups fought effective actions in keeping other raiders at bay and away from the bomber boxes. Strafing attacks also added seven locomotives destroyed and two more damaged. One 357FG pilot returning alone, on the deck, discovered several large oil tanks and poured a withering stream of fire into them — only to see his bullets bounce off harmlessly from their armoured shells.

Jerry, "but we only got as far the name, painted in a Disney-style — red on a yellow back-ground. We also had our jackets painted likewise by a guy on the base"

The crew's combat tour in *Wells Cargo* also took them to many tough targets including Hamm, Hanover, Augsburg and Zwickau. Charles Wells earned the DFC and later commented about his plane to an local newspaper, "*Wells Cargo*

always brought us back and, like its predecessor Wells Fargo, carried and delivered the goods successfully." The Wells crew finished their combat tour in late June 1944 and returned to the States — *Wells Cargo* soldiered on for another full year before returning to Bradley Field on 24th June 1945. In December of that year, the plane was finally despatched to the smelters furnace at Kingman, Arizona.

> "I picked an Me109 and followed in pursuit.... I was unable to close for about 10 minutes.... indicating 370-375mph. Finally the Hun throttled back and I pulled up within 200 yards of the plane.... one short burst and the plane went up in flames.... Me109 rolled over and hit the ground."
> ENCOUNTER REPORT, Col Gabreski, 56FG

Arthur Mack smiles down from the cockpit of *Four Leaf Clover*, he survived four missions to Berlin in this plane but its fifth raid on the city was its last and it went down with another crew on board. (A. Mack)

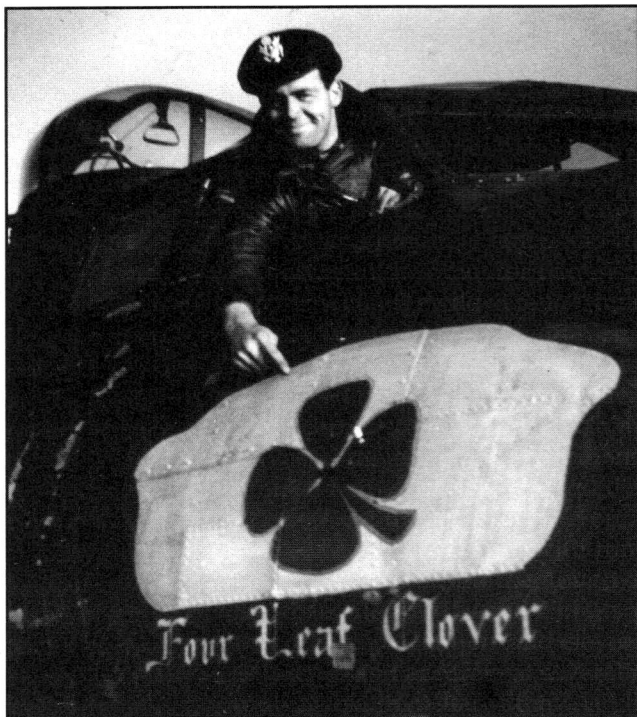

Nature as deadly as any foe

The 306th Bomb Group lost five of their Fortresses on 8th May, one ditched in the cold waters off Sweden after leaving the formation just before the IP with an engine failure. Its crew was interned. Another went down from unknown causes after falling behind north of Nienburg, all on board perished.

The biggest loss came from a single terrible incident brought about not by the Luftwaffe or mechanical failure but by Nature. Massive air turbulence caused by prop wash created an unseen force which, combined with the tight defensive formations which the bombers had to maintain, was to cost the group three planes and 30 men.

Flying over Wittstock, northwest of Berlin, a 92BG Fortress jettisoned its load and rose up through the formation of the 306th to disappear into dense contrails above. The result of this unexpected passage up through the formation forced several 306th aircraft to pull out of their positions. In so doing they hit the massive prop wash turbulence of preceding planes. Two ships were thrown together by this overwhelming force.

Eyewitnesses reported seeing that one ship had lost part of its left wing in the resulting collision. "The aircraft seemed to do a circle around the fuselage of Jacob's ship," reported one observer, "knocking the entire tail off the latter aircraft." Another man reported, "It turned over so that two aircraft were back to back and disintegrated, falling onto the wing of another." The severed tail slammed into the right wing of a third Fort, *Four Leaf Clover*, chopping out an entire engine. The sky became a mass of whirling, twisted planes which spilled out their contents of bombs, fuel, guns, ammunition, parachutes — and men! Somehow, four men from the two crews survived the mass destruction to become prisoners of war.

Six times to Berlin and good luck turned to tragedy

The 306th Bomb Group received a new camouflaged B17G (42-37942) on 19th December 1943 and assigned it to their 367th Bomb Squadron. Ten days later, 2Lt Arthur Mack's crew took over the plane. "I was issued the plane on 29th December, I still have the memorandum receipt," recalled Arthur Mack. "My first mission with her was my second trip to Ludwigshaven the next day. My crew decided on the name *Four Leaf Clover* as my wife had sent a clover encased in a clear plastic locket just a few days before."

"The next two missions were flown to Bordeaux and Kiel on 31st December and 5th January. There had been no time to arrange for nose art. On 11th January I was scheduled for my 5th mission, to Halberstadt. Losses were high and the 'Clover' sustained much damage, wounded crew, an engine fire and shot out controls. I landed at Kimbolton in a 'pea-souper' and press photographers were there. The aircraft was photographed and stories written. 22nd January 1944 issue of 'The Sphere' ran a full page of pictures, other London papers covered the story as well as most newspapers back in the States."

One of the millions of people who read the story of *Four Leaf Clover*, was Patricia Perry, a 14-year-old school girl in the USA who had been cultivating four leaf clovers for some time and mailing them to servicemen as good luck charms. "Patricia Perry, whom I never met, sent me ten four leaf clovers, one for each of my crew members.... I returned to my base but *Four Leaf Clover* took several weeks to repair. While at Kimbolton an unknown artist painted the nose art on the right side of the ship. A green clover leaf on a white ground"

Arthur Mack regained his plane in time to strike Frankfurt on 4th February. Other missions followed in quick succession including four of the first five raids on Berlin in early March. After the recalled mission of 3rd March, Arthur wrote in his diary, "Got ten miles inland and called back. Got credit for the mission. One tail gun, both waist guns, radio operator's gun and chin turret guns froze out of action." Three days later he wrote, "Berlin — heavy and accurate flak en route and over target. No fighters. Hit overcast east of Berlin. Target ball bearing plant covered — hit suburb of Hohenschoenhausen. B17 hit in tail on way out by flak — wing with engines whirling fell like a rock". Then on the 8th March, "Berlin — little flak en route. Bombed visually. Destroyed ball bearing works. Fighter escort good, saw Berlin for first time — immense. Milk Run." The following day, "Milk Run again! Bombed PFF overcast over continent. Flak low and behind over target. Threw chaff out to deflect AA gunners."

Arthur Mack set out for Berlin twice more, but on those occasions he did not fly in his *Four Leaf Clover*. His luck held but the 'Clover's' did not. The plane's fifth raid to Berlin on 22nd March resulted in severe battle damage for the crew who took the ship that day. More extensive repairs were needed and yet another crew climbed aboard on 8th May to take *Four Leaf Clover* back to Berlin for the sixth time. Caught by tumbling debris from other colliding planes its luck finally ran out.

Slaughter at 10 o'clock – for ten Falcons in just ten minutes

On 8th May the 96BG, known as the Snetterton Falcons, was experimenting with a smaller 14 ship box formation. In theory the smaller box still yielded the same bombing pattern but to the ever-watchful Luftwaffe pilots it simply showed up as being a smaller, therefore less well defended, formation. The combination of this and their precarious position when they became detached from the main formation, brought about by the appalling snarl up over Dummer Lake, was to cost them dearly.

In the aerial traffic jam over Dummer Lake, the B24 formations pulled back a little but continued to fly parallel to the 96th's 'A' and 'B' boxes. This prevented them from returning to their assigned position in the bomber stream. The 96BG was severely exposed and carnage followed. The sequence of the losses is difficult to establish and group records state, "First attack came at 09.55hrs knocking down approximately five aircraft; second attack coming at 10.05hrs and knocking down five

more. Chutes were seen but could not be identified to any particular aircraft..."

Thirty to forty German fighters struck from dead ahead and out of the sun, holding their fire until they were almost on top of the bombers. Other attackers dropped parachute bombs into the formation and succeeded in striking at least one Fortress.

Burning and crippled aircraft soon filled the skies. One B17, *Reluctant Dragon* (42-38133), had its entire nose section blown away and almost stalled out but still managed to limp back to land at Snetterton Heath. Only three survivors were still aboard when it landed. Six had bailed out over Germany and another had died at his guns from cannon fire in the midst of the attack by the FW190s. After the left stabilizer was shot away, pilot 2Lt Jerry Musser wrestled with the plane's controls as it plummeted 10,000ft before getting it back under control. Together with his copilot and engineer, Musser then nursed the plane back to England.

Another Fort (42-97782)

was hit by 20mm cannon fire and rammed by the incoming V/JG3 Staffelfuhrer's FW190. The ball turret was blown away but the lucky gunner had just left his position to get more ammunition. As the crew leapt from the blazing wreck it exploded into fragments. A lead Fort was also hit in the attack. It was 42-97631 with 2Lt John White's crew on board together with Major Shoemaker in the copilot's seat. They had taken over the lead position of the 'A' Group after the designated lead ship aborted. Hit in the first pass by the fighters, one engine on White's plane caught fire immediately. Several attempts to extinguish the fire failed, even a control-

mission with the 96BG was the crew of Flight Officer Leo Green. Their ship, *Smilin' Thru* (42-102444) was also another of those caught in the vicious German attacks. The tail gunner, Sgt Harry Shirley, sustained bullet wounds in both of his feet but stayed with his guns as the rest of the crew bailed out from the blazing plane. This heroic act was brought to an abrupt end only when *Smilin' Thru* exploded in mid air and blew him clear. Parachuting down, Sgt Shirley became entangled helplessly in a tree until cut down by German soldiers. His bravery cost him several toes and a spell in a German hospital.

Laura Jane (42-38062)

"We could hear the 45CBW leader cursing the B24s for being too fast and ahead of their schedule. The B24 leader responded that we were too slow and late!"

---

led dive refused to blow out the flames. A second pass by the fighters brought an order to abandon ship but it exploded as the crew were leaving, blowing several men clear.

Captain Milton's Fort (42-39998), leading the 'B' Group, was also damaged and forced to peel away from the formation. It crashed near Clappenburg but all survived.

Other B17s were hit in the onslaught and fell from the shattered formation. 42-102482 went into a steep dive with its No.2 engine and the left wing burning furiously. Although injured, the pilot Lt Harold Eye maintained control of the plane and attempted a crash landing near Wolfenbuttel. It cost him his life, and that of his copilot. James Fitzpatrick's 42-38190 exploded within seconds during the first attack and only one man survived.

Flying their sixth

had its tail fin and stabilizer shot to pieces by the fighters as they raced past. Five chutes emerged from the plane as it descended still, amazingly, under control. Pilot Frank King refused to abandon the plane because the remaining crew still on board were wounded. Bellying the plane in near Ostenholz saved their lives but lost Lt King a leg in the crashlanding when he was catapulted from the wreck.

Between the two fighter attacks, thirteen 96th Fortresses from the 'A' and 'B' groups bombed the Brunswick area with the B24 formations and began the withdrawal. When the skies had finally cleared, ten 96BG aircraft and their crews had gone. The 96th Bomb Group had suffered 40% of the 8AF's losses for the day. One third of the B17s they had fielded for the mission did not return to Snetterton Heath. Forty-three men from the group were dead.

Three quarters of a Flying Fort

"It was just as though a hacksaw had cut off the tail assembly..... We were about half an hour from the target. Someone called out, "Flak to our left", I swung my turret around in time to see a Fort catch a direct hit behind the waist guns. The whole tail assembly went hurtling off into space. The plane immediately went into a nose dive, plunging 7,000ft, pulled out, came up into a bank, fell over on its back and started down again — this time disappearing through the clouds. We thought he had crashed, but after a couple of minutes our waist

gunners called on the interphone they could see through a cloud break and the wounded Fort was still flying.... from the job I saw him doing with just three-quarters of his ship, I wouldn't be surprised if somebody tells me he landed down OK. It was difficult keeping our eyes on the plane because the tail assembly was fluttering down like a falling leaf. It disappeared through clouds several minutes after our last glimpse of the stricken ship."

Press Release statement by DAVID ARMSTRONG, 91BG, Engineer on *Outhouse Mouse* (42-31636)

Eleven combat wings in two forces struck the heart of Berlin — 588 B17s in all. A third force of 300 B24s was also sent to strike Brunswick. Cloud, haze and heavy contrails caused difficulties during assembly and some formations were up to 45 minutes behind schedule on leaving the English coast. The 3BD made a 360° turn to get above the cirrus cloud and 4CBW, for example, lost their low group and part of the high group flying through the persistent contrails. 45CBW had two aircraft collide during the assembly. Moderate to heavy cloud over the Berlin area made it necessary to use PFF bombing techniques although several groups did find breaks in the cloud cover to bomb visually.

Luftwaffe controllers concentrated two large 200-strong formations of fighters west of Berlin and Brunswick but effective escort and support diverted much of their effort away from the bomber stream. In all 28 heavy bombers were lost, with the heaviest fighter opposition being encountered by the B24 formations heading for Brunswick.

Many of the combat wings attacking Berlin with the 1BD reported no contact with enemy fighters at all although fifty Me109s and FW190s did make two passes at the IP, followed by a head-on pass by another 25 fighters. The 3BD force fared even better and only reported seeing 40 fighters on the return flight, described as inexperienced and disorganised; initiating attacks from all points of the compass, singly and in small groups.

"We figured we would have to go to Big B sooner or later but we kept hoping it would be later..... say two or three years later! Since we've been lying around and haven't pulled a mission since April 27, it was a blow something like a sharp right in the stomach when we heard the briefing officer say very solemnly "your target for today is the center of the city of Berlin"."

Diary extract, Preston Clark, gunner 94BG

The Luftwaffe fights back

The Luftwaffe's main assault struck the Berlin bomber force in the Wittenberg area with 150 fighters, and again over the target. The fighters swept in, 15 to 25 aircraft at a time in tight formations, supported by top cover.

Although many of the attacks were not pressed home, some after action reports recorded a few enemy fighters as 'suicidal', heading unwaveringly straight and level at the selected bomber; while others employed the standard slow roll through the formation. The bombers harvested a share of the attacking fighters as they swept through their own tight defensive formations.

Crew men from the 'Bloody 100th' described some of the action on their Combat Reports. Top turret gunner S/Sgt E Rogers flying in *Latest Rumor* wrote "2 FW190s came in at 12 o'clock and just a little higher than level. I opened fire at 600

yards and gave him one long burst and one short burst, on the first FW190. He began to smoke badly as he passed by." Another top turret gunner, in *Royal Flush*, stated "Four FW190s came in single file from level and 1'o clock and then turned off left to high at 150 yards. I started firing at #2.... fired five bursts as enemy aircraft passed to 5'o clock. It went up in a stall, fell off on its right wing and down in a tight spin. Smoke and flame were coming from cockpit and engine."

As two more FW190s barrelled in from the rear the tail gunner, also on *Royal Flush*, described one peeling off to the right while the other roller coasted to within 700 yards before coming straight in on the tail. He squeezed off 150 rounds and watched as the fighter slid away on its left wing into a spin, tracing a flaming spiral as a wheel fell off and other debris tore from the blazing engine.

Lucky ship! Lucky shot?

Superstitious Aloysius (42-31982) was assigned to the 91st Bomb Group at Bassingbourn having rolled off the production line at Boeing's Seattle plant in January 1944 — one of the last camouflaged Fortresses. Assigned to the 91st in late February, the B17G set out to raid Berlin no less than seven times as part of the 1st Air Division, flown on four of those occasions by 1Lt Charles Bell and his 322BS crew. It eventually fell victim to Luftwaffe fighters over Leipzig on 20th July 1944.

"London newspapers often quoted a source referred to as a Swedish eyewitness visiting Germany. We called him the 'Swedish Traveller'. We were loaded with 1000lb bombs and were told to release one of them over the North Sea to save gas. Our bombardier prepared to do this but we did not as our calculations showed plenty of gas. However, when we opened the bomb bay at the Initial Point, one bomb fell away. This annoyed me greatly until I read the newspaper account next day. The 'Swedish Traveller' told of being just north of Berlin when he saw a flak tower open fire on American planes flying above the overcast. Almost immediately, a single bomb struck the flak tower, destroying it. He marvelled at the uncanny accuracy and effectiveness of the American bombers. I like to think this is what happened to our wayward 1000 pounder!"

Charles Bell, 91BG

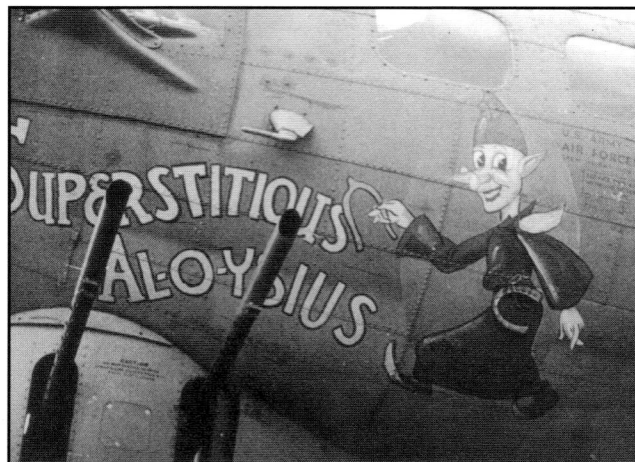

91BG's *Superstitious Aloysius* lost on 20th July 1944 over Leipzig (R Murphy)

Only three B17s in the Berlin force were lost to aerial opposition but 11 B24s attacking Brunswick were lost to fighters. Flak, however, extracted a high toll, being described as moderate to intense over the target with both barrage and continuous following fire being experienced. A further eight Forts from the Berlin force were known to have been brought down by the flak. Others received mortal damage and limped back towards England; three B17s ditched in the North Sea and another crashlanded in Sweden.

Only 495 Fortresses actually bombed Berlin, dropping 367 tons of high explosive and 547 tons of incendiaries. German records of the attack could not be located but analysis of strike photos reveals two heavy concentrations from the 3BD fell in the built-up Mitte area, the central section of the city just east of the Tiergarten, hitting the Friedrichstrasse rail station. Another dense concentration fell into the Horst Wesel area with hits on the Reichbahn, Aussbesserungs Werke railway works and the Schlesischer passenger/freight car repair shops, sidings and warehouses. A fourth concentration hit the Weissensee industrial area where many small industrial and commercial factories were sited. Much of the bomb load dropped by 1st Division appears to have fallen into open fields but some struck the Lichtenburg district, 6kms east of the city centre and at least one bomb scored a direct hit on a bridge over a rail yard. Several concentrations of incendiaries fell into the Blankenfelde and Schonhausen districts and along the west bank of the Spree River in Kopenick.

Paddling in the Baltic

Shortly after the escorting fighters left, Doug Hiley's 100BG Fort (42-97607) was hit by Fw190s. Unable to make it home Lt Ralph Horne, the pilot, turned for Malmo in the hope of making it to neutral territory. As they struggled towards safety their B17 came under attack again from a another lone Fw190. Doug Hiley told what happened, "It shot off most of our port horizontal stabiliser. Our tail gunner got the 190 and the bombardier and I both hit it, taking off its left wing — but it was already a goner. Our No.1 engine was damaged in the exchange and we began an unavoidable descent. There was confusion for a short time as to whether we would bail out or ditch... we ended up ditching in the Baltic about 3 to 4 miles off the coast of Sjaelland, Denmark."

"We reached the shore in the late afternoon... the water was very shallow to about 50 yards off the beach. We sank our dinghies and Mae Wests before reaching the shore but noticed that they were still quite visible from the top of the sand bluff behind the beach. We broke into pairs but soon learned we were on a very small island. We crossed a causeway to the mainland when it got dark and were helped by a local family who showed us a map."

Doug continued, "It was our intention to locate the road north... we reconnoitred and found an area of haystacks and decided to use one of them. The four enlisted men crawled into the bottom of the stack and

The fighter battle

In all, nineteen fighter groups were despatched from 8th and 9th Fighter Commands, totalling 833 fighters. Twelve groups, comprising 670 Mustangs and Lightnings, were assigned to protecting the Berlin formations while the remainder escorted the Brunswick force.

357FG encountered 150 German fighters in the Wittenburg area and another 50 in the vicinity of Potsdam, claiming ten shot down for the loss of one of their own. Three of those destroyed were claimed by Lt Bob Foy in his P51 Mustang *Little Shrimp*, making him the group's 13th ace.

352FG , escorting the 1BD along with the 4FG and 355FG, claimed eleven victories over Wittenberg, but this was later revised to 7.5 kills. One of their pilots, Lt Carlone, was killed however when he shot down an Me109 at low level. The enemy fighter bellied in at 250mph and exploded. Carlone pulled up but snap rolled into trees and crashed his Mustang.

Eleven more were downed by P51s from 359FG in the same combat melee, west of Wisnat. Three of their P51s were lost in the action.

During the withdrawal, Mustangs from 4FG surprised three Me109s near Wisnat and then another six, shooting down four of them. The melee was so intense that two German fighters collided as they made sharp turns and sliced the tail from a third — adding three more to the enemies losses.

For the 364FG it was a costly mission. Two Lightnings strafed the airfield at Jubeck and destroyed an He111 on the ground but were caught by flak and forced to belly in. Both pilots became POWs. Another P38 was also lost after being hit by flak, heading home on one engine, and was abandoned over the sea. Yet another made it as far as five miles from the English coast before the pilot, too, was forced to bail out. Neither survived.

"The Fw190s aimed at our lead element but actually hit us. A great gash was made between our No.3 and No.4 engines... both were put out of action... the top of our tail was shot off." Douglas Hiley, navigator 42-97607, 100BG

Jack McGrath and I got up on top. We woke up to the sound of conversation from six men pitching the hay stack. The boss spoke a few words of English and told us to stay put... he then led us to a barn and we were given bread, eggs and cigars. We were starting to feel hopeful but then the man returned with the local town's Burgomaster.

With tears in their eyes they informed us that they had reported our presence to the Germans. They explained that too many people had become aware of us and that they feared reprisals. The Wehrmacht took about 90 minutes to arrive and when they did they burst in through all the doors and windows — just like in a movie. We learned later that the German troops had been there all along, starting from a circle of about one mile from the farm and closing in."

Doug Hiley and the rest of the crew were taken into captivity to begin a year-long incarceration as prisoners of war.

19th MAY 1944

Berlin – wrong place... wrong time!

Not all the aircraft lost over Berlin were as a result of direct enemy action by fighters or flak. Tragically, some were unlucky enough to be in the wrong place at the wrong time to be struck by bombs dropped by aircraft flying in a higher formation.

On 9th March a 384BG Fort named *Silver Dollar* (42-37781) was hit by bombs which completely severed the plane's tail section. On 22nd March, it was the turn of a 96BG Fortress *Winnie C* (42-6099) to fall victim to 'friendly' M47 incendiary bombs which sent it, too, into a fatal dive from the skies over Berlin. On 7th May, *Ragged But Right*, a 385BG

Fort (42-97790), was also struck by falling bombs but managed to return to England. So too did a 452BG plane, 42-32087, but it would fall victim to Berlin later on 6th August.

Then, on 19th May, 94BG's *Miss Donna Mae II* (42-31540) was knocked down by American bombs, having already survived Berlin previously on 6th and 9th March. *Miss Donna Mae II* , flown by Lt Marion Reid's crew, was below the high squadron just as the formation passed over the target. One ball gunner spotted the plane below him just in time to call a delay to their bombing but another Fort positioned above them did not see it

and released five 1000lb bombs.

As the string of bombs tumbled away, one struck the left stabiliser of *Miss Donna Mae* smashing it down vertically and sending the damaged plane earthwards. The Fortress fell into a steepening dive and at 13,000ft one of its main wings tore off as fellow crews watched in vain for parachutes. While this went on, the crew of the Fortress which had released its bomb load at such an unfortunate moment were totally unaware of the tragic consequences.

It was not until he had landed back at Bury St

Edmunds did pilot John Winslett learn of the tragedy. He was handed eight photographs from his plane's camera. "Take a look at these pictures and tell me why this plane didn't fly to home base", asked Lt Col Creer. John Winslett noted in his diary that by chance... "The cameraman had set the camera to begin making pictures when the bombs were released instead of when the first bomb hit the target, Berlin. Just before 'bombs away', the ball gunner said 'clear underneath'. The ball gunner in the squadron lead plane said it was clear also.... (the struck plane) was No.5 in the lead squadron and I

94BG's *Miss Donna Mae II*, one of two Fortresses struck by American bombs over Berlin on 19th May 1944 (USAF)

was No.3 in the high squadron. The pictures reveal that the doomed plane was turning to the right when he flew under us, he should have been flying straight ahead on the bomb run."

Navigator Abel Dolim was in the aircraft leading the second flight of the lead squadron and recalled "At bombs away over the target, our group leader began his right turn to the rally point while we were still dropping bombs, and as we lagged in the second flight, the high squadron

leader banked into our overhead space and a 1000lb bomb clipped the horizontal stabilizer of the aircraft on our left wing."

Crew members in the plane flying on Lt Reid's wing recalled that as the high squadron passed over the top of them they too were narrowly missed by the tumbling bomb load. Two bombs fell in front of their No. 3 and 4 engines and two more went aft of the right wing, another just missing the tail guns.

Men in other crews in other groups on 19th May

also reported near misses and a B17G from 398BG (42-97339) was struck in a separate incident by several 100lb incendiary bombs which bounced all over the doomed plane. The waist gunner in a nearby Fort reported on return, "Most of them hit over the cockpit, top turret and front part of the radio

hatch. One bomb hit the No.3 engine and flamed up but the fire went out. The plane went into a wide sweep as though out of control and came back into formation.... then went down." Two planes were downed and another twenty men were lost as a result of these 'friendly' bombing incidents.

> "The fighter attacks came in from 1 o'clock and lasted about five minutes, mostly Me109s. There was one German pilot who rolled under our ship and, I have to say, if I ever see him again I will recognise him – he was that close!" Marshall McKew, pilot 91BG's *Jezebel* (42-38144)

Fever Beaver survives friendly bombs, falling Forts, flak and fighters!

The tragic incidents which caused the loss of the 94BG's *Miss Donna Mae II* and the 398BG Fort were part of a chain of events which could so easily have proved even more disastrous by bringing down other ships in other groups. Flying 100BG's *Fever Beaver* was John Massol, already a veteran of four previous raids on Berlin. He recalled the event clearly, "On the bomb run, a group got above us and started dropping bombs in front of us. One of their planes had half its horizontal fin knocked off.... the bombs fell so close to us that we could read the markings on them. Then the plane came down nearly on top of us. We took such violent evasive action that our bombs slammed around and the machine gun ammo jumped out of the bins. I don't know what this did to the men in the back of our plane but it threw the ammunition out of the cans and it had to be put back so the guns would operate."

Fever Beaver survived that near miss but the problems of the day were only just beginning. John Massol continued, "Flak

Ed Stern (right) stands below the nose of 100BG's veteran *Fever Beaver*, with copilot Hal Granger (left) and navigator Ed King (J Massol)

knocked a hole in one engine and the oil started to seep out and freeze. My oxygen was knocked out at my elbow, (CP) Granger hooked me onto his supply and he used a walk-round bottle. Flak also hit the armor plate beneath the cockpit and damaged radio equipment above it. That armor plate probably saved us."

The radio gunner, Asa Sprengler was not so lucky and he recalled, "I got shrapnel up the back. I had the radio room door open plus the bomb bay doors were open, and when the shell went off the concussion and stinging pain was

so bad I wanted to scream but blacked out.... I came to on my feet but could not see. Flak smoke and dirt from the floor filled the air, plus I could not hear out of my right ear. The stinging pain was so bad — I know it was just a second but it felt like it lasted a week... I can still hear McCartney yell 'Ace got blown out of the radio room!'."

John Massol picked up the tale. "After bombs away we headed more or less for Denmark. As we got close to the North Sea the fighters hit us. An engine was set on fire and a chunk of the vertical fin was blown away." Unable

to stay with the formation, they had no choice but to relinquish the lead. "For some unknown reason, I had decided that if the fire did not go out on my count of 7 we would have to bail out." Fortunately, the fire was extinguished.

All loose equipment was jettisoned from *Fever Beaver* as it drifted below the group seeking what little protection it could get. "I had the men move up to the radio room to give the plane the best balance," continued Massol. "We started a slow descent with the two remaining engines adjusted for maximum fuel economy... flak had caused leaks. It was a long lonesome trip over the North Sea but we made it to our base... the ground crew told us later that we had about 10 minutes of fuel left in the tanks and that they had quit counting holes after 500! The plane required a new wing, all new tanks, two engines, rebuilt radio room, all new electrical equipment, new armor under the cockpit, repairs to the oxygen system, 13 replacement machine guns and assorted equipment including a new Norden bomb sight."

24th MAY 1944

616 B17s in ten combat wings escorted by 18 fighter groups were despatched to Berlin and a further six wings of B24s struck out at airfields around Paris. Scattered clouds over Berlin forced some groups to use radar for bombing but others identified their targets visually, achieving fair to good results.

Escorts encountered 200 enemy fighters and claimed 30 shot down, but a hundred still managed to get through to attack the bomber formations and 18 B17s were lost. The 100th Bomb Group once again suffered severe loss when it became detached from the rest of the bomber stream in heavy contrails. Nine of its number were shot out of the sky by vicious and determined attacks from about forty

fighters between Kiel and Hamburg. Later a large concentration from JG3 caught the bomber formations over Berlin itself immediately after bombing and made massed head-on passes with considerable effect. The 381BG lost six of its Forts when it, too, became detached from the main stream after deciding on a second bomb run. Losses, equipment failures and poor weather reduced the number of B17s actually bombing Berlin to 464 aircraft. Heavy and persistent contrails made formation flying very difficult, forcing following groups to bomb from a higher altitude than briefed.

Some 1080 tons of ordnance tumbled down on Berlin with a large concentration striking just north

A ducking for *Sweaty Betty*

94BG's *Sweaty Betty* (42-31252) led the group on their first assault on Berlin on 6th March. Over the city yet again, it was badly damaged by the intense flak which shot out both engines on the left side.

John Whorton was the pilot and he recalled, "I was unable to feather either of the props due to the cold oil in the prop dome and I could not maintain air speed or altitude using No.3 and 4 engines. After quite a battle, Willie (co-pilot Louis Williamson) and I got her levelled off at 120mph and 200fpm descent and we fell into the undercast. Ellis gave us the heading to fly and when we broke out of the clouds we were over the North Sea just west of Cuxhaven. A few flak barges in the area shot at us but were

out of range. We sent out an SOS but no one would answer us."

High fuel consumption and the continued loss of altitude soon had the crew jettisoning over the side all the equipment they could prise loose in an attempt to lighten their plane — but to no avail. "We threw out everything we could: guns, ammunition, flak helmets and even dropped the ball turret."

Finally out of altitude, John Whorton ditched *Sweaty Betty* into the North Sea. "The impact was an instant stop. We had never practised a ditching procedure before but we all got out without any injury. Both life rafts inflated and we all got into them." *Sweaty Betty* floated for 15 minutes before sinking below the waves."

Within minutes a P51

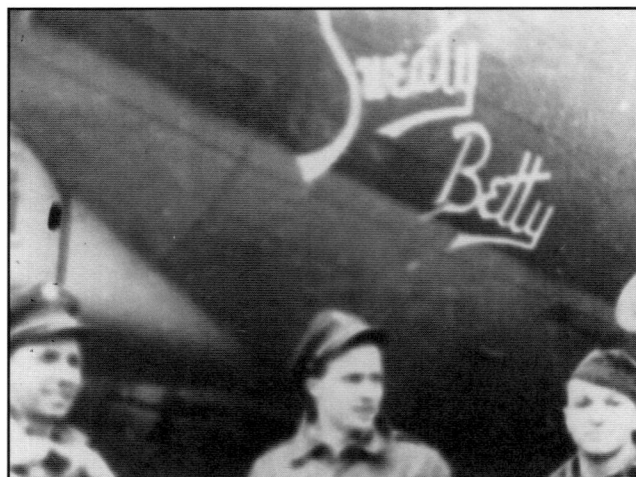

swooped low overhead and soon after an RAF Walrus amphibian arrived on the scene closely followed by a high speed Air Sea Rescue launch, HSL 2678 from Gorleston, which picked them up. "They took us aboard and, when they were sure none of us was injured, said they would continue their patrol until 30 minutes

after all the bombers had passed over. We were in the water for less than half an hour. They told us they had heard all of our SOS signals and had plotted where we would hit the water but did not answer us because it would give their location away. They took us back to Yarmouth where we spent the night and treated us royally."

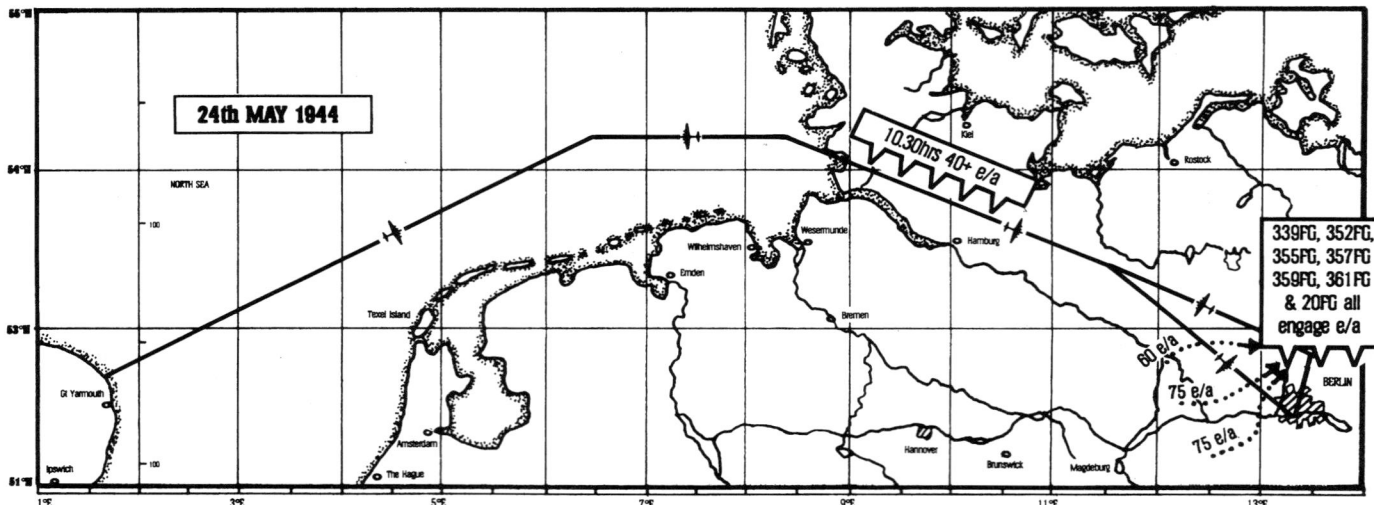

of Tempelhof airfield into the Kreuzberg district. Here the military and police barracks took hits as well as a gasworks. In Mitte, the town hall, law courts, main post office as well as the Air Ministry building were hit and extensively damaged. So too were three hospitals and several churches. Other bursts struck the Schlesischer passenger station and surrounding commercial buildings to its west and south, with heavy loss of life. Weissensee, Lankwitz, Lichtenfeld and Reinickendorf districts also suffered considerable damage. A training school in Zehlendorf and flak barracks in Steglitz took hits. A flak position in Hohenschonhausen was straddled by bombs. At Tempelhof the administrative offices of Rheinmetall Borsig, Daimler Benz and Siemens AG were all badly damaged.

Anti-aircraft fire over Berlin was described as intense and accurate, resulting in five Fortresses being lost. In all, 33 B17s failed to return along with twenty fighter escorts. One 398BG Fortress exploded in mid-air and debris damaged almost every aircraft in the group's formation.

"...the flak just made a carpet of black over the city.... saw four Forts go down at once. As we left the target, about 50 Me109s hit us.... one flew into a Fort and cut it in two."
Diary extract, Gilbert Bradley, 91BG

One way *Return Ticket*

381BG's *Return Ticket* (42-39890) had arrived with the group in late December 1943. A month later it suffered considerable damage when its tail fin was chopped off in a taxi accident. Repaired, it was reassigned to the crew of Lt Emil Urban and taken over Berlin twice during March. The bombardier, Cliff Hermann recalled: "Many names were suggested during a shake down flight prior to being scheduled for combat. The crew had a saying that *Return Ticket* would never get punched and would always bring us home."

Although true for the Urban crew, who returned safely to the USA, *Return Ticket*'s luck finally ran out over Berlin with the crew of 2Lt Carl Dasso. After completing the bomb run the 381BG formation turned and made a second pass over the target. Detached from the main force it fell victim to a large group of German fighters striking in a single, sudden and devastating pass. Sixty to seventy German fighters swept through "wing tip to wing tip, shooting frantically". Four 381BG planes were shot out of the formation and two more Forts collided in a huge ball of fire, almost bringing down another.

Return Ticket received a mortal blow from the fighters which sliced off its right wing, outboard from No.4 engine. As the plane rolled, its left wing tore away sending it tumbling from the sky, trapping many of the crew by centrifugal force in an aluminium tomb.

Carolina Queen (42-97214) flown by John Wardencki's crew was reported to have been run into by Clarence Wainwright's 42-31698 as aircraft juggled evasively in their formation. Both aircraft crashed in the vicinity of Tempelfelde-Gratze with only two men surviving from Wainwright's crew. *Avengress* (42-31291), flown by Carl Gardon, crashed in Wilmersdorf and may also have been a victim of the mid-air collision.

Also caught in the devastating attack was *Spam Can* (42-31878). Heavy damage caused Walter Higgins' to order an immediate bail out while he held the ship steady but neither he nor any of the enlisted men in the rear of the ship, except the engineer, survived after the plane exploded and crashed near Melchow. Four crew, including Higgins, were veterans of 30 missions flown with the 15AF in Italy, plus a further 7-10 flown from Ridgewell.

The final 381BG loss, 42-38010, fell away from the formation with one engine smoking and chutes blossoming below. Another two men died as the plane crashed into Berlin's sprawling suburbs below.

Joanne – what a scorcher!

The huge fireball which engulfed two 381BG Forts when they struck in mid-air while taking evasive action created an unavoidable sheet of flame for John Williams' crew as they followed close behind in *Joanne* (42-97174). The searing heat blackened the shiny silver exterior and burned away much of the fabric on the control surfaces on the tail of the ship. The tail gunner, believing the plane to be doomed, bailed out over Germany. To make matters worse, thick black soot caked the pilots' windshield, making visibility extremely limited. The co-pilot was forced to open the side window and scrub away at a small area to enable him to see out. The flying skill of the pilots and the rugged construction of the B17, brought the scorched Fort safely back to its base at Ridgewell.

Joanne was repaired but the reprieve was short-lived however, for less than one month later, on 21st June, the ship returned to strike Berlin. This time it was the flak that was unavoidable over Wagnitzer and the plane and crew of 1Lt Roy Pendergist went down. Returning crews reported seeing the No3 engine ablaze with the trailing edge of one wing and the ailerons blown away but the aircraft was still held under control as several chutes blossomed from it.

24th MAY 1944

Another disaster for the 'Bloody Hundredth'

This mission to Berlin was to prove to be another costly one for the 100BG which had already earned an unenvied reputation for high losses. Assembly was beset with difficulties and the group set out across the North Sea desperately trying to catch the Wing formation. Penetrating enemy territory they were soon spotted by the waiting German fighters and their straggling formation made them highly vulnerable. Circling round, the Luftwaffe pilots roared in to make a mass attack on the strung out low squadron, cutting out four B17s and leaving others damaged and detached still further from the protection of the group, to be picked off in later attacks. Nine 100BG Forts failed to return.

One of those caught in the slaughter was Emil Siewert's *Nelson King*, named by the crew of Frank Lauro back in November in honour of their radio man. During a freezing mission to Bremen Sgt King had removed his heated gloves to assist a gunner whose oxygen mask had frozen. King's own oxygen supply froze up and he lost consciousness, still without his gloves. This act of bravery towards a fellow crew man was to cost King the loss of all his fingers to frost bite. *Nelson King* (42-31306) had been lucky to survive a previous trip to Berlin on 6th March. An FW190 had smashed away the entire fin and rudder. But in spite of the appalling damage, Frank Lauro had maintained control of the plane and completed the mission. Now the Luftwaffe

fighter pilots had returned to claim their belated prize.

Caught in the intense flak over Berlin, another of the victims was the unnamed lead plane (42-97845), shredded by 20mm shells and flak fragments. Ed Stern, who had flown so many of the early Berlin missions in *Fever Beaver* with John Massol's crew, was bombardier on the lead ship. The luck which had stayed with him over Berlin so many times before finally ran out.

The lead crew was an unusual combination of men. The command pilot was the 350th Bomb Squadron CO, Major Fitzgerald and the pilot Capt James Geary had already completed one

---

"Fighter support was good. The enemy fighters made their attacks by sneaking up out of the undercast and then cutting back in." Extract, 13CBW Mission Critique

---

tour with the 390BG before being assigned to the 100BG. The formation commander, sitting in the tail of the ship was Lt A J Harris, a pilot who had previously been interned in Sweden but repatriated and, most unusually, had been allowed to continue combat flying.

Ed Stern recalled what happened, "We were leading the 13CBW and, as we approached Berlin there was a solid black cloud of flak over the entire city. It seemed impossible that any plane could fly through that ominous, inky morass. My target was a specific building in downtown Berlin. What it contained was never divulged at briefing. In spite of continuous close bursts of

flak, I located the target and set about lining up the crosshairs of the Norden bombsight."

"Almost immediately after bombs away, and closing the bomb doors, a flak shell exploded directly in front of the plane. A shower of steel shattered the plexiglass nose, a big chunk lodged in the bombsight, another tore out my oxygen and intercom lines, and a third plowed into our No.3 engine. Geary feathered the prop. Flying on three engines, we could not maintain enough airspeed to continue to lead the formation."

"Forced to leave the protection of the group," Ed continued, "we limped behind and were soon attacked by about fifteen fighters, who proceeded to make a lace curtain of the plane." Both the radio man and a waist gunner were wounded and Ed gave first aid to them before taking over the waist gun position. Still under heavy fire, a gas tank erupted into flame and the pilot gave the bail out order. "Oddly enough," commented Ed, " we bailed out right over a Luftwaffe fighter base near Ludwigslust. As we descended in our chutes, the Me109s in the traffic pattern dipped their wings in salute. Once rounded up we were taken to the airbase and put into cells. It was fortunate that we were found by the Luftwaffe as the local villagers threw stones at us and were screaming "luftgangster" and "terrorflieger", as we were being marched through the town. To mollify the enraged villagers, the accompanying soldiers would kick us in the rear

from time to time."

As the lead plane fell away, the position was taken over by *Powerhouse* (42-31534) but, while the group struggled to reform, it too was hit by a stream of 20mm shells from a fighter coming in behind. The ball turret took a direct hit but the wounded gunner managed to bail out. Soon the entire right wing was a mass of flames threatening to explode the aircraft. As crew men exited from the waist door they jumped through an inferno which streamed back, causing grievous facial burns, but all survived. The pilot Lt Frank Malooly struggled to hold the plane steady while his crew bailed out, barely escaping himself before *Powerhouse* exploded into fragments.

Henry Jesperson's *Times Awastin* (42-102528) was caught in a withering stream of 20mm cannon fire from FW190s as they swept past. The radio room was blasted, killing the occupant, the ball turret was also hit and jammed trapping the gunner within. The navigator was killed instantly by more 20mm fire just as he bailed out and two other men also died as the aircraft exploded in mid-air.

Delbert Pearson's 42-97095 also exploded, one minute after being hit by FW190 fire, and Robert Roeder's *BTO in the ETO* (42-102648) broke apart at the radio room and tail wheel leaving three men dead in the plane and two others thrown out without chutes. Two other crews flying their first or second mission, in 42-102635 and 42-102624, suffered the loss of 17 men killed in the attack. All bailed out safely from the ninth loss, Lindley Williamson's (42-31941), but two men were thought to have been lynched by civilians.

"Two Me109s led by one FW190 came head on in line for our right wing. I opened fire on the FW190 and as all three passed under our wing, this aircraft spurt flames. It pulled up sharply as it cleared the tail of our ship and exploded" Combat Report, Bombardier, *Superstitious Aloysius*, 100BG

The Cannonball's home run

"Approaching the target, the group behind us cut the IP too close and overran our outfit. As a result there were 108 bombers where only 54 should have been — what a mess! Then the 190s jumped us, coming in from 12 o'clock. One of them went right under the tail of our ship, a gunner in the group behind us killed the German pilot who crashed head-on into a B17. That plane went down and hit several more. Flak shot out our No.3 engine and it could not be feathered, the prop broke free on the crankshaft and windmilled. The gears in the nose of the engine were chewed to bits, several pieces flew through the side of the plane and hit the hydraulic system pump. The ring cowling on No.3 engine was torn loose. It blew off and was held on by just one bolt. All the way back it kept banging against the leading edge of the wing. After leaving Berlin we were alone, the plane was in bad condition so I had Bailey (navigator) plot a course for Sweden, just in case. Things held up OK, we came down to 10,000ft through broken clouds just north of the Frisian Islands. Visibility was low in East Anglia and we called the base and had them fire some flares and a mortar until we spotted the drome."

Dave Hanst, 91BG Pilot, *Wabash Cannonball* (42-29947)

"Didn't see any bandits and had good fighter support all the way. Flak was about the same as on our other Berlin raid, a lot of it as far as the eye could reach in all directions.... A ship from the high squadron threw a scare into us, almost ramming down on top of our ship just before bombs away." Diary extract, Preston Clark, gunner 94BG

The dome of the Franzosische church, just south of the Unter Den Linden and the Friedrichstrasse station, blazes from incendiary hits. (Bundesarchiv)

Catching the Berlin trains

The escort for the Berlin bound force was composed of Mustangs, Thunderbolts and Lightnings drawn from both 8th and 9th Fighter Commands, over 700 fighters in total. The opposition they encountered from intercepting Luftwaffe fighter forces was considerable.

As an experiment, 4FG's Colonel Blakeslee controlled and directed four separate fighter groups escorting the 1BD. Flying parallel to the bomber stream for an hour and a half with a force of eight Mustangs it proved to be a frustrating and unproductive experience. The rest of the 4FG meanwhile encountered forty Germans in two groups between Hamburg and Lubeck. One enemy group bounced the escort of the rear bomber box, in fours, while the other attempted to hit the bombers. They were bounced by 334FS in a combat which ranged from 35,000ft to ground level, claiming ten victories for the loss of one pilot.

20FG encountered twenty of the enemy soon after rendezvous with the bombers near Bernau and Capt Ilfrey bagged two Me109s, but the group lost one of their P51s. They also reported "one long-nosed Fw190 with American markings". 361FG suffered more severely and lost three of their pilots in a series of combats. Over Berlin, the group engaged 75+ enemy fighters and dispersed them through the bomber formations.

One unfortunately collided with a B17 on the way. Northeast of the city they were themselves bounced by eight Me109s and then tangled with twenty more.

While escorting the 3BD, the 339FG's Mustangs encountered 75 enemy fighters of JG3, north of Berlin — they claimed eight fighter kills for no loss. Returning pilots reported "four entirely black P51s made one pass on Red Flight". These may have been mistaken for 355FG Mustangs who also detached one squadron to attack the same group of Germans, leaving two squadrons to carry out their primary role of protecting the bombers. Led by Lt Col Myers they roared straight in for a head-on attack which drove the enemy clear of the bombers and made Myers the group's sixth ace. One of the group's P51s was lost when it was caught by flak south of Hamburg.

Blue-nosed P51s from 352FG also joined in the action between Perleburg and Berlin and sent a further two Me109s plunging down in flames. Thirty minutes later over Osterberg, 50 miles west of Berlin, they added two more to their tally. Two of their P51s were caught by ground fire as they strafed an airfield near Stendal during the withdrawal. Meanwhile others in the group streaked earthwards to strafe ground targets — destroying a total of 17 locomotives on rail tracks leading to Berlin.

"My 5th mission to Berlin. I am now in the habit of tuning in the German Air Raid Warning Service. Their announcers are women who call out their messages hysterically – *Achtung, Amerikanischer Grossbomber wegen nach Osnabruch, Hannover, Braunschweig und Berlin*. They know exactly what we are up to...." Diary extract, Abel Dolim, navigator 94BG's *Florencia* (42-102574)

The first strike against the Nazi capital since the D-Day landings in France, two weeks earlier, sent sixteen combat wings of B17s over the centre of the city with a further seven wings of B24s aimed at an aero engine works and a tank engine factory on the outskirts. At the same time a smaller formation of two wings of Fortresses struck a synthetic oil production plant 75 miles south of Berlin at Ruhland. More than 1300 heavy bombers were involved, supported and escorted by 850 fighters from 8th and 440 from 9th Fighter Commands. Initial plans for the raid had also scheduled additional forces from the 15th Air Force based in Italy reinforced by another 900 RAF Lancaster bombers to be used in their first large scale daylight role. These two additional forces were withdrawn from the operation as a result of insufficient escorts being available to cover adequately the huge number of bombers and the 8th Air Force went alone.

The attacking force comprised four separate formations, the first broke away as it approached Berlin, headed south for Ruhland and then continued on to Russian territory as part of Operation Frantic. The second force, nine combat wings of almost 500 B17s, hit the centre of city. A third force of 368 B24s aimed at the Daimler Benz works at Genshagen and the Dornier works to the south of the city. Finally, seven wings of Fortresses headed for the aero-engine

Close shave over Berlin for the *Ramblin' Rebel*

As the 1st Bomb Division, second in line, approached the city it was hit by a massed attack from the rear. Between fifty and seventy-five Me410s struck at around 09.30hrs in the vicinity of Muritz Lake, 60 miles north northwest of Berlin. The attackers swept through the bomber boxes in tight elements of two or three aircraft. It was the 91BG 'A' Group that took the brunt of the attack and lost four of their B17s in the first assault. A 91st PFF pathfinder ship which was on loan and carrying part of a 398BG crew on board was also lost.

All the enemy fighters came in from 6 o'clock, mostly level, with others diving down through the formation and then sweeping up to attack from below. After cutting through the bomber box, the attacking elements broke up into individual fighters which then continued to strike from all quarters. The attackers were persistent and continued their assault on the 'A' Group for twenty minutes, joined by other single-engine fighters, until the formation was due east of Berlin. Six to ten of their number were reported shot down in flames.

The 91st's 'B' Group, flying behind, escaped the fighter attack completely but experienced problems of their own. Four minutes past the IP, still 8 miles east of Berlin centre, bombs began tumbling from the lead ship. A mechanical failure had released the load too early and fifteen ships dropped their bombs as a consequence — only four held their load. Realising what was occurring, the bombardier on the lead ship closed the bomb doors in an attempt to correct the situation. One 500lb GP bomb and one M17 smoke marker were caught up as a result.

As the formation processed over the city centre the lead ship opened its bomb doors again to shed the remnants of its load onto the target. Tucked in tight, behind and below, flying as deputy lead, was Walt Pickard in *Ramblin' Rebel* (43-37540). It was his first time to Berlin. An earlier attempt on the 3rd March had seen him shot down into the North Sea when the entire 8AF had turned about as a result of the appalling weather. Half of his crew perished that day. This second trip was to be almost another disaster for him. "When that smoke marker came tumbling out over my head it either hit a glancing blow to the fuselage directly in front of the windshield and spewed out its acid; or it was spewing out the acid as it passed...." recalled Walt. "It covered the windshield with an opaque liquid... I could not see a thing through it — and we were only feet away from that lead plane! I asked my copilot if he could see... there was a small corner in the upper right of the windshield that was clear and he took control. I opened the side window and stuck my gloved hand out to try to wipe that gook off the glass in front of me. Good thing I had on my gloves. After a couple of ineffectual swipes, I pulled my hand back in. It was 'Look Ma, no glove!' The acid had burned out the palm of the glove. I don't know what happened to the 500-pounder. If it had hit the same spot it would have ruined the whole afternoon for us!"

The dense contrails at 27,500ft, which had been so persistent since the IP, now proved to be a saviour for the *Ramblin' Rebel*. The trails were so heavy with condensed water that they washed the windshield clean after a while and enabled the pilots to see more clearly. Lt Pickard made it safely back to Bassingbourn, notched up his 20th combat mission and took a well-earned spell of leave to London.

Walter Pickard (front right) with members of his crew and their B17G *Ramblin' Rebel*. The 'Rebel' returned to Berlin on 5th December and again on 18th March 1945 before heading back to the USA with almost 100 missions accrued. (W. Pickard)

plant at Basdorf, 15 miles to the north, and other targets in the centre of Berlin.

Two of the heavy bomber forces encountered severe opposition in the air. An estimated 250 German fighters were reported with more than half of them pressing home attacks. Although there was little activity en route to the target, as the first Berlin force approached the city it was struck by an attack of about 75 fighters, mainly Me410s. Small groups of fighters struck from the rear but usually broke off several hundred yards away. Their tactics were sufficient however to bring down six B17s.

Once again it was the B24s who experienced the most extensive assaults as they approached their target. Several groups sustained attacks in the form of single passes by packs of ten or more fighters, a mix of Me109s, Me 410s and Fw190s, sweeping in level to low from the forward quadrant. Attacks continued well into the target area with escorts intervening and engaging the enemy from 23,000ft down to the ground. The final force struck lucky and reported no enemy air activity at all. But once again the flak over the city was intense and accurate.

More than sixteen hundred tons of high explosive and incendiary bombs were dropped on the city and its immediate area. Thirty concentrations burst in the heart of the city and at least six major fires were started among industrial, mercantile and residential areas. Several direct hits were achieved on the Friedrichstrasse rail tracks and mainline station. In Tempelhof, heavy concentrations scored hits on an electric motor factory. Incendiaries blanketed the Schlesischer rail station and adjoining marshalling yards. Other direct hits were recorded on the Anhalter rail station in Kreuzberg and also the Reich Chancellery. Six concentrations hit four miles east of the centre and the onto marshalling yards and factories at Lichtenburg.

The northwest section of Karlshorst, six miles southeast of the centre, also received hits, as did the important rail junction and yards at Rummelsburg. Other concentrations fell across residential areas to the southeast at Elsengrund, and Hohenschonhausen to the east in the heaviest daylight pounding the city had experienced so far. Returning crews reported that smoke over the city had risen to 30,000ft.

At Basdorf, the aero-engine plant took large

portions of three concentrations amounting to more than 80 high explosive bombs which scored twenty direct hits on the main heavy machine shop. Others fell on the main workshop and across all four engine test-beds. The boiler house, offices and smaller machine shops also suffered severe damage from blast and the subsequent fires, several buildings being totally demolished. Two of the six important test-bed buildings were damaged. The Daimler Benz plant at Genshagen, however, escaped almost intact with no hits in the targeted area from those aircraft which passed over it. Generally, bursts fell into the wooded area 900 yards north although one burst did hit rail tracks to the south of the plant.

The Berlin forces returned to England with 45 heavy bombers less than had been despatched and more than five hundred of those that did return had sustained varying degrees of battle damage. But the final cost of the day's total operations, including the ill-fated Operation Frantic to Russia, would become much higher.

"A IX Fighter Command group reported 1 B24 decoy encountered over Berlin with 'P' on the side and 'Z' on (its) tail. The B24 made a right turn, and the fighters were immediately bracketed by heavy flak and bounced by 2 Me109s from rear and above."

Extract from INTOPS Summary NO. 52

The fighter battle

The first force to attack Berlin, 1BD, was escorted by 277 fighters drawn from six groups from both 8th and 9th Fighter Commands. 339FG tangled over Neubrandenburg with a 25-strong Luftwaffe force and knocked down two Me109s and two twin-engine Me410 fighters for no loss. Elsewhere, strafing runs destroyed one large flying boat and a train.

The B24s heading for Genshagen received support from nine fighter groups, totalling over 400 aircraft. Combats by 354FG Mustangs claimed eight Me109s and 410s, and six more damaged, from a force of fifteen which threatened the bomber boxes near Dahme. 355FG, covering the Russia-bound 'Frantic' force, added another three victories from a second force of attackers. Over the city itself, another Me109 went down when 363FG, investigating a strangely marked B24, were bounced by two Me109s.

In the vicinity of Magdeburg, 352FG tangled with a force of Me410s and 109s, destroying two. Ground strafing by 353FG accounted for one locomotive destroyed and nine more damaged. One P47 pilot from 56FG made a fatal error while making a low level attack on a train, powered into the ground and exploded.

The final force of B17s aimed at Berlin and Basdorf was escorted by 280 fighters from six groups. No enemy opposition in the air was encountered and only one locomotive was damaged by strafing runs. But two P47 Thunderbolts from IX Fighter Command were lost when they collided while over England.

"The operation had been staged for maximum fighter cover for this raid. However, owing to operations in France it had not been found possible to give this maximum fighter cover and therefore the cover available would be insufficient, C-in-C Bomber Command felt that it was unwise to take so deep a penetration into Germany in daylight inadequately protected. It was therefore ruled by Air Chief Marshal Tedder that Bomber Command should not participate in the raid. With this decision the Americans agreed, since it meant that they had more adequate cover for themselves."

Memo: Asst/Chief Air Staff (RAF) to Under Sec. of State, 22 June 1944

21st JUNE 1944

A Frantic diversion which led to disaster for the 8th Air Force

Many of the major missions on German targets were carried out in conjunction with smaller diversionary raids, launched in an attempt to confuse the Luftwaffe fighter controllers and draw off at least some of the defending forces. Sometimes these diversions were carried out by medium bombers, sometimes by small formations of heavies. On occasions they amounted simply to feints which approached the enemy

Mirgorod and Piryatin.

15AF bombers made the first Frantic shuttle on 2nd June with about 60 bombers. It was a success, no bombers were lost, and two days later they returned to Italy via the target of the day. 21st June was chosen as the debut for the 8th Air Force's involvement. A force of 114 Fortresses drawn from 3rd Bomb Division's 13CBW and 45CBW, and 70 of their Mustang escorts, accompanied the main Berlin attackers but

"21st June 1944 saw the 8th Air Force's highest loss of aircraft to the Luftwaffe on any single day of the war – 89 heavy bombers destroyed!"

coast and then turned back for home, hoping to have drawn up some of the short range fighters who would then have to land again to refuel, losing vital interception time. On 21st June the role of the diversionary force was reversed. On this day the larger part of the bomber force was launched towards Berlin, still considered to be a target the Luftwaffe could not afford to ignore. It would act as a diversion for a politically and strategically important secondary mission — part of Operation Frantic.

Frantic was the code-name for the shuttle operations designed to utilise Russian air bases to enable the USAAF to strike deeper into German territory, without the need for a return flight. Such attacks could stretch the Luftwaffe defenders still further as well as strike at the vital industrial targets previously out of reach. Three airfields within Russian held territory were selected and developed to take the American heavy bombers and their escorting fighters: Poltava,

then separated en route and struck at an oil plant at Ruhland, continuing eastward to the airfields around Kiev.

The diversion proved successful, at least in the short term. The main force returned to England having lost 44 bombers, a heavy but acceptable toll, considerably less than the 69 lost on 6th March. The crews of the Frantic force were pleased with their apparent success as 73 Forts touched down at Poltava, another 41 at Mirgorod, while the Mustangs made for their field at Piryatin.

Unknown to those crews, the Luftwaffe had despatched a Ju88 from its Fernaufklarungsgruppe 100 (long range reconnaissance) to shadow the force as it passed across Germany into Russia. High overhead, the German reconnaissance plane turned for home to report its findings.

On the ground, exhausted by the long flight, the American crews turned in early and slept beneath the wings of their planes, mostly drawn up in a huge curve on the

western edge of the Poltava field. At 23.35 air raids sirens sounded and the men leapt into slit trenches and took what cover they could find. Just after midnight, Ju88s and He111s from KG4, KG53 and KG55 dropped flares over the field and began a leisurely bombing of the American planes for a full hour. Russian defensive fire was totally ineffectual and soon B17s were bursting into flame while nearby fuel dumps exploded. When the high level bombers finally withdrew they were replaced by Ju88s at low level dropping anti-personnel bombs and strafing with machine guns and cannon fire, setting yet more Forts ablaze.

At 02.15 the bombing stopped as suddenly as it had started. Five minutes later flash bombs, dropped from high flying photo reconnaissance aircraft, illuminated the airfield to enable the Luftwaffe to record the night's success. Fires burned on for hours and in the cold light of dawn the extent of the disaster became apparent. 44 Fortresses had been

completely destroyed and, of those remaining, 26 bombers had sustained damage. Two C47 transports were also destroyed together with two other aircraft and a further 25 Russian planes damaged. Almost half a million gallons of aviation fuel had gone up in flames; two Americans and thirty Russians were dead.

Added to the forty-five heavy bombers lost on the Berlin mission, the total for the 21st June became 89! It would be the highest loss as a result of a single day's fighting that the 8th Air Force would ever suffer. Not one German aircraft had been brought down by the defenders of Poltava — it was a master strike.

In an attempt to repeat their success, the Germans hit Mirgorod airfield on the following night but the Americans were fast learners — the B17 Fortresses had gone. But the official embarrassment at the Poltava affair was acute and went largely unreported, even in confidential and classified Air Force publications such as 'Impact', until months later.

Hair raising ride for *The Wild Hare* and the *Sleepytime Gal*

"Nearing Berlin our group was straggling and strung out. Off to the left we saw a large gaggle of bandits going towards the rear of the bomber stream... five minutes later 20mm shells began bursting all through our formation... the pilots of those fighters certainly had nerve, they flew right through our group then rolled over and dove away. Every gun on our ship was going full blast, the whole ship was shaking, the noise was terrible, and the cockpit was thick with powder smoke. One went under our left wing less than 20 feet below, its right engine was streaking smoke and flame, it rolled over and went straight down. On the first pass the bandits got three of our Forts... all had their gas tanks on fire from 20mm bursts.

Ahead of me was Ed Waters (*Sleepytime Gal*), to my left another ship, in one glance I could see huge sheets of flame coming from the wings — down they went.... on the second pass the 410's got another Fort, a PFF ship, that left two of us, four B17s down in four minutes! Short of the target we encountered an overcast, here the fighters broke off their attack, then the flak started.... contrails were heavy, visibility very poor.... the krauts were tracking us with flak....

I opened all four throttles to the limit. We flew for half an hour and then No.1 shot all its oil out through the breather, we feathered it. Near the coast P38s picked us up and herded us across the Channel."

Dave Hanst, Pilot,
91BG's *The Wild Hare* (42-31515)

Kismet – Fate!

"Big 'B' as it was called, was a psychological target as well as a real one because there were 800 to 1000 flak guns for defense as well as the ever present fighters. The flight was as usual with some fighters or 'bandits' coming through, though not real mean. But the flak at the target was immense and accurate. *Kismet* (42-102605) was taking a beating. We could feel and hear the 'wumps' of the exploding 88s and 155s. You don't see the one that blasts you out of the sky and these were so close that I expected each time that the very next one would be it.

"The sounds of shell fragments hitting and ripping the skin was nerve shattering. Upon reaching the IP, the pilot asked for a damage report. There was plenty. Holes everywhere but nothing serious, yet! I had expected to bail out, so I positioned the turret guns straight so I could open the turret door quickly, if needed, climb out, grab my chute and follow the waist gunners out. It was that bad!

"As I switched the power on again, I noticed a stream of liquid streaming out behind No.2 engine. I quickly raised the turret guns up and level to see fuel flooding down through the No.2 turbine wheel. I called for prop feathering to cool off the turbo — it was done. Saved the day and us. Why didn't it blow? Should have. I also noticed that the right tire had a split in it, but we landed OK. *Kismet* needed another left wing, a broken spar. Everywhere there were holes, large and small, the proverbial sieve. To top it off, as I picked up my chute to put it in my flight bag, I could see flak splinters had torn through it. 'Kismet' — Fate!"

WILBUR RICHARDSON
Ball turret gunner, 94BG
Kismet (42-102605)

20mm shells tore into the leading edge of the left wing of Ed Waters' *Sleepytime Gal* (42-102527), peeling it back like an orange skin. Other shells smashed into the No.3 engine and it started to burn. Fed by leaking fuel, the fire increased its intensity as the plane peeled away from the formation before exploding in a huge fireball. Burning wreckage filled the sky and three parachutes blossomed among the falling debris. An Me410 curved down and fired a burst at one of the chutes but it is not known if the unfortunate crew man was hit or not.

Fate decided which of the crew would survive the massive explosion and the subsequent strafing from the Luftwaffe. Almost miraculously, five men did reach the ground safely to become prisoners of war.

"...they cued up on us and started loosing 20mm at us. Then started in... I poured lead at a Ju88, he was on fire in his left wing then he exploded... I started firing on a 410, he caught fire and dived down to earth..."
Diary, Gil Bradley, top turret engineer, 91BG's *Old Faithful* (42-37958)

21st JUNE 1944

Slaughter over Genshagen

As the B24 formations turned onto the IP to begin their run in towards the Daimler Benz plant at Genshagen enemy fighters disrupted their assault by a series of vicious attacks. Planes went down so rapidly that returning crews were unable to give much detail regarding their loss. 389BG suffered more than any other group and it is impossible to establish which of their planes was the first to go. German records indicate five of the aircraft struck the ground within a few minutes of each other at around 10.30hrs.

All went down fighting but one caused the Luftwaffe problems even after it had slammed into the ground. A waist gunner on *Fightin Sam* (42-52579) later described the events that had overtaken them. "About 20 minutes before we were shot down we were going through intense flak. There were twin engine enemy aircraft going in the opposite direction and our escorts

were going after them.... in a few minutes we were getting direct flak hits. Two of our engines were shooting out flame and smoke. Then we started to get a nose attack from Me109s, we got a hit around the ball turret and the ship lurched.... The oxygen tanks were punctured on the side of the waist and were throwing a flame over the ball turret where the cable was broken and shorted," described Don Serradell.

"I looked back at the tail and it was in flames.... finally located a fire extinguisher and had some difficulty getting it open, perhaps because of the extreme cold." Serradell succeeded in putting out the fire and in assisting the tail gunner from his position before both of them bailed out. The ball gunner was trapped in his turret and went down with the plane. The engineer had been hit and slumped onto the narrow catwalk through the bomb bay, without any parachute.

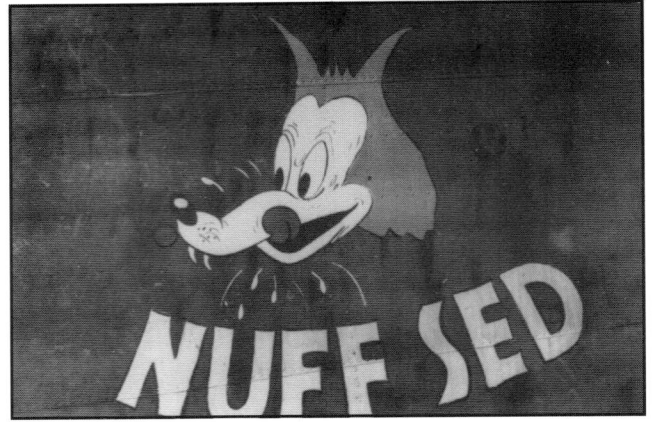

One of six 389BG Liberators lost over Berlin on 21st June, another eight of the group's B24s returned with battle damage. (T. North)

".... attacked at target... by approx. 20-40 single engined enemy fighters. Six of our aircraft were shot down during the period of these attacks which lasted from 10-15 minutes. Since our crews were engaged in warding off these attacks it was impossible to distinguish each aircraft as it went down...." 389BG Mission Report

Before anyone could assist him the plane went into a spin and threw other crew members out. One such lucky crewman later reported that after he had landed he saw the engineer "bail out at about 200ft and strike the ground with his chute half opened." Don Serradell landed on the

roof of a small building in Johannisthal but was not hurt — yet! "There were civilians waiting for me and they gave me a working over..." Eight survivors were quickly rounded up but *Fightin Sam* was still troubling the enemy. It had crashed directly onto a runway at Johannisthal airfield and German reports stated "Because the plane is lying on the runway of the airfield it disturbs the fly-traffic (sic) if west-wind..."

Another 389BG Liberator caught by the fighters was the un-named 42-50371 flown by George Schukar's crew. It too suffered from flak hits which fatally injured a waist gunner. The fighter attack later shot them down to crash near Luckenwalde after exploding in mid-air into five parts. *Nuff Sed* (42-109794) received a burst of 20mm cannon fire which smashed the nose turret and exploded ammunition. The aircraft caught fire in the forward section and bomb bay. Those still able to do so after the fighter attack began to bail out. The copilot exited through the nose wheel door but

A 2nd Bomb Division Liberator passes over Berlin's smoke covered rail yards on 21st June 1944 (USAF)

became entangled. Kicked loose, he was followed out by the engineer. The radio man went through the top hatch and the tail gunner, wounded in the legs, bailed out of the tail hatch. *Nuff Sed* crashed into the centre of Teltow killing the other six men on board. Survivors were rounded up by men from a nearby flak searchlight battery.

Six kilometres south east of Teltow another B24 crashed to earth. Carl Hartquist's crew were flying in *The Magic Carpet* (42-95122) when it too was struck by 20mm cannon fire from fighters. Fire erupted in the bomb bay and the bombardier went back to try to extinguish it but without success. As the crew began to leave the burning plane, another fighter pass riddled the ship and fatally injured at least two of the crew. Another man also died when the plane, still under constant fighter attack, exploded in the air.

The fifth casualty was 42-95145, flown by William Core and his crew on their eleventh mission. The first pass by the fighters was so sudden that one crewman was killed in mid speech as he yelled a warning of the attack. A subsequent pass killed at least one other man before the plane went out of control and crashed south east of Berlin. Only the radio man survived.

The sixth and final victim from the 389BG did not go down immediately after being hit. A P51 fighter pilot reported seeing two men bail out over Steglitz but only one chute opened. The damaged plane left the formation but limped on losing altitude. The pilot, 2Lt Albert O'Steen, had been severely injured and was pushed out by others at 3000ft — his chute also failed to open. Seven survivors and the plane, with the tail gunner still on board, came down near Magdeburg.

Steady nerves for well trimmed *Florencia*

Navigator Abel Dolim, a veteran of the Berlin battle, flew in 94BG's *Florencia* (42-102574). His diary recorded: "My sixth Berlin mission. At briefing we were told that this raid was to be carried out in retaliation for the indiscriminate V-1 bombing of London and that the RAF, previously scheduled to participate, had scratched themselves off the mission list. During takeoff I was alarmed by the drag on our left wing but I checked my strong desire to say anything on intercom for fear of unnecessarily alarming other crew members.... Our bomb run was 40 miles long at 90 knots ground speed due to a stiff headwind.... We unloaded our delayed action GPs and incendiaries over the Charlottenburg district

"The 500lb incendiary canisters are designed to disintegrate after dropping about 1000ft and spew out approximately 200 two and a half pound thermite bombs. They explode on contact with water and can only be put out by smothering with non-combustible material. Under no circumstances are we allowed to return and land with a load of delayed-action bombs as they are sensitive to shock which may cause them to explode prematurely."

Diary extract, Abel Dolim, navigator 94BG's *Florencia* (42-102574)

while heavy flak from the 900-odd 88mm cannon around Berlin gave us the most accurate and sustained fire we have encountered to date.... As we turned away from the target, we saw many brightly blazing pinpoints of fire in the heavily built-up residential area below.

"At interrogation, I asked Joe Hamil (pilot) what went wrong on takeoff.... with his usual

deadpan look he told me that we took off with our controls locked and that we were only saved from a likely crash by well-positioned trim tabs. Hamil and I were the only members of our crew at interrogation and there were 10 double shots of whiskey lined up on the table. He started on one end and I started on the other. We met in the middle for a draw."

The Feather Merchant takes a beating

Jim Long had been a 'feather merchant' before joining the 381BG. He explained, "The name derives from a popular comic strip of the era whose characters were Barney Google and Snuffy Smith. Civilians employed by the Army Air Force in the depots and repair facilities were sometimes called 'feather merchants' by service personnel with whom they worked."

Having enlisted into the AAF and finally arrived at 381BG base at Ridgewell, Jim's crew were assigned to a new plane. "As I recall, our crew was afraid that some HQ staff officer would come down to the hardstand one day and paint something we might not care for on our brand new shiny plane. In the event, I got some paint and did the job."

As bombardier on

James Parkman's crew, Jim flew to Berlin in the silver B17G he had embellished himself with the title *Feather Merchant*, 43-37553. "We took some damage coming off the target and had an engine shot out, lost power on another. We flew on two and a half engines and fell way behind the rest of the formation. We were scouring the sky for

fighters and pretty soon one came in towards us. It turned out to be a P38 in trouble, with one engine out. He tagged in close to us until we neared home and then peeled away towards his own base. We were losing a lot of gas and had to land on an A20 field, downwind with hydraulics out and tail wheel flopping... almost out of fuel."

The thirteenth raid on the German capital saw the 8th Air Force split its forces, sending the Fortresses to Berlin and the Liberators to attack torpedo factories at Kiel and oil refinery installations around Hamburg. A small force of two combat wings of B17s also struck the Focke Wulf assembly plant at Gdynia and proceeded on to Russian bases as part of Operation Frantic.

The first daylight strike on the German capital since June was carried out by 74 B17s from the 1st Bomb Division. They struck the Daimler Benz Motoren aero-engine plant at Genshagen just south of the city, dropping almost 400 tons of ordnance. The flak was intense and seven B17s went down from the 1BD with four others badly damaged and finished off by marauding German fighters. Other groups from this first force, totalling a further 200 B17s, hit primary targets of aircraft assembly and pilotless aircraft plants in the Brandenburg area 30 miles west of Berlin.

Seven concentrations of bombs hit the Genshagen plant and damage was severe with only three workshops out of 17 escaping unscathed. Seven of them were completely gutted as a result of the incendiary bombs which blanketed the east end of the plant. Three out of 18 of the important engine test beds were also hit as were nearby rail tracks and sidings.

Underground Farmer goes down in the sea

The 381BG's *Underground Farmer* (44-6020), in the hands of 1Lt Allen Webb and this crew, was one of those to be hit by the heavy flak barrage shrouding the city. At around 12.37 the aircraft was observed to be hit in its No.2 engine. Soon after, Lt Webb was heard over the VHF saying that he was unable to feather it due to lack of oil and was falling back from the formation. The Wing leader, Major Briggs, broke in and instructed him to try to head for home — promising fighter support. The last contact the group had indicated that *Underground Farmer* was 40 miles west of Berlin covered by friendly fighters but they didn't make it home.

Less than an hour after leaving the formation, *Underground Farmer* crashed into the Baltic Sea between Neustadt and Pelzerhaken, near Lubeck. The crew had just agreed to try to get their battered ship to Sweden but flak batteries around Lubeck caught them again — this time fatally. All the crew bailed out successfully but were subjected to continued intense ground fire as they descended in their parachutes and to considerable abuse on reaching the ground. The tail gunner died and three others of the 9 man crew sustained injuries from flak fragments.

Flak and fighters catch the 351st

As the 1BD approached the enemy coast , the six formations preceding the 94CBW overshot their final turn. This error unexpectedly placed the 94 CBW 'A' group (351BG) in the division lead. As they closed towards the Initial Point, the 351BG formation passed directly over flak batteries to the east of Berlin. Two ships, *2 and 6* (42-97216) and *Linda Ball 2* (42-97381), were hit immediately but managed to struggle on with the formation.

The flak continued to tear into the group as it went along the bomb run and Lt Strange's Fort (43-37533) was hit, caught fire and blew up. As the 351BG made a ragged turn off the target, twelve Fw190s and six Me109s struck from the rear — flying directly through their own flak in their eagerness to get at the bombers.

Screwball (42-107046) was caught by Fw190s and 20mm shells sliced open the leading edges of the wings, smashed the top and ball turrets, killing the lower gunner. As 2Lt Boyd's crew began to tumble from the stricken plane it exploded, killing the pilots and the radio man. One lucky gunner was blown clear of the wreck with only one parachute clasp connected — it was sufficient.

Damaged by the flak, three other B17s became victims of the fighters which sped through the formation, picking out stragglers, concentrating their attacks on the low group. 2Lt Petty's *Twinkle Toes* (42-31509), also limped away from the target but headed for the safety of neutral Sweden where the crew were interned by the authorities.

Also caught by flak was another 351st Fortress which was hit on the No4 engine, bursting it into flame. Salvoing the load the pilot, Lt Woodrum, side slipped the huge Fort 12,000ft and succeeded in extinguishing the fire. Alone, the plane was picked up for a while by two P51s but fuel shortage forced them to abandon their escort. The ship limped on, under sporadic flak fire from a series of batteries, until finally they emerged out over the North Sea, at 4000ft. With instruments smashed, the navigator kept track of the dwindling fuel on the back on an envelope until they finally made an emergency landing at Leiston.

By the end of the day the 351st had lost six of its Fortresses with sixty aircrew listed as missing. It was the highest number of planes and men the group would ever lose over Berlin and the greatest casualty total from any group for the day.

Marshalling yards in Tempelhof were also attacked and more incendiaries fell across the locomotive and repair facilities; the goods yard sidings and the mainline through-tracks were also hit several times. German reports indicate the greatest damage and casualties occurred in this area.

Industrial plants were also attacked at Marienfelde by a following force of three combat wings totalling 154 B17s, amidst moderate to intense flak. This force sighted 15 jets near Helmdstadt but they were no threat. A small force of Me109s and a single Fw190 did launch an ineffective attack on the lead group in the target area. Two days previously the Luftwaffe had experienced heavy losses from Allied aircraft when they tried to assemble in the Fassberg area. On 6th August the German controllers decided to assemble their defensive forces east of the Elbe. Aircraft from the 2nd Fighter Division flew to Perleberg and then doubled back to attempt interception in the Hamburg and Neumunster region — with little success.

Flak cut three Forts from the 3BD formation, another was totally wrecked in a crashlanding back in England; two others failed to return, but one made it to Sweden where the crew were interned for the duration of hostilities.

Over a hundred tons of explosive and incendiary bombs were dropped onto the Miedersciwie tank engine factory and almost two hundred tons fell on the Daimler Benz Marienfelde aero-engine plant. The main workshop building there was destroyed and the machine assembly shops and offices received several direct hits. The nearby Fritz Werner machine tool factory also took direct hits on its power plant and pattern storage buildings. The communications equipment factory of Siemens Haske AG suffered severe damage to work and machine shops.

Two main buildings of the Norddeutsche Motorenbau tank engine plant were gutted by a concentration of over 100 bombs. The testing and assembly building took nine direct hits; the machine shop another four. Strikes were also made on a zinc smelting works as well as the sulphuric acid plant of Kali-Chemie AG in the Treptow district. Heavy damage was reported on the Deutsche Telefonwerke plant nearby.

> "We'd been to Berlin once before, Hamburg and the oil targets like Merseburg were just as scary but it was a psychological thing, every time you sat in the briefing room and saw that red string stretch out to Berlin it was a bit of a shock.... we were nearing the end of our tour and weren't too happy to be going back to Big B!"
>
> Jim Long, bombardier 381BG's *Queenie* (42-97828)

The pilot bails out of a doomed Me109 – to fight another day. (M Sams)

Aces high! – the fighter battle

Four groups of escorts were despatched to protect the first bomber force attacking Genshagen, 168 Mustangs. A force of about fifteen Me109s and Do217s was seen near Schonfield and Strausburg airfields. Another group of thirty single-engine fighters were engaged by 352FG near Hamburg in a combat from 27,000ft down to the deck.

20FG encountered ten Me109s over the Berlin suburbs but failed to engage. They did catch two Me109s south of Brandenburg and destroyed them for the loss of one. A Do217 and four other single-engine fighters were also claimed by the 20FG who went on to add two locomotives to their tally with ground strafing runs. In all, nineteen fighter kills were claimed by the escorts for the loss of just two Mustangs. The 352FG scored twelve of them, with Major George Preddy claiming a staggering six victories.

The 4FG escorting the Marienfelde force shot an Me410 and an Me109 out of the air twenty miles southeast of Berlin, near Prenzlau. Another Me410 was destroyed on the ground, three Ju52 transports and a Ju88 were damaged, during strafing runs as well as two more locomotives and over 70 wagons and tank cars destroyed. The 4FG almost lost their most successful ace, Captain John Godfrey, after he had claimed the Me410. Flak ripped through his fuel system and he prepared to bail out, jettisoning his canopy. Finding that he could stay in the air by using the hand priming pump, Godfrey limped back for two and half hours to make an emergency landing at Beccles, nursing a bloody and bruised hand. He would eventually finish the war with 18 aerial and 12 ground victories.

The three escorting groups for the 3BD claimed four more kills in the air northeast of Bremen, plus two on the ground, for the loss of a single P51. The 355FG, passing below the bombers, was bounced by six to eight Me109s from JG5 as they dived through the B17s between Hamburg and Bremen. Captain Bert Marshall, leading the 355FG in his *Jane II*, became an "ace" when he brought down one attacker after a low level chase. The German pilot is thought to have been Lt Auguste Mors, a skilled pilot with 60 kills to his credit.

A second Me109 was shot down by 355FG's Captain Lenfest, flying his *Lorie III*, the victory also made him an "ace". A third was claimed by Lt Martin but the 355FG also lost one Mustang in the melee.

359FG covering the withdrawal strafed ground targets and added two locomotives and 55 wagons to the day's tally.

6th AUGUST 1944

6th AUGUST 1944

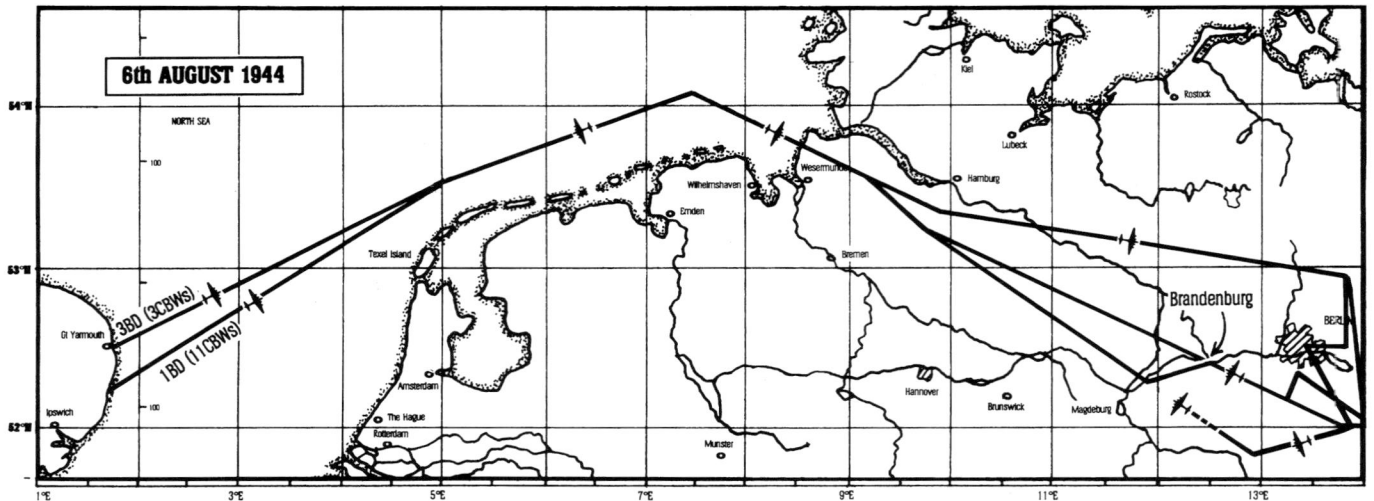

"... observed solid wall of flak over the target..."

The following account was written by Lt Jay Hatfield, pilot of 487BG's 43-37805, shortly after his capture on 6th August. It was concealed throughout his confinement and filed with the USAAF authorities upon his return to the United States.

"6 August 1944: Early briefing; one hour delay before usual instrument take-off. Normal assembly above overcast. My position in formation: deputy lead of high group. Left England at 12,000ft, climbing over the North Sea to 20,000ft at Heligoland; 23,000ft at German coast. Light but accurate flak from time to time. Two squadrons of Me163s (jet jobs) at 12 o'clock high about 45,000ft which hung around but did not attack. Made IP on time (1231 hrs).... observed solid wall of flak over target, at least 10,000ft thick. We were the third group over and the first two groups disappeared from view in flak. Informed crew on intercom to check flak-suits and chute harness.... started riding into heavy barrage of flak at 1235 hrs.

"Bombs away at 1239 hrs. Bombardier closed bomb bay doors; Group lead started to break to right instead of left, as briefed, and thus brought us into heaviest flak zone. At 1240 a direct hit on No.3

engine knocked off No.3 prop, which went through the nose of the ship, making a large gash. No.3 engine was blazing from the cowling; No.4 knocked out, prop windmilling, oil all over both engine nacelles. Shut off gasoline to No.3. and No.4 immediately; copilot, on orders, closed cowl flaps, pulled CO2 controls and extinguished flames in No.3. Flak hit in pedestal of cockpit, striking me in left shin; knocking out generator panel, jamming alarm bell switch. Direct hit blew all of plexi-glass out of the nose of ship; bombardier and nose gunner left at this time, not known if blown out or bailed out on faulty alarm bell signal. Tail gunner reported that two chutes opened....

"Copilot's window smashed, pilot's window cracked. Unable to feather No.4 as all of oil gone. Prop control cables on No.1 and No.2 shot away, rpm dropped to 1850. Trim-tab controls shot away, autopilot inoperative. Losing altitude rapidly, dropped out of formation, going down about 500fpm. Compass shot out, headed in general direction of WNW, rest of crew all at stations. Released excess weight of ship, started to jettison ball turret, which had been shot out.

Realised could not return to base, so decided to get as far away from the target as possible. Half of oxygen shot out, crew using emergency supplies.

"Check on condition of ship showed that half of right stabiliser and elevator gone; top part of rudder gone; large holes in fuselage of ship; radio man had flak in left leg, not serious.... Right wing-tip gone, all radios out; flaps partially shot away and vibrating in slipstream; right landing gear hanging down; nose of ship starting to buckle and sheets of metal tearing off in the slipstream.

"At 10,000ft more flak coming up, tried evasive action but unable to shake off the flak, which was beginning to hit us more frequently. Told crew to stand by to abandon ship. Sent co-pilot back to waist of ship to check chutes of crew... copilot checked chutes and then lined crew up in waist compartment, aft. At 6,000ft, I left seat, to give signal to crew and returned to seat to level ship off.... Crew all left ship from main waist door, at about 4,000ft. Flak very heavy now, No.4 engine and wing on fire and ship starting to break up.

"Headed ship towards open country, feathered No.2 engine, put ship in left back, climbed down through hatch, went

forward to nose hatch and stepped out of ship, being hit in the head by flak at that time. Made delayed jump, finally pulled rip-cord, was in air about 10 seconds and then landed hard, slightly dizzy, at 1310 hrs. Chute canopy had several holes in it from ground fire. Ship piled in, about 1500ft away and exploded, almost disintegrated. Crew still coming down and landing. Got out of chute and boots, started across the field toward the crew; saw armed civilians had surrounded us; stayed with the crew and surrendered.

Civilians, who had ropes, guns, pitchforks, clubs, etc, at that time started knocking the crew around and placed a rope in a tree nearby, making preparations to lynch us. Before this was done, members of a flak battery of the Luftwaffe appeared and took us from the civilians."

Hatfield's ship crashed near Zietz, south west of Berlin. The unfortunate bombardier who had fallen from the shattered nose of the ship over Berlin itself had been hit by the severed propeller from No.3 engine. Although hospitalised in the city he died soon after. The remainder of the crew spent the rest of the war as prisoners of the Germans.

Cripes A'Mighty – six in one day!

When Major George Preddy took off to lead the 352FG on the escort mission to Berlin on 6th August there were serious doubts as to his ability. The previous day he had taken the group over Germany and indulged in a dogfight near Hamburg. Sweeping in behind an Me109 as it lined up to attack the bomber force, Preddy had sent it down in flames from 400 yards. The dogfight developed into a brawl as 40 more German fighters, flying top cover, roared down to join in. Another Me109 was sent away smoking but Preddy was forced to break off by another bandit. Other 487th Squadron Mustangs pounced to the rescue and sent three of the enemy down.

The Major and his colleagues understandably celebrated the day's triumphs in the Officers Club. The weathermen had predicted appalling conditions for the following day so they celebrated long and hard. But 'the best laid plans...

The camera gun ensures there is no mistaking the score. Scratch six Me109s. Ironically, in December, Preddy's Mustang would be mistaken for an Me109 and shot down by friendly fire. (352FG Assn)

oft go astray' and within an hour of getting to bed Preddy was awoken to be told that a mission was on!

Although many around him felt he was in no fit state to fly, Preddy insisted he would lead the group and climbed, somewhat unsteadily, into his P51, *Cripes A'Mighty*. High over the North Sea, the Major threw up in this cockpit and felt sick as a dog but in less than an hour and a half he was ready for the enemy.

Approaching Hamburg, a force of thirty Me109s threatened the bombers and Preddy led his White Flight into the attack. Opening fire on a fighter near the rear of the group from 300 yards dead astern he sent it spinning down enveloped in flame. Another target crossed his sights and hits into the wing root sent it too spinning away in flames with the pilot bailing out. As the melee continued, another Me109 began to break up from Preddy's close range fire; then another started to burn

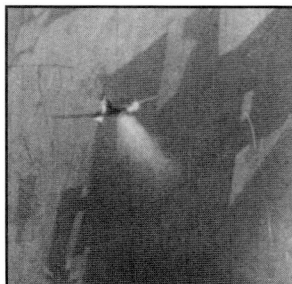

Major George Preddy poses for the cameras and indicates his victory score for the day (352FG Assn)

after just a short burst. As the entire enemy formation continued on in a diving left turn, taking little evasive action, the Major sent another down on fire.

At 5,000ft one German fighter pulled away to the left. This one proved a little more evasive. As Preddy fired a short burst and pulled up the German climbed after him. *Cripes A'Mighty* was pulled round as tight as possible in a 150mph climb with machine gun fire flashing

past. As the German then fell away to the left, Preddy dropped astern and fired another burst into the plane. As he roared past, its canopy was jettisoned and the pilot leapt from the stricken machine. It was Preddy's sixth victory that day. Having lost contact with both friend and foe, he headed *Cripes A'Mighty* towards Bodney and the award of a Distinguished Service Cross.

Tragedy finally overtook Preddy in December 1944, on the day he scored his 24th and 25th victories. His P51 was shot down by US fire in mistake for an Me109.

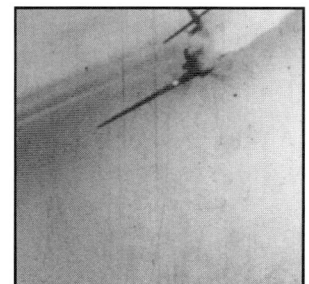

Munitions dumps, aviation and tank industry plants in the Berlin area were the chosen targets but only for the Fortresses of the 3rd Bomb Division. The 1BD struck the Stargard Luftwaffe Training School and the Stettin Armoured Force School while the 2nd Division's Liberators headed for a selection of oil processing and aviation industry targets in northern Germany.

The 3BD assembled 418 B17s for its strike, formed up in eleven combat wings. Their targets were the BMW aero engine plant and the Neustadt military depot at Spandau together with the ordnance depot and the Alkett tank factory in Tegel, the biggest of its kind in Germany. The weather was good with only a handful of scattered clouds below, making it a near perfect day for visual bombing.

Approximately 50-75 enemy fighters were encountered between Nauen and Berlin; these struck the trailing 4th Combat Wing on their bomb run. The entire formation was flying about one thousand feet below a high cirrus cloud layer but above that shroud were massed several Gruppen of German fighters from JG4 and JG300. As the trailing group, the 385BG, turned on the IP its high squadron became separated from the rest of the formation — the Luftwaffe pounced!

Seventeen bombers fell away from the formations in spite of five groups of escorts becoming embroiled

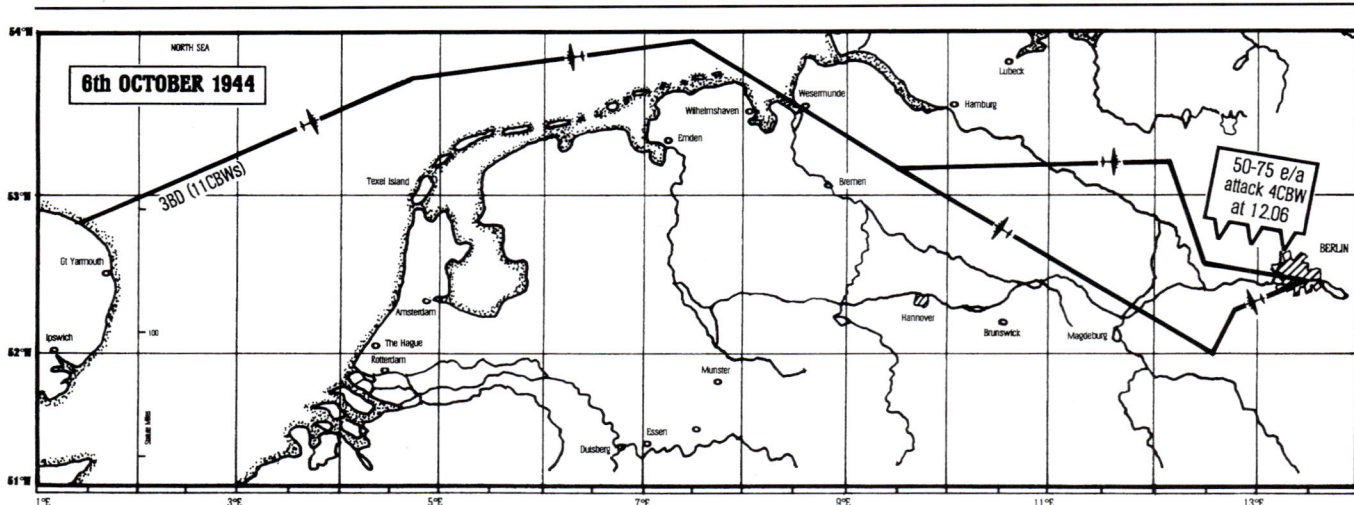

The fighter battle

Eight groups of P51 Mustangs, totalling 414 fighters, took to the air as escorts for the Berlin force. Several of the groups engaged a large force of Luftwaffe fighters, including some long-nosed Fw190s, in a protracted melee as they made saturation attacks on the bombers between Nauen and the target.

As the 355FG and 4FG escorted the bombers from Wesermunde towards the target, fifty to seventy enemy aircraft attacked the last five or six bomber boxes. The company front attack was devastating and cut about 15 Fortresses from the formation of the 4CBW in the first pass. Three of the Fw190s were shot down by two squadrons from the 355FG after the group had turned back from further ahead in the column to assist the 4FG in breaking up the assault.

On its way in to rendezvous with the bombers, the 4FG had already claimed an Me410 over Heligoland. Near Nauen they also chased away eight Me109s which had attempted to draw off the escorts. They then turned their attention to the attackers hitting the 4CBW. One 4FG Mustang chased an Me109 at such speed that as the enemy plane turned to port it simply shredded itself to pieces. Another Me109, caught about 15 miles east of Berlin, brought the 4FG's total for the day to three kills for no loss of their own.

The 357FG's Mustangs also joined in the melee around the 4CBW with part of two squadrons and

> **"6-7 solid black P-51s with white invasion markings observed at Oranienburg, 12.30 at 24000ft – believed enemy operated..... P-51s seen firing at American fighters. Believed that attacking enemy aircraft landed on landing strips in dispersed areas in woods just north of Magdeburg."** Extract Intops Summary #297

helped to separate the attackers from the beleaguered Fortresses. They later engaged another group of 50 fighters northwest of Berlin, shooting down five Fw190s and two Me109s. Two 357FG pilots, Lts Martinek and England, both scored double victories, the latter flying his P51 U've Had It! and upping his victory total to twelve. The group lost none of their Mustangs in the encounter.

The 479FG also became embroiled in the confused dogfights west of Berlin. The Mustangs of 479FG turned directly into the enemy, who were attacking in waves of 8-10, and were met by many aggressive, head-on combats. They succeeded in shooting down an Me109 and Fw190 without loss. Twenty minutes later, the 361FG engaged another sixteen German fighters northwest of the city and destroyed one Me109. Unfortunately, debris from the destroyed plane smashed into the victor's Mustang and Capt Brubaker went spiralling down with his victim. The group returned from the mission with another of their pilots missing from an unknown cause.

The camera on a 490BG Fortress shows the bomb load hitting the target – the Spandau Neustadt Ordnance Depot (top left) situated just east of Berlin's Tegeler See (M. McKenzie)
Damage assessment of a photograph taken the following day indicates two-thirds destruction of the three main buildings (1,2 & 3) and numerous hits across the vehicle park (4) (USAF)

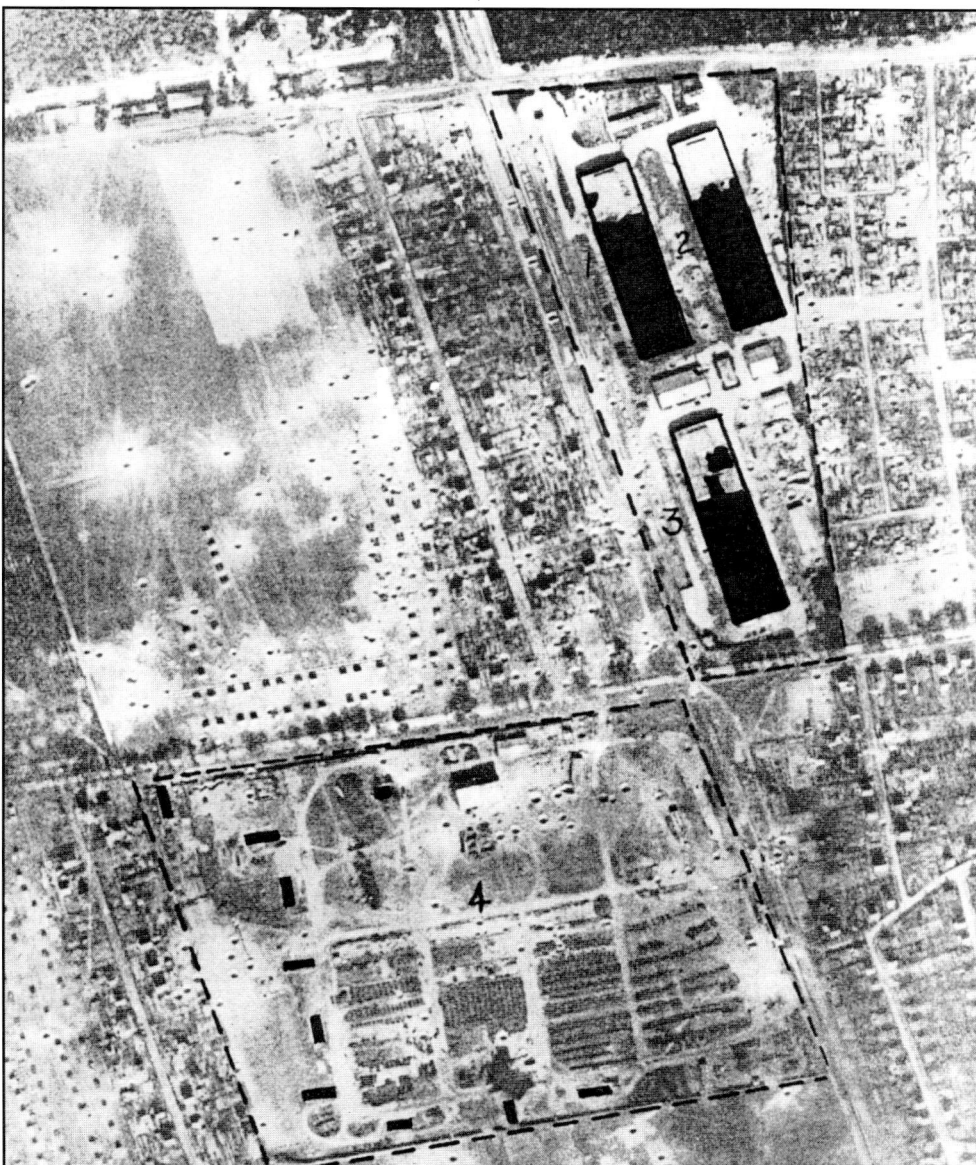

in defensive combat. The 385BG suffered its worst losses of the war, with eleven of its bombers shot down, including a PFF lead ship on loan to the group. The 94BG also lost another three planes, one of which was forced to ditch into the North Sea.

All of the primary targets were hit visually with almost 1000 tons of bombs. Returning crews from 390BG reported seeing the smoke rising from their target, the aircraft engine plant at Spandau, as far away as Bremen as they withdrew. High explosive bursts had blanketed the north end of the plant and a 490BG Fortress also crashed into the parking area and added to the destruction. An adjacent aircraft instrument factory and residential areas took further hits.

The giant Alkett tank assembly plant suffered a concentration of high explosive bombs which extended on into the nearby gas works. The plant's main machine shop and assembly buildings took several direct hits and numerous structurally damaging near misses. The Spandau-Neustadt ordnance depot was also severely hit by more than 130 high explosive bursts and a carpet of incendiaries which followed. Three of the large standard ordnance buildings each received five direct hits and equipment stored at several locations in the vicinity was also destroyed and left burning as the last bomber passed over.

6th OCTOBER 1944

Sudden devastation for Van's valiant tail-enders

6th October 1944 proved to be one of the worst days of the entire war for 'Van's Valiants', the 385th Bomb Group flying from Great Ashfield, and once again Berlin was the target. The 385th's 'B' group was flying in the high position of the 4CBW, scheduled to be last over the target. Their 549th Squadron was the last squadron in the group — tail end Charlies to the entire 8th Air Force.

After taking off in dismal, gloomy conditions progress towards the target was uneventful. Some anti-aircraft fire was thrown up by a flak train somewhere in Holland and ahead of the 385BG a plane went spiralling down. At 12.06 hrs the formation peeled off at the Initial Point to take its position on the bomb run and about 1000ft below the very high cloud layer. At this point they were some 60 miles short of Berlin. Making a rather wide turn, the formation became slightly separated from the rest of the bomber stream. One minute later it was struck by a mass of fighters sweeping down to attack

from both the rear and above their formation.

It was a sudden and devastating assault. Fighters from Gruppen JG4 and JG300 charged out of the clouds directly through the formation in waves of four or five fighters abreast and in that first pass reduced the high squadron's strength to just two aircraft. Fortresses exploded in the air or spun down cutting a trail of greasy flames. Observers described those first attack waves as coming through on their backs then looping round to make a second and third pass. Using the same tactics, the successive waves shot two surviving Fortresses to pieces with 20mm cannon fire before split-essing away for the safety of the deck. The whole thing took less than 90 seconds according to one eye witness.

Another witness described seeing the fighters pouring in their devastating fire and working their way methodically through the formation from the rear. The sky was full of burning planes and falling

debris — just a few chutes were seen but stunned observers had no way to tell from which planes they might have come. The onslaught was too sudden and too overwhelming. Even German salvage crews complained that so many aircraft (probably more than 12) had crashed between Rathenau and Nauen that they were too hard-pressed to begin all their salvage work before darkness fell. Establishing precisely what occured during the terrible onslaught is complicated by a further twist of fate. The next 8AF raid on Berlin, on 5th December, reportedly destroyed almost all the accumulated Luftwaffe records relating to the aircraft downed on 6th October in the Nauen area. What records did survive indicate that almost all of the lost aircraft struck the ground at 12.14hrs

Hell's Bells (43-37548) was flying on only its third mission, as tail-end Charlie, and was one of the first to take hits. The fuselage was riddled and the right wing was hit — flames licking back through and below the stricken aircraft. It went into a steep dive, pinning the unfortunate crew inside unable to move even their heads. Suddenly it levelled out in a roller coaster movement, the bombardier jettisoned the load and the crew worked their way to their bail out positions. Two crew men were already dead from the cannon fire and others were wounded but the pilot Lt Hyman Kaplan held the plane steady enough to enable survivors to jump. Kaplan then made his way to the nose to bail out. Fate intervened, as a survivor explained, "Before he could bail out, the ship exploded and threw Lts Kaplan and Mulder (bombardier) into

> **"35 e/a attacked the last formation of 11 aircraft of the 385BG.... The entire squadron was wiped out."** 8AF Mission Report

the nose of the plane. The nose section fell separately with both men in it. The bombardier fell, or was thrown, out of the nose at about 8000ft..." Kaplan was still inside when *Hell's Bells* crashed into the ground near Liepe but his action to hold the plane steady saved six men.

Yet another B17 fell away with Nos. 1 and 2 engines burning and a waist gunner killed by 20mm fire. It went into a slow, flat spin streaming a spiral of greasy smoke as the crew bailed out.

Lt Courcelle's *Texas Bluebonnet* went down, then Ray Noiseau's *West Virginian*. The latter aircraft exploded in mid-air, blowing the navigator and pilot clear. Lt Noiseau later stated, "Lt Waggoner (copilot) and myself were both in the cockpit. Our ship was afire and blew up. I came to in the air and opened my chute... was in hospital in Berlin for a month... most of the crew were killed while in the ship by 20mm fire." Everett Isaacson's *Dozy Doats* (42-97079) was also caught in the first attack which killed the tail gunner and put shells into the mid-section of the plane. It too exploded in mid-air and fell to earth in two pieces with five men dead. Bill Leverett's *Roger the Dodger* (42-97275) fell away, *Wee Willie Wilbur* (42-102465) went down with the loss of all on board. Three other B17s, together with their 94BG lead PFF ship, tumbled out of formation in quick succession. When it was all over, eleven aircraft and one hundred men were gone.

> **"Top group of each combat wing flew directly beneath cloud layer – perfect for attack. Enabled enemy aircraft above clouds to pick his time and place."**
> Extract, 55FG After-action Report

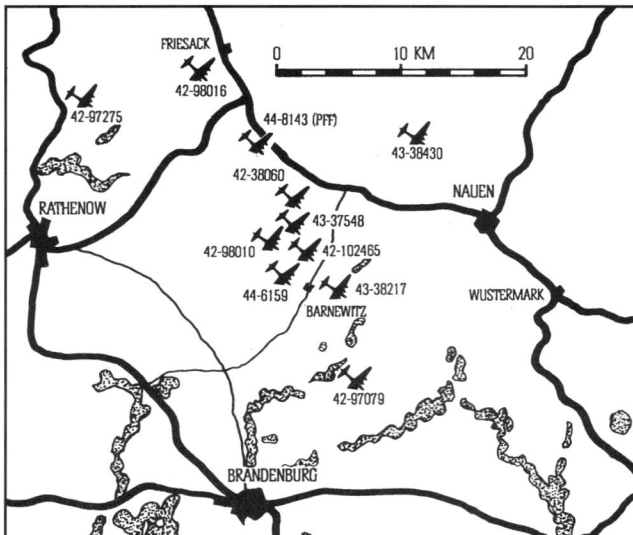

Raise your hat to dear old Mag... *The Filthy Hag*

"She looked beautiful to all of us except co-pilot Harold Harpootlian, " recalled radio man Jack Miller. "B17G, 42-31599 was assigned to our crew (Lt Gordon Hendrickson), at Scott Field, Illinois. Harpootlian had taken his original training as a P38 pilot and was very disappointed to find himself assigned to a bomber crew. When we flew into Valley in Wales, we lost #599 but this was only temporary. We were given five days pre-combat training and sent to the 94BG at Bury St Edmunds,

"She looked beautiful to all but one of our crew..."

Jack Miller, radio operator 94BG

where #599 awaited us."

"Hendrickson was lost flying with another crew and 'Harpo' became our 1st pilot and had the honour of naming the ship. In letters written to a friend in the States he had expressed his feelings towards bombers and was sent a cartoon by his friend. This became the artwork for *The Filthy Hag*.."

Stephen Najarian added to the story, "The name originated from a song which served as a toast at Harpootlian's local bar in Brooklyn. *Here's to dear old Mag... The Filthy Hag...*" etc, etc. Sometime later, before Harpo completed his tour of missions, HQ brass ordered that the 'Hag' be clothed and so a black dress was added."

Jack Miller recalled a humorous note regarding *The Filthy Hag*, "On one of my trips to London I acquired a top hat. As a lark, I took it with me on the remaining missions I flew. Some of these were as a togglier and when we

were on the bomb run, when the flak was at it heaviest, I would sit in the plexiglass nose and tip my hat to each wing ship. This relieved some tension."

Completing his tour in April '44, Harpootlian passed the plane onto other crews — she had proved lucky for him. By October, the 'Hag' was a veteran and, on the 6th, the crew of Jesse Brashers was on board to watch with horror the slaughter of their colleagues flying with the 385BG. By that time the 'Hag' had been re-named as a result of instructions from higher authority. Jesse Brashers explained, "We knew the ship strictly as *Boots and her Buddies*. Someone took exception to some of the names on the noses of our airplanes and they had to take off the old title. In fact, I never knew

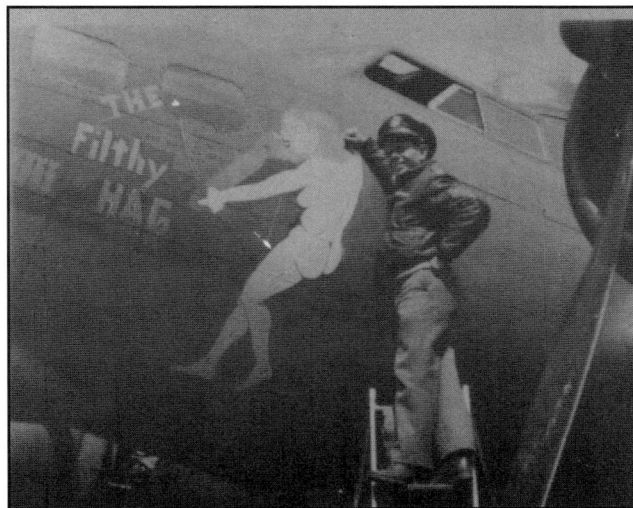

Capt Fraser Burbank, 410BS Engineering Officer, takes a closer look at the original 'hag' before she was dressed in black – by order. (S. Najarian)

what the original name was. She was affectionately known as 'The Old Bitch!' On 6th October it was a beautiful morning in Britain and when the sun came up there wasn't a cloud in the sky. Over the North Sea one of the turbo chargers over-sped and the engine ran away but we got that under control... just before reaching Germany a prop ran away. We got that under control

too but by rights I should have aborted then but it was our 33rd mission and we were eager to finish our tour. The bird ran beautifully all the way to Berlin."

As the determined attackers swept through the 4CBW they also knocked down a PFF aircraft which was actually assigned to the 94th but loaned to and partly crewed by the 385th. Within seconds the sky was filled with exploding Forts and others dropping away trailing smoke and flame. Barely a handful of chutes were observed at this time, witness to the suddenness of the attack.

After the initial onslaught, some of the fighters broke away and picked off the damaged stragglers. Before long they turned their attention to

the 94BG and swept in from 6 o'clock low and level to knock three more Forts from the formation.

Jesse Brashers continued the story, "We saw no fighters until just as we turned on the IP... the sky was filled with Me109s. We had not seen fighters for a month — suddenly they were everywhere. The first pass hit the high squadron, the second pass caught us in

the lead squadron. The No.1 engine was shot completely off its mounts, there was nothing left, the No.2 was windmilling and No.3 was only pulling half power. We went into a roll and dropped from 35,000ft to 20,000ft before regaining control. We then flew north east towards Sweden for approximately 25 minutes. The fire in the wing and cabin became so

"We affectionately referred to her as the Old Bitch!"

Jesse Brasher, pilot 94BG

bad that I decided to bail my crew out and take our chances with the Germans, which we did. All crew members survived."

A silver B17G *Our Baby* (43-37630) also peeled away under heavy fighter attack from the rear. The third Fort (42-38207), carrying 333BS C.O. Major Blount as command pilot, was badly mauled and was forced to lag behind the formation with two seriously wounded men on board. Somehow the plane made it to the Channel, and almost back to England, but was forced to ditch into the sea one mile off Lowestoft. The plane floated for barely a minute before sliding below the surface and although air sea rescue planes and high speed launches had been alerted, only two bodies were recovered from Lt Davis' crew.

Jesse Brashers evaded capture for almost 3 days, no mean feat in the midst of Germany itself! "First few days they treated me like an officer and a gentlemen but then they let me know real quick... I was a prisoner! They took us to Berlin and threw us in a cell at Tempelhof airfield... then to Frankfurt, Oberusel and finally Stalag Luft 1."

When *Roger the Dodger* didn't !!

42-97275 arrived with the 385BG in the spring of 1944. In August the plane, coded R-Roger, was assigned to Lt Jarman and his crew for the latter part of their tour. "We did not fly all our remaining missions in the ship but when it was available we flew it," recalled Wallace Jarman. "The name and painting on the nose was my decision. I must admit that I did not have total crew agreement with the choice of *Roger the Dodger*."

Mike Pappas was a tail gunner and it was he who was 'commissioned' to paint *Roger the Dodger*. "I did the nose art work on the plane and also on her crew's flight jackets," wrote Mike. "Some 551BS crew men were walking behind me and one of them noticed my jacket, which I had painted with our bomber's name — *Big Gas Bird*. One of them asked if I would do the same for their ship and said that each of the crew would contribute one Pound apiece — $40.00! Big bucks at that time! I never did get paid!"

"I wasn't too keen on their choice of a name... I suggested a feminine name and image — I wanted to indulge myself in a nudie-cutie painting. But they were adamant, so I reluctantly agreed — *Roger the Dodger* was born."

Wallace Jarman's crew took 'Roger' to Hamburg, Bremen, Stuttgart, Coblenz and Kassel among other targets. Finally, they flew to Munster on 5th October to complete their combat tour. *Roger the Dodger* had successfully dodged fighters and flak and brought them safely through. Meanwhile, Mike Pappas had a lucky escape and was not flying on the day his regular crew were shot down over Munster. Put into the replacement pool for gunners, Mike became frustrated by the

delay before he could add more missions and complete his tour. He checked out as a toggler, trained to drop the bombs on the lead ship's signal. "The nose, compared to the cramped and freezing tail gunner's position, was a dream," said Mike. "Now I could see where we were going, but I'll readily admit that it was sometimes a terrifying sight up ahead."

On 6th October, assigned to Lt Bill Leverett's crew who were to fly *Roger the Dodger*, he took his position in the nose beside the colourful artwork he had painted weeks before. It was an unfortunate quirk of Fate — what had proved lucky for the Jarman crew would now bring misfortune to their replacements.

"The Germans attacked from 6 o'clock high, coming in waves of four or five on each Fort. The first wave raked the fuselage... the second bored 20mm incendiaries through our wing tanks. Our waist gunner was killed instantly," recalled Mike. "The tail gunner was severely injured and almost had his arm torn off. I later heard that another crew man snapped on his chute, pulled the cord and threw him out. Upon landing he was unable to dump the chute or even stand and a civilian shot him. Bill Leverett witnessed the entire tragic episode and he later told me that enraged civilians, armed with hammers and shovels, had beaten to death many of the airmen — some of them already wounded in the air.

Lynn White was a photographer and also a stranger on the crew. He recalled, "I had my chest chute right beside me. I stood up and tried to put it on... I couldn't co-ordinate, I couldn't put the thing on.

Wallace Jarman and his crew with *Roger the Dodger* (W. Jarman)

I realised I didn't have oxygen and grabbed a walk-around bottle.... After a minute without oxygen at mission height you pass out.... I bailed out at 25,000ft. My walk-around bottle was ripped off from the airstream and I was 'out' for some time. When I came to this German fighter was circling me. My understanding at the time was that they had orders to 'strafe' airmen in parachutes. After about the third time he circled I gave him a salute. He saluted me back and took off!"

"As for myself," continued Mike Pappas, "I was stunned by the suddenness of the attack and was thrown upside down over the control post of the chin turret. It felt as if the plane had made a sudden stop in mid-air — the result of having Nos 1 and 2 engines abruptly knocked out.... I was unaware that my oxygen supply had been severed and I passed out. When I finally came round I was horrified to see how low the plane was. I could see tiled roofs on the houses through the nose...1,400ft... the plane must have

drifted 20 miles or so, in a steep glide, tilted to the left. The entire left wing and engines were blazing furiously, as well as the left side of the fuselage. I lunged for my chute, snapped it on and made a dash for the escape hatch but one of my harness straps caught on a floor fixture.... then I realized that I had forgotten to fasten my leg straps... 800ft.... I felt something snap and tighten and hoped it was the catch.... 600ft.... I dropped out of the hatch, waited two or three seconds to clear the flames and pulled the rip cord. The pilot chute jammed and I clawed at it with my left hand tearing two nails away. It popped out and the chute blossomed above me."

Mike landed in a field near Vehlgast and was greeted unemotionally by a civilian with a rifle who kept his distance and ushered him towards a nearby house. "He reached the house first, apparently unconcerned that I might have shot him in the back with my service pistol. I had, in fact, deliberately left it in the plane. A girl

---

"I have never seen such devastation in all of my life. We drove through miles and miles of rubble where it looked like they pushed aside some of it with a bulldozer in order to make a path to get through. There was not one living thing, not anything anybody could live in..."

Lynn White, photographer, 385BG *Roger the Dodger*

came out and asked in English *"Where did you fly from to bomb our country?"* New York City, I replied straight-faced."

The local Volksturm eventually arrived and took Mike into custody. He was taken to the Burgermaster's house where he received a tirade of abuse and a black eye for a second, unwise, wise-crack. Luftwaffe soldiers then transported him to Tempelhof air field and threw him into a concrete cell. "Written on the door," Mike recalled, " was *Kilroy was here too, dammit!*"

Lynn White was also quickly spotted after he landed. Two school girls shrieked with alarm and soon others arrived with a farmer holding a fearsome pitchfork. "I reached down and handed him my knife, handle first. That seemed to cool the situation," wrote Lynn. Kept under guard until the following day, he was then collected by the military and transported to the very place he had been sent to bomb. "They put us on a train with one guard. Pretty soon we had to get off the train as most of the stations had been bombed out and we went to the underground (subway)…. if looks could kill, we would have been dead from the looks the civilians were giving us. We were still in our flight gear so there was no mistaking who we were. We were in Berlin…. we got off the subway and onto a bus…. got caught in an air raid and had to go into a shelter with all of these Germans. When the raid was over we got back on the bus…. This big burly guy starts towards us…. he comes walking towards me, turns around and slips me a cigarette and continues walking." Taken to Spandau air base for an initial questioning, Lynn was then taken on to Frankfurt for a more thorough interrogation.

Smoke billows up from the giant Alkett (Altmarkisches Kettenwerke GmBH) tank assembly plant in Tegel. (USAF)

An estimated 10% of the Luftwaffe's total of more than 17,500 flak guns were positioned in and around Berlin and its suburbs. They claimed the majority of casualties caused to the 8th Air Force. (J Ramaker)

5th DECEMBER 1944

Munitions factories and a tank assembly and flak gun plant were the targets of this daylight raid on Berlin. Tegel on the western edge of the city was the more precise location and the attacking force was split into two almost identical formations. The first was comprised of Fortresses of seven groups from 3BD, 229 aircraft; the second was six groups from 1BD, 222 aircraft. Liberators from 2BD were assigned the rail yard at Munster as their primary target for the day.

Solid undercast over the entire breadth of Germany is believed to have prevented a maximum effort by the Luftwaffe fighter force. Aerial opposition against the bomber stream was virtually nil, although a large number of enemy fighters did attempt to make contact with the first formation as they came off the target. At least 230 fighters came from the northeast in an effort to engage as the bombers exited the flak area. These attacks were not pressed home and escorts kept the enemy at bay, claiming an impressive score of victories in the running dogfights. Even when some jets appeared later during the withdrawal, threatening battle damaged and straggling bombers, these were also driven off by P51s.

Flak over Berlin was described as only moderate and largely inaccurate with several rockets seen to rise and explode near the formations. Three B17s from the first force, with nine more from the second,

A field day for the fighters

Almost three hundred and fifty Mustangs, from six fighter groups, escorted the leading 3rd Bomb Division. Numerous successful combat actions were fought against an estimated two hundred German fighters, with claims of 65 destroyed for six lost. Another Thunderbolt was declared as scrap after crashlanding back in England.

Sweeping ahead of the leading Berlin force, the 339FG encountered small groups of enemy aircraft and chased them through heavy cloud layers and a solid undercast. Only one FW190 was claimed as damaged in the action but the group lost two of its own pilots before the day was out. Lt Col Henderson, the 503FS CO, and his wingman were bounced by three FW190s as they climbed back to escort altitude after the melee. His plane was badly shot up and was last seen upside down going into clouds 25 miles north of Berlin. The other pilot experienced engine failure and bailed out west of Steinhuder Lake, but did not survive.

In an attempt to reach the bomber boxes, the German fighters attacked from out of the flak areas. Escorts, however, were effective in keeping them away and engaged in combat from 27,000ft down to the deck, completely breaking up the enemy formations. 357FG had five pilots each score double kills, adding nine Me109s and one Fw190 to the tally. By the end of the day the group claimed a total of 22 enemy fighters destroyed. Capt Zetterquist was flying Colonel John Storch's *Shillelagh* (44-13546) and he downed an Fw190 but was himself hit and forced to bail out, as was another 357FG pilot.

355FG also engaged seventy of the enemy near Berlin. Led by Major William Hovde in his P51 *Ole III* (44-13531), the group swept into the enemy as they formed up for their attack on the bomber boxes. In just two minutes thirteen German fighters went down and their assault plans were completely disrupted. Major Hovde shot down five, shared a sixth before his ammunition ran out and doubled his score to date, becoming the second highest scorer in the 355th Fighter Group. Hovde was awarded DSC for his action which prevented even a single a attack on the bombers.

A similar sized force of escorts was also assigned to protect the second bomber formation, 1BD, and it too succeeded in engaging the enemy with considerable success. Twenty five destroyed in the air were claimed for the loss of nine more Mustangs.

Some fifty enemy aircraft were engaged in the Berlin area near Neuruppin by elements of 364FG. Still carrying their drop tanks when bounced by the escorts, the German planes continued to fly slavishly on in formation even after the attack had begun. These were 'rooky' pilots and the 364FG Mustangs destroyed eleven of them for no loss. One of the group's aircraft, however, later crashed in Belgium, killing the pilot who had been wounded in the action. The 364FG engaged the enemy again over the target when another force attacked the formations as they were on their bomb run.

Thirty-five German single engine fighters were also encountered towards Lake Muritz and these proved to be more aggressive. Another similar sized force was engaged, by an unidentified flight of escorts shepherding a straggler, just as they were grouping into an attack formation south of Steinhuder Lake.

In all, some twelve jets were sighted, mostly flying parallel to the bombers during the withdrawal without pressing an attack. Two Me262s did try for a straggler but were easily driven off before they could be effective.

353FG also had a successful day and raised their total group victories to date to over 250 by claiming nine kills — but lost two of their own in the battle. The 479FG lost four of their Mustangs, one ditching into the North Sea. But their bag during the action contained four times as many destroyed enemy aircraft.

At the end of the day the Mustang pilots escorting the 8AF's Fortresses to Berlin had returned to claim a total of 90 enemy aircraft destroyed and another thirty as probables or damaged — all for the loss of fifteen of their own.

"We were lucky on this one – P51s drove off enemy fighters which tried to get to our formations – saw numerous dog fights.... Don't know what we'd do without those P51s, P47s and P38s. Can't give them enough credit..."

Diary extract, Duane Vieth
radio operator with Brown's Clowns crew, 100BG PFF

---

were lost — mainly to flak. A further 169 bombers returned with battle damage.

Arriving over their target in the late morning (the sirens sounded at 10.28am) the first force carried high explosive bombs. Following formations were loaded with a mix of GP and incendiary loads in the hope of starting fires amongst the shattered buildings. Dropping through almost complete undercast using H2X radar guidance, with some visual assistance, the results were generally only rated as fair to poor.

The primary target of the Rheinmetall Borsig AG plant in Tegel was blanketed with incendiary bombs, especially east of the forges. Serious fires were started throughout the factory buildings, workshops and offices. The bulk of the high explosive bomb load, however, missed the target and fell short into open fields and spread on into a residential district to the north, just on the edge of the tank plant.

A large cluster of bombs fell to the north east of

"..on the train, our guard told us we could get off if we wanted to, he was only there to *protect* us – we had, after all, only just bombed the place a couple of days earlier! We went through Berlin on the subway, which was operating normally, to Tempelhof airfield.... later by truck to a rail station – total devastation for mile after mile. Like London but far worse..." Don Freer, pilot 91BG's *Easy Does It* (43-38234)

"The enemy today attempted to oppose the heavy bombers attacking Berlin with 275-300 single engine aircraft... from north east in an effort to attack as the bombers exited the flak area. Escorts effective from 27,000ft to the deck, completely breaking up formations and preventing them getting near the bombers."
8AF Mission Summary, 5th December 1944

---

the target area into the Reinickendorf district and into Wittendau where the main stores and repair buildings for the Berlin tram and subway trains were situated. Many buildings were set ablaze in these districts, destroying or badly damaging more than 500 buildings and killing over 170 persons. Hits were reported on the Nordbahnhof rail station, several buildings of a flak barracks in Borsigwalde and an engine gear-box factory. A number of bursts also fell into Pankow, a few into the marshalling yards there but most onto residential buildings.

Some aircraft evidently overshot their target and unloaded their bombs as far away as Neukolln, south east of the city centre, possibly aiming for the Tempelhof airfield. German air raid reports reveal a number of fatalities and "many buried" in that area and indicate that several heavy concentrations also fell into the Weissensee district on the northeast outskirts of the city.

Fortresses of 452BG plough their way through the Berlin flak heading for the tank plant at Tegel (L. LaHood)

A milk run turned sour for some

Losing only twelve bombers from the day's operations, involving almost 600 B17s and B24s including the attack on Munster, might have been considered by some as a 'milk run'. A veteran of the 100BG recorded in his diary, for example, "Good results, Flak not bad — no fighters on the 100th for a change. All okay!"

But for some crews from the 91BG's 322nd Squadron it proved to be their worst mission of all. *Easy Does It* (43-38234) had joined the group back in August 1944 and was assigned immediately to Lou Walton. His navigator Donald Almon recalled, "It was a new aircraft and my crew got to name the plane and agreed on my choice of *Easy Does It*. The nose art painter interpreted this as a girl repairing her seam but to the crew the emphasis was in our minds that this bomber *does* it! It was also a unique way to incorporate the bomber's nomenclature in the title. The circle was dark blue, the letters red, lingerie black and the model was a red-head."

Almon and the rest of his crew took *Easy Does It*

to some tough targets : Hamm, Kiel, Kassel, Nurnberg, Schweinfurt but not Berlin. Over Cologne on the 14th October they had almost stalled and gone down but five days later they finished their tour. Their original copilot Donald Sparkman, now the first pilot on the crew, continued on to fly three further missions in *Easy Does It*, bringing the plane's total to 27.

On 5th December, however, it was the crew of Don Freer who climbed aboard. They had taken the ship to Misburg on the 29th November and now it was to be Berlin. The plane's veteran status at that time meant that it handled "Loosey, goosey" according to Don's recollection, "Real lazy on the controls. When we started out, I was told that two guns wouldn't operate — but even if you had no guns, you still flew the mission. It was my first time to Berlin and there was a thick undercast all the way in. On the bomb run there was a clearing through the cloud and the lead bombardier headed for it — hoping to make a visual reference. Through

that gap was a constant barrage of heavy flak. As we headed for it I could see I was lined up with that barrage — dead nuts!"

As the formation crossed the target, the Borsig Steel Works, a direct hit from 88mm flak blew away the No.3 engine cowling and shattered the engine. "Blew it right off," continued Don Freer. "Knocked out No.2 which windmilled and also hit No.4 which ran away. I couldn't feather either. The under-fuselage was shredded and looked like a cabbage grater. The nose was hit bad and the togglier injured; the bombardier severely wounded and knocked unconscious; the copilot was dazed. I put the plane into a dive to help maintain flying speed. The bomb doors were open but the bombs were jammed up so the engineer eased his way out on the catwalk and prised them loose — bravest man I ever saw."

"The window glass was all cracked, we were on fire and gas was streaming from the wings. After 5-10 minutes I realised that there was no way I could control the plane — the flight controls were all shot out. So I ordered that the unconscious bombardier be hitched up to a static line and dropped out, then I gave the crew one minute to bail out. After that period there was still one man left in the ship and I

gave him another minute, then dived for the escape hatch. I was wearing a long back pack chute and the top of it hooked up on something and I was left dangling through the hatch. Somehow I managed to get a foot hooked on something and hauled myself back into the plane." On the second attempt, Don was more successful and as he floated down, the plane went out of control and spun past him, exploding almost immediately in a fireball. "I came down through the cloud and popped out about 500ft above a pine forest. There was a small clearing and I tried tugging at the risers to direct me towards it. I almost made it but hit the last few trees and slammed into the ground. I dislocated both knees and twisted my ankles. It was real painful but there was no point in crying for Momma so after a while I snapped my knees back and hobbled 4-500 yards. There I was met by a group of civilians carrying axes, picks, etc — but they were quite friendly." Taken later to Templin, Don Freer was reunited with the survivors of his crew. Two men had died. Soon after, he was moved to Staaken airfield, then Tempelhof, Oberusal and finally Stalag Luft.

Another 322nd Squadron plane, *Bride of Mars* (43-38360) was also flying its first Berlin

> ## "At briefing we were told we would catch a lot of workers at the target, a flak gun factory. It was the first time I heard that said as part of a briefing – 'a meat run' they called it."
> Don Freer, pilot *Easy Does It*, 91BG

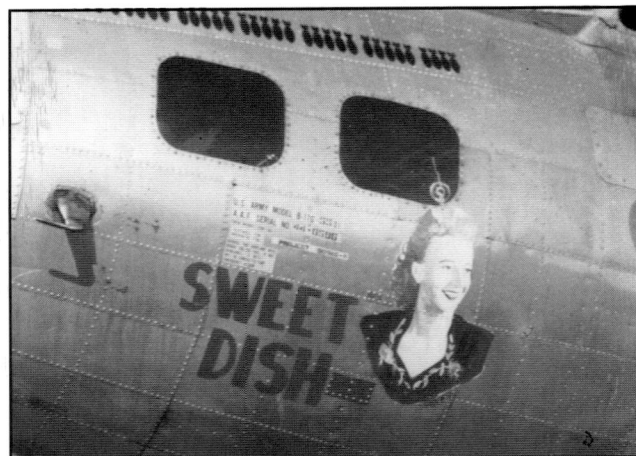

mission, its 28th sortie. It too was hit by flak just prior to bombs away forcing the pilots to feather the No.1 prop and slowly drop away from the formation. All of Ralph Blanton's crew bailed out safely and were taken prisoner. The third aircraft from the group for which the 'milk run' would turn sour was an un-named B17G (43-38693). With three engines feathered it was last reported as dropping away from the formation with six chutes blossoming below, another victim of the flak.

A fourth 91BG plane for which the day would prove 'eventful' was called *Sweet Dish* (44-6596). It had arrived at Bassingbourn just one month earlier and was on its 8th raid. It had been assigned to Bob Roach's crew as brand new. "We had a crew meeting to discuss names — nothing came from this gathering so I suggested *Sweet Dish*. My wife was known to all the crew and as 'Dish' was her nickname they all concurred on the title. The portrait was painted by Tony Starcer from a small pocket photo I carried."

Flak slammed into *Sweet Dish*, just as it had done to her fellow travellers. "The result", recalled Bob, "was fire in No.2 engine as well as the loss of No.1." As the plane plummeted 3000ft, F/O Roach gave the 'Standby to bail out' warning. "During this dive to eliminate the fire, the engineer jumped out, the navigator and togglier apparently also jumped when they saw him leave."

Roach and his co-pilot pulled *Sweet Dish* back under control and found themselves without a navigator, bombardier or top turret engineer but with 365 flak holes peppering the entire plane. Using great skill, both pilots managed to get their aircraft back to England on the remaining two right-side engines.

Patched up by ground crew, *Sweet Dish* went on to become a veteran of 46 missions, 24 of them with Bob Roach at the controls. The three missing crew men became prisoners of war for the duration of hostilities but *Sweet Dish* survived and returned to the USA via Valley in Wales on 8th June 1945. What the Luftwaffe had failed to do, the smelter's torch then achieved by turning her into scrap.

Three sweet 17s lost to Berlin flak

At 11.08 hours, as the 305BG approached the target and passed through the dense cloud of flak, Charles Todd's *Chiquita* (42-39947) caught a 88mm burst. The tail section broke off and the remainder of the plane rolled away to the left before plunging down. Observers in the formation saw 7-8 objects, which they believed to be crew men, tumble from the ship before it went into a death spin and disappeared into the undercast. The shattered plane crashed into the State Forest on the northeast edge of Berlin. There were no survivors.

Hit at about the same time, Lt Richard Funkhouser's 43-38074 turned over in a steep bank and plummeted to about 10,000ft before being brought back under control with No.4 engine windmilling. The whole crew bailed out once they were well clear of the formation but the pilot was blown clear when the plane exploded before it crashed just east of the Berlin-Nord rail yards. The engineer, T/Sgt Garland Williams, later reported, "The complete crew were rounded up and were together late that afternoon, except for the navigator Lt Augustine. The pilot had been beaten badly but other members were OK". Lt Funkhouser also recorded, "An officer of the SS stated he had killed one of the 'Luft Gangsters'... I was beaten unconscious by civilians."

The third 305BG loss was Richard Pounds and crew in *Sweet Seventeen* (43-37827). Not knocked down immediately, the plane lost one engine over the target and then two more later due to excessive power. The crew bailed out and *Sweet Seventeen* crashed 16km north of Braunschweig. All were captured but the radio man died in German custody when an over-enthusiastic guard, waving a pistol about, shot him.

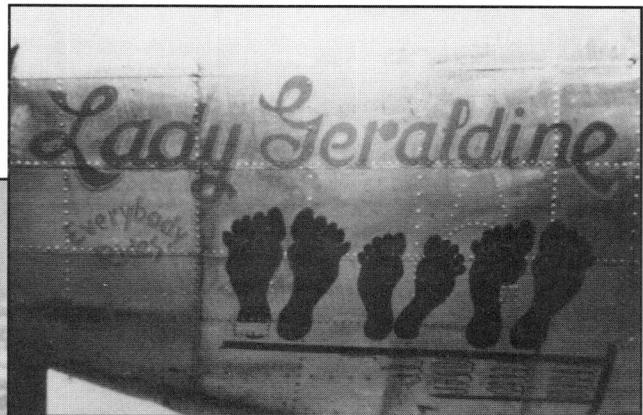

Lady Geraldine avoids 'little men'

As 100BG's *Lady Geraldine* (42-102649) ploughs her way towards Berlin it is easy to see why the flak was described by many as 'little men' – head, shoulders and legs seem to form from the smoke bursts. On both occasions when *Lady Geraldine* made it to Berlin, 5th December 1944 and 18th March 1945, she sustained category A battle damage from the flak. (D. Rock)

Assistance to the Russian offensive by disrupting vital transport centres had been planned for some time but bad weather thwarted the 8AF until now. Air crews were briefed that the 6th Panzer Army was redeploying through Berlin and were thus given an added reason to strike this bottleneck.

The raid was originally conceived as an attack by 8AF day bombers followed by an RAF night attack, guided by the expected fires. The weather, however, rarely allowed such co-ordination and 3rd February proved to be no exception. Unfavourable weather prevented the night assault by the RAF.

The Tempelhof yards were designated as the primary target for this first daylight raid on Berlin of

1945. The ability of the Fortresses to climb above the towering weather fronts enabled twelve groups from the 1AD, 467 bombers, to form the initial stream. A second force followed, 536 aircraft from fourteen 3AD groups, making a total of one thousand heavy bombers. The 8AF's B24s were sent to Magdeburg to strike the synthetic oil plants.

Considerable under-cast was experienced en route to Berlin but over the city the weather was CAVU (Clear and Visibility Unlimited) for the first force enabling visual bombing. A few minutes later the following 3AD found increasing cloud and some groups had to use H2X radar for bombing.

Flak was described as moderate to intense and

Strafing through the flak

1st Air Division was escorted by five groups of Mustangs totalling 280 aircraft, including 44 from 352FG which was by now based on the continent. No aerial engagements were reported but two Mustangs were lost to flak or other causes. The 2nd Scouting Force flying ahead of the formation sighted 30-40 Me410s flying low near Stendal but they chose to stay with the bombers rather than seek combat.

The five groups escorting the second bomber stream had better luck. Six pick-aback lumbering He-111s carrying their Fw190s on their backs were caught near Hamburg and two Fw58 trainer/transports were attacked near Augermunde. Total victories for these escorts amounted to four single-engine and eight twin-engine aircraft destroyed. Six Mustangs were reported lost but none to aerial combat; three to flak, one from engine failure and two from unknown causes.

Eight of the escort groups strafed ground targets and some accounts record that the strafing was carried out even while the bombing was still in progress. Pilots exchanged the danger from the non-existent Luftwaffe for that

of their own falling and exploding bombs. Screaming in across the city at roof top height they achieved devastating results.

The totals for the day included more than fifty locomotives destroyed and sixteen others damaged along with 160 box cars. Twelve oil tank wagons were left blazing and more than fifty trucks destroyed or damaged. 339FG Mustangs caught one train with a string of flat cars each carrying two large military trucks, blasting it to pieces. Lt Bruno Grabovski in *Duchess*, and his wingman from 352FG, also spotted rich targets on the ground and destroyed seven locomotives and damaged five others before starting on their cargos.

Mustangs from 78FG found numerous aircraft on the ground near Luneburg and made several passes amidst intense flak, losing two of their planes to its withering fire. Another 78FG Mustang took a 20mm hit behind the cockpit and one through the tail which blew away most of its rudder and stabilisers. With a weird cock-screw motion the plane lurched towards home like a bucking bronco, 450 miles and two and half hours away. The P51s title? *Bum Steer*.

> "I was lining up at 500 yards in a turn on one Fw190 and he was lining up on a P47. I opened fire, but observed no hits.... the Fw190 fired at the P47... (it) burst into flames. At this time I gave the Fw190 a second squirt and observed no hits. As he sliced the half roll into a steep diving turn, his right wing tore off, he flipped to the left and hit the ground, exploding."
>
> After Action Report, Major Conger, 56FG

In addition to the escorts, Thunderbolts from 56FG conducted sweeping operations. It was the first planned mission to Berlin by P47s and the 56FG was the only group not assigned for escort duty. Sweeping ahead of the bombers they encountered fifteen Fw190s and Me109s near Friedersdorf, southeast of the city. Nine

enemy fighters were shot down for the loss of only one P47. One Me109 was chased at very low level across the suburbs of Berlin until it eventually hit some trees and crashed, giving Major Paul Conger in *Bernyce* his second victory of the day. He would finish the war with a total of 11.5 confirmed aerial victories.

56FG pilots, Major Paul Conger (left), Captain Cameron Hart (centre) and 2Lt Philip Kuhn, caught several Luftwaffe fighters just as they took off to attack the B17s. These three men accounted for five out of nine victories in the ensuing melee which took them across the suburbs of Berlin. (USAF)

accurate. Sixty B17s from the 1AD and a further thirty-three from 3AD suffered major damage, all due to flak. A total of 31 bombers were lost but six of them managed to reach the safety of Russian occupied territory, now not far from Berlin.

Aerial opposition to the 1000 strong bomber force was nil and gunners on the Forts made no claims at all having barely sighted the enemy. Only two Me109s made a single pass through the 1AD in the Berlin area.

Sixteen clusters of bombs from the 1AD fell into the centre of the city to the south of Unter-Den-Linden and adjacent to the Tiergarten. At least eight direct hits were scored on the massive Air Ministry building. Tight patterns fell onto the government district hitting the Reich Chancellory, Foreign Office, Ministry of Propaganda and the Gestapo headquarters. The damage caused to the Reichstag is believed to have forced Hitler to move his headquarters to the underground bunker, where he largely remained for the rest of the war and where he finally committed suicide.

Friedrichstrasse station was blanketed with strikes and Gorlitzer station took at least two direct hits.

> **"Finally, you could recognize Berlin in the distance... It wasn't that you could see the city. What you could see was the black cloud of smoke from the spent 88mm and 105mm anti-aircraft shells and the smoke rising from the ground below."** Mike Banta 91BG, Pilot of *Yankee Gal*, (43-37844)

Potsdam station was hit as well as the adjacent sidings, repair buildings and rail lines leading to the area. Tempelhof marshalling yard and airfield also received their share.

The attack by the 3AD added a further 1200 tons of bombs to the west of the centre, by then shrouded in dense smoke. One and a half square miles of the Mitte area was totally devastated. Due to the dense smoke, twenty-five B17s by-passed the city and bombed Gatow and Luneburg instead.

It was the 8AF's greatest bombardment of Berlin and there was a heavy loss of life. 25,000 casualties were reported by neutral sources; Swedish newspapers carried detailed accounts. Study of secret German reports on the air raid casualties suggest that the loss of life, although great, was not as high as reported. But the news reports undermined the morale of some of the aircrews. Many were unsettled by their orders to unload hundreds of tons of ordnance into a city centre rather than the pinpoint bombing of precise military targets. But Berlin was still the administrative centre of the, as yet undefeated, Nazi war machine and that meant that its fate was sealed.

Final flight for *Blue Grass Girl*

486BG's Lewis Kloud's crew were on the final mission of their tour on 3rd February. It must have seemed like a blessing when they returned from the 'Big B' with barely a scratch, having sighted none of the Luftwaffe's fighters and survived the flak barrage with only superficial damage. They were flying in *Blue Grass Girl* and, as they began the descent over the North Sea, the gunners in the rear of the ship went forward to celebrate with the officers up front.

Suddenly and inexplicably, flames engulfed the whole of the rear fuselage and *Blue Grass Girl* fell out of the formation. The gunners found themselves unable to get back to the rear where their chutes were stored. Lewis Kloud and his co-pilot gave them theirs without hesitation.

One, two, three, four parachutes blossomed from the plane as it powered down, trailing flame. A fifth man jumped but too late. The fireball which had been the B17 slammed into farmland at Reydon, near Southwold, killing five men.

> **"I remember as we made our way to Berlin I could look ahead of us for 100 miles and see nothing but airplanes, and look behind us for another 100 miles and see nothing but airplanes... we were bombing from 30,000ft and the smoke came right up through the clouds. When we dropped our bombs, the bomb doors froze open, so I had to walk back without a chute holding an oxygen bottle and hand crank up the bomb door, standing on a six inch wide walkway with the doors open over Berlin."**
> DAVE DAHLBERG, 487BG, *Picadilly Lilley* (43-38044)

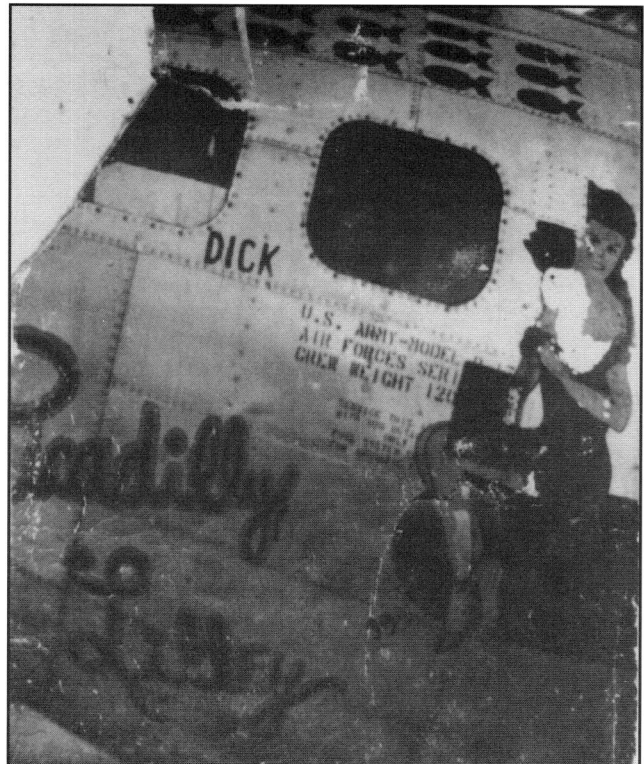

The photograph may be tattered and torn but it is still treasured by a crew man, like a picture of a favourite girl. 487BG's *Picadilly Lilley* was lost only three days later on a mission to Chemnitz. The plane had taken off as a spare, joined an unknown group and was never seen again. (D. Dahlberg)

3rd FEBRUARY 1945

Under a reign of terror

A direct hit smashed right through to the tunnel of the Underground rail station at Hausvogteiplatz, just east of the Tiergarten. (Bundesarchiv)

"Before we left Germany I tuned into a propaganda broadcast from Berlin. The announcer said 'every man, woman and child is out fighting the flames, with the Russians only 70 kms away'." T/Sgt Clifford Whipple, radio operator

One of the first news correspondents allowed to leave Nazi Germany since 1943, Herbe Granberg, worked for the Swedish press. He filed a story in Stockholm on 23rd February which was widely published, including appearing in "Stars & Stripes", and which revealed what it was like to be in Berlin and under the one thousand heavy bombers of the 8th Air Force on 3rd February.

Taking shelter in the subway tunnel, thought to be one of the "safest" air raid shelters, Granberg found himself amongst thousands of terrified people caught below the city's biggest daylight raid. The eerie darkness, flickering lights, the clouds of chalky dust billowing along the tunnel.... the rumbling and quaking like huge footsteps getting ever closer... ear shattering explosions and bulging, crumbling concrete as high explosive bombs hit right above pushing out the walls and caving in the tunnel only a few hundred yards away. They all became familiar sensations to the citizens of Berlin, just as they had to others across Germany. Just as they had to the citizens of London and Coventry and Warsaw and Rotterdam before them.

Deep underground, he was still shaken by the destruction of upper floors of the station above as they crashed down after being hit by several bombs. Whimpering and muffled sounds, flashlight beams and darkness.... the long wait in silence, choking in the thick swirl of dust. The "All-Clear" siren and the sudden rush to get out.

Above ground, on the streets, a fire storm of smoke and flame, limiting visibility to a few yards, soot caked eyes.... multi-storey buildings collapsed like playing cards, deep craters pocketing the roadways. Everywhere people pushed their way through with suitcases and bundles, past fractured water pipes, burning gas mains and sparking power lines, twisted and torn telephone wires, through the tangled mess that had been the city. Delayed action bombs detonating, and continuing to erupt for the next two days.... street after street cordoned off, waiting for life convicts to remove the explosive charges or die in the attempt.

25,000 persons were reported in the Swedish press to have perished in the raid. In just one of the subway stations, it was said, 320 had been caught by a direct hit. The city was packed with hundreds of thousands of refugees which must have made it difficult to establish definitive casualty figures. However, detailed archive records marked 'Geheim!' (Secret) reveal a German thoroughness, as well as the official figures as being somewhat less than those 'leaked' at the time to the neutral press. It should be noted that such figures do not generally include military casualties, nor is it clear if they also included foreign slave labour or POW workers, of which there were many at work in the city in factories and clearing bomb damage. However, it should also be noted that the German High Command War Diary yields a figure of less than 1000 fatalities for the raid.

Official archive figures, recorded on 8th February, indicate about 1500 dead and 2000 injured in the raid with a large number missing. A week later these were revised upwards to 2541 killed, 1668 injured and 714 still missing. A vast number, some 119,000 people, were recorded as being made homeless as a result of the bombing of 3rd February.

The blitz which devastated the cities of Poland, Belgium, Holland, France, Greece and Britain, and preceded a reign of Nazi terror, had returned from whence it was spawned. The citizens of Berlin and tens of thousands of refugees, the innocent and the guilty, now suffered the same dreadful fate their leaders had brought to the world.

Wrecked street cars litter the centre of the devastated Oranienstrasse in Berlin after the raid. (Bundesarchiv)

Naval shells fall on Berlin

Berlin lies more than 200 miles from the nearest stretch of Atlantic coast, far beyond the reach of the Allied navies and their heaviest battle wagons. And yet, naval shells fell on Berlin on 3rd February as part of the daylight assault on the city.

In their attempt to penetrate and disrupt German underground installations, the Allies experimented with several different weapon systems. The Berlin subway, which operated for most of the war almost immune to the day and night bombing, received an extraordinary piece of ordnance, designed to penetrate to considerable depth before detonating.

Merrill Stiver, pilot of 303BG's *Jackie*, recalled, "We dropped modified naval shells. The target was Berlin's rail lines, above and below ground. The bombs I remember had regular tail fins, were long and lean with chemical fusing for irregular explosive time. The length of the bomb was critical due to the bomb bay length. They had no wings; and my bombardier said the drop tables were different, due to the configuration. I remember asking what the bombs were called and someone said they were 16 inch naval shells, adapted for our use."

The weapon was one of the fore-runners of the

Lt Stiver with his 303rd Bomb Group Fortress *Jackie* (Stiver)

"Disney" rocket bomb, developed during late 1944 and first used operationally in March 1945. 14ft long, the "Disney" was developed by the Royal Navy for use against the German U-boat and E-boat pens along the Atlantic coast. Weighing some 4500lbs, after release, it was propelled by a rocket motor which ignited at 5000ft and yielded an impact velocity of about 2400ft per second. Detonation occurred approximately twenty feet below ground. The RAF had no suitable launch aircraft for the weapon or development trials and the USAAF was approached

for a B17G for test dropping.

The use of the naval shell bomb on Berlin's underground rail network preceded operational deployment of the "Disney" rocket bomb. The US Navy had also been developing several bombs including the Mk1, 1600lb armour piercing weapon which was 14 inches in diameter and 83 inches in length. This may have been the weapon deployed over Berlin on 3rd February with such success in disrupting the under-ground rail network. German records indicate that the subway tunnels collapsed, or were badly damaged, in at least 30 locations and that 30 subway coaches were completely destroyed. Merrill Stiver reflected, "I remember the Swedish Red Cross saying later that there were large numbers of casualties in the subway system."

> **"As a result of the raid of 3 Feb, sixteen machine construction firms.... were put out of commission on account of total damage to factories.... caused a 40% production loss in the leather industry... 35-40% in the paper industry and a 65% loss in the printing trade... 14% was noted in the iron, steel and sheet metal industry..."**
>
> Extract from Situation Report, Berlin Chamber of Commerce, February 1945

At least three bombers crashed into the very centre of the city on 3rd February. This wreckage of a B17 Fortress lies at the corner of Franzosischestrasse and Kanonierstrasse, close to the Propaganda Ministry (Bundesarchiv)

"Report of captured enemy aircraft... place of crash, Berlin - Tiergarten Bellevuealle in direction of Treptow, is added that two enemy aircraft crashed.... 2nd enemy aircraft has place of crash Berlin-Alexanderplatz to Treptow...."
German Report SSD LBGW77 6/2(231C) on loss of Fortresses from 91BG (42-97632) & 306BG (43-38407) which crashed in the centre of Berlin, together with 100BG's 44-6500.

> **"My seventh Berlin mission. The Germans now have about twelve hundred 88mm guns around Berlin. The flak seems to be more accurate and the barrages more effective than some months ago. Today's bomber stream seemed endless and we were literally surrounded by P51s."** Diary extract, Abel Dolim, navigator 94BG (43-38662)

The *Yankee Belle* meets the Hitler Youth!

"I had hardly closed my eyes when the orderly's torch hit me like a bolt of lightning..... Breakfast 0400, briefing at 0500!"

So started the day for one navigator with the 91st Bomb Group, Lt Asay Johnson. It would prove to be a day he would never forget — the start of a nightmare. The surprise awakening had come after air crews had been told only a few hours previously that the following day's mission was scrubbed. The news had heightened their evening's bar room entertainment and now hundreds of men trudged muddily towards their mess huts, bemoaning the raid's resurrection.

Other 91BG pilots were also attending the briefing including Mike Banta who recalled, "We were told that this would be the greatest 8AF attack of the war on the German capital with over 1000 heavy bombers participating.... it seemed as if every heavy bomber in England was in the early morning sunlight. As we flew towards the target each succeeding battery of flak burst closer to the squadron. This is where the sweat begins... it seemed like an eternity...."

'Ace' Johnson recalled, "We were flying in *Yankee Belle* (42-32085) that day, as wingman to Col Lord's lead ship. Over the target we encountered heavy, accurate flak. We were on the bomb run when all hell broke loose... the lead plane took a direct hit and exploded, spraying debris all over the sky."

Mike Banta, flying nearby in his *Yankee Gal* watched in horror. "Before the lead ship (42-97632) could take evasive action, it received a direct hit where the edge of the wing meets the fuselage. It was blown cleanly in half. The nose went immediately

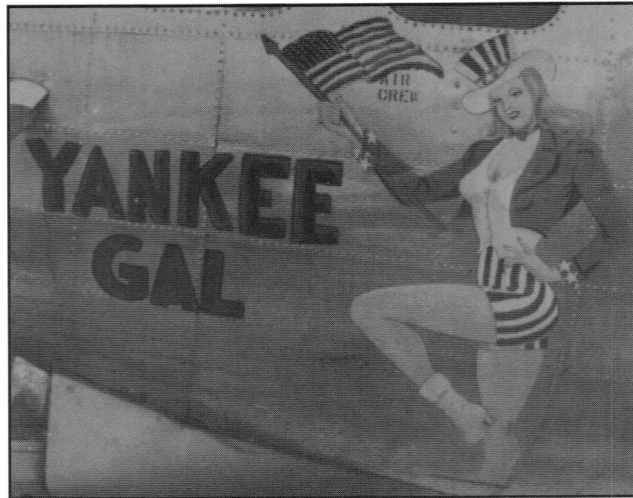

"It seemed as if every heavy bomber in England was in the early morning sunlight." Mike Banta, pilot 91BG, *Yankee Gal*

into a dive with engines still under power... the tail appeared to fly along with the formation for a split second before fluttering back over the rear element." Cliff Schultz also had an eye-witness view from the radio room of the ship on the right wing of the lead. "The aircraft broke in two and the Mickey Operator leaned right and fell out without his chute. The radio man was face down on his table... paper, ammunition and equipment just poured out of the front section." The remnants of the lead

ship plunged into the centre of Berlin killing all on board.

Ace Johnson took up the story again, "Moments later, our *Yankee Belle* took several hits, which knocked out Nos. 3 and 4 engines — both on the same side — which put the plane into a slow spin." The pilots were able to feather the No.4 prop but

the No.3 windmilled causing a tremendous drag, increasing the aircraft's spin. The shaft on the prop became red hot and burned through, sending it spinning over the top of the plane into the rest of formation behind. When the prop severed, it reduced the drag and allowed the pilots to pull out of the spin — but too close to the ground to bail out! We were about ten miles from the coast by now but were covered by German fighters. I plotted a course for Sweden but the plane was so badly damaged that we were forced to crash land. We came down in an open field and narrowly missed a barn just before hitting the ground".

Some returning crews reported the ship had dropped away from the formation ten miles north of Berlin, then fallen into a spin and exploded — disintegrated completely! In fact, *Yankee Belle* bellied in about 20km south of Altentreptow and was

"As we flew towards the target, each succeeding flak battery burst closer to the squadron. This is where the sweat begins... it seemed like an eternity."
Mike Banta, pilot 91BG *Yankee Gal*

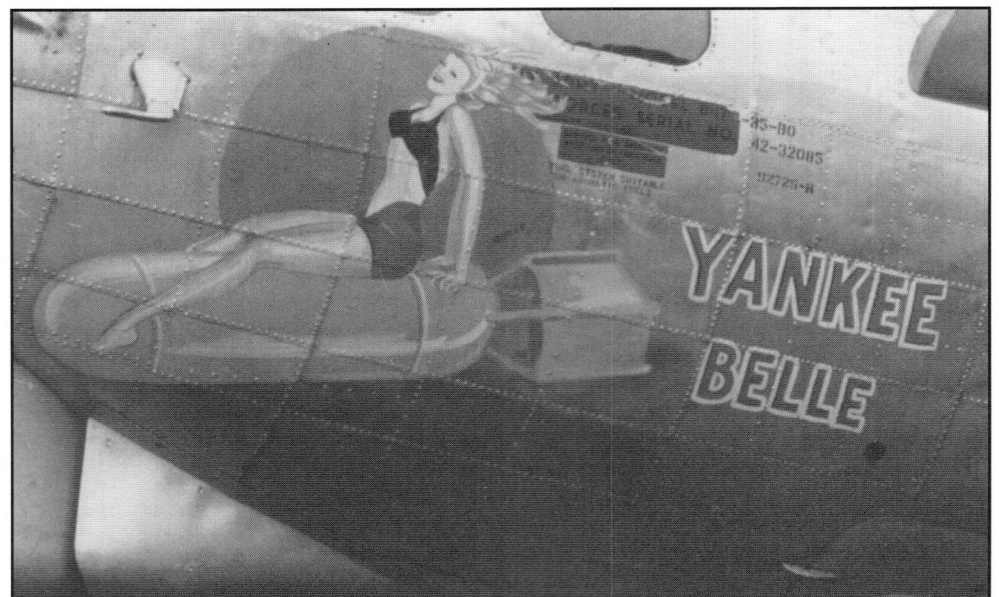

Uncle Sam's lost *Jewell*

claimed by flak gunners from 1st Flak Division. They reported "Crew captured in woods by People's Guards'. George Miller, the pilot, was also caught nearby and re-called, "We were warmly greeted by a group of German WWI retreads carrying ancient rifles that I thought they might shoot off by mistake." Ten hours after being woken for the mission, Lt Johnson stood ankle deep in mud, in front of his crippled Fortress, surrounded by a gang of brown-shirted Hitler Youths brandishing long daggers and making very threatening movements. "I hurt all over from being tossed around inside the plane during the crash-landing", he recalled. "I had blood oozing from flak wounds in both legs, my right arm and hand."

"After being harassed by the menacing youths for what seemed like an eternity, we were taken to a civilian jail and fed a meal of red cabbage, tasteless porridge and black bread. This was the last 'decent meal' I was to partake of for a long time. Next morning we were moved to Frankfurt.... back through Berlin which only a few days before had been our target. We sat overnight in the marshal-ling yard while the British bombed Berlin, a terrifying and never to be forgotten experience."

A long, harrowing spell of interrogation and internment followed during which 'Ace' was struck by the extraordinary detail that his captors apparently had, not only about his Bomb Group but also about him personally. "I was amazed by the effort that they had expended to impress me and I was puzzled as to how and where they had obtained all this detailed information."

The US heavy bomber lost on a Berlin raid with the highest number of missions accrued was undoubtedly 379BG's *Birmingham Jewell* (42-97678). Built by Vega and delivered to the USAAF in late January 1944, it arrived in England about three months later. Over the next ten months *Birmingham Jewell* was despatched on raids over Germany and Occupied Europe at a rate of over one mission every three days. By 3rd February 1945 it was over Berlin with 127 mission markers painted on its side but the city's flak defences finally claimed it and the 'Jewell' never returned.

About 20 minutes prior to the target, pilot William Webber experienced problems with one engine. Unable to maintain altitude or formation Webber opted to turn the veteran plane back. The Luftwaffe caught up with the 'Jewell' near Hamburg. Waist gunner, Norman Scarffe, recorded later, "We were attacked by two or three Me109s. On the first pass the enemy aircraft scored hits which put out of action one engine and set the bomb

Celebrating 100 missions completed – happier times for the *Birmingham Jewell*, before becoming a victim of Berlin flak (USAF)

bay on fire." Copilot James Kiester added that hits were also scored in the nose section and three engines were shot out.

Scarffe continued, "On the first pass, I was struck in the back by 20mm cannon and knocked to the floor. At this time the fire in the bomb bay got out of control and swept back towards the waist."

Tail gunner, Bennet Howell confirmed, "The plane had been hit by a fighter from the tail.... prior to that No.2 engine was out and the intercom system was not functioning... I was the last to leave the ship and it was in level flight losing altitude fast, the whole

ship looked to be on fire."

Both pilots stayed at the controls for as long as possible to allow others to bail out. The copilot then pushed the fatally injured nose gunner out of the escape hatch and followed. Lt Webber tried to set the autopilot controls but the electrical systems were shot out and the plane went into a dive before he could escape. One chute was seen to go down burning — probably the radio man, last seen fighting the fire. Another crew man also died.

German reports indicate the plane exploded in the air before crashing near Rendsburg in Holstein. One body and two prisoners were, according to a German report, "removed from the site by unauthorised persons." They were later recovered but the escape kits of those involved had, by then, been looted and emptied of all their money. A furious Luftwaffe major commanding the area demanded that those guilty of the crime be punished but they could not be identified.

When its combat career ended, the *Birmingham Jewell* was the 8AF's highest scoring and most successful B17. Purchased at around $204,300, each of the B17's 127 raids represented an investment by Uncle Sam of just $1609.

Another victim of Berlin's flak defences was 384BG's *Challenger* (42-102501). Despite losing both starboard engines just before bombing, 2Lt Robert Long continued on to drop with the formation. *Challenger* was eventually ditched into the North Sea and the pilot swam 50yds to catch one of the dinghies blown away by the wind. Exhausted, he died soon after. The radio man was swept away and, although rescued two and a half hours later, another man also died before the ASR launch could reach port. (USNARP)

3rd FEBRUARY 1945

Approximately 2300 tons were dropped by two Air Divisions.

Estimated tonnage: within 1000ft of Aiming Point = 90 tons : within 1 mile of Aiming Point = 720 tons

"The degree of concentration can be visualised by comparing an acre to an American Football Field. Approx. 72 football fields encompassed a 1000ft circle – on average each football field received five 500lb bombs." (8AF Statistical Summary)

Below: Bomb plots of the 3rd Air Divisions formations. First Air Division concentrations were, reportedly, even more condensed due to better visibility for the first waves over the target (USAAF)

1st Flak Div claims a *Joker* and downs *Hitler's Hoe Doe*

As the 381BG passed over the city they were subjected to intense and continuous flak thrown up by the guns of the Luftwaffe's 1st Flak Division which tracked them for a full seven minutes. John Anderson's *Joker* (42-102873) was hit on the bomb run and its No.2 engine started burning. This was not the first time that Berlin's flak guns had ripped into *The Joker*. More than seven months earlier, the plane had been badly damaged over Berlin on 21st June. Now, as the fire took hold, Anderson valiantly held the plane on its run for five minutes before the crew abandoned it. Moments later the

Fortress swerved right, then left, reared up in a climbing turn and exploded. All of the crew escaped the plane, and nine chutes were seen, but Lt Anderson was killed possibly as a result of the explosion. Wreckage of the shattered plane fell to earth in the Jagen forest near Eichhorst, 11km northwest of Finow. All eight survivors were caught, although at least one man, Sgt Curtis Wallace, remained at liberty until 24th February.

Paul Pucyleuski's Fort, named *Hitler's Hoe Doe* by the crew, did not seem to observers to have been hit by the flak — they could see no fires or outward

signs of damage. However, immediately after the target, at 11.23hrs, as the group began a swing away off the bomb run, *Hitler's Hoe Doe* made a sharp turn and slid underneath the formation.

Although the plane appeared to be under control, it began a slow spin down from 27,000ft and out of sight of the group. Forty minutes later, as it skirted the airfield at Tutow, 6km west southwest of Jarmen, it crashlanded. The Luftwaffe report No. KU3639 simply states, "At

12.05hrs, 1500 metres south of the border of D. airfield Tutow... Fortress crashed. 45% destruction... 8 men captured, rest unknown. Claimed by 1st Flak Div."

2Lt Pucyleuski and five of his crew were rounded up in nearby woods almost immediately. Two men, Sgts Mitchell and Green, managed to evade for three days before they too were caught at Hohn-mocker. Navigator, 2Lt Kellcher, was recorded as missing by the German authorities and may have become a victim of a local lynch mob.

Nazi propaganda condemns 8AF and General Spaatz

The wartime propaganda campaign had raged long and hard, pursued by both sides of the conflict. Now, as the final days were drawing closer, the campaign reached a vicious fever pitch. The Germans had long since accused the RAF of conducting a "terror bombing campaign" against the civilian population. Now it turned on the 8AF and its commanding General.

High power radio transmitters beamed Goebbel's latest message across the Atlantic to the American public, referring to the 3rd February attack on Berlin. "General Spaatz knew that it was taxing the ingenuity of German organisation to cope with feeding and housing of non-combatant refugees," it stated, "of whom hundreds of thousands have fled before the organised savagery and terrorism of the communist Red Army invading East Germany."

The report continued, "General Spaatz also knew

that the available German air forces were concentrated on the Eastern front to combat the Red flood which threatens to destroy Germany and all Europe." Before completing the broadcast, the announcer went on to say that the German Army had awarded the General the "Order of the White Feather".

Most listeners dismissed the broadcast for what they knew it was — propaganda. However, after an even more devastating RAF-USAAF raid on Dresden, later in February, a most extraordinary Associated Press dispatch seemed to almost confirm that the Allies had indeed indulged in 'terror raids'. The dispatch was issued through Paris Radio and, although banned in Britain, received wide circulation across America.

The report had resulted from a SHAEF press conference held at Supreme Headquarters in Paris. An RAF Intelligence officer outlined the new

Kaiser Wilhelm church near Lust Garten, 800m east of Friedrichstrasse rail station and 2000m northeast of the aiming point (V. Edwards)

Allied air plan 'to bomb large population centres' to 'bring about the collapse of the German economy'. During the questions and answers which followed his submissions the officer inadvertently referred to the German propaganda usage of the word 'terror-bombing'. This term was quickly picked up and was included in the consequent dispatch. "Allied air chiefs have made the long-awaited decision to adopt deliberate terror-bombings of German population centres as a ruthless expedient of hastening Hitler's doom," ran the copy. "....The all-out air

war on Germany became obvious with the unprecedented daylight assault on the refugee-crowded capital...." it continued.

Generals Arnold and Eisenhower were taken aback by the report and by the wide publicity it received. General Arnold cabled Spaatz for clarification and received an assurance that the USAAF had not departed from its well tried precedents. Although somewhat vague, Arnold took this as a reassurance that the USAAF was still only attacking military targets, albeit within cities.

The transportation network was, yet again, the target for the 8AF's heavy bombers. It was the heaviest daylight raid on Berlin so far carried out by the USAAF. The rail stations and their surrounding marshalling yards, sidings and repair facilities would receive the full weight of all three Air Divisions on the 26th February.

Three forces were despatched, the first 377 Fortresses were from the 1st Air Division, directed at the Schlesischer rail station, followed by another 446 from the 3AD, targeted on the Alexanderplatz station, and finally 361 Liberators from the 2nd Air Division aimed at Berlin North station. The entire aerial procession formed a bomber stream that was 300 miles long, taking a full hour to pass over the city. Once again, the Luftwaffe was nowhere to be seen — poor weather and the constant attacks against oil production and storage facilities kept them on the ground. No airborne enemy aircraft were identified as such although a few scattered contrails were spotted over Holland and over Berlin itself. These probably indicated some jet activity but it came to nothing.

Flak was now the bigger threat, officially described as moderate to intense, but even this seemed a shadow of its former strength with some groups recording it as being almost absent. Generally inaccurate, it did account for the loss of three

---

"The attacks of last February on transportation targets ruined the message service of the railroads which paralyzed them far more than the material damage which could be repaired quickly."

Extract from US Strategic Bombing Survey Report postwar interview with Colonel General Jodl

Call it a day!

Just one of millions of propaganda leaflets thrown out in bundles from USAAF bombers over Berlin and the surrounding area in the closing weeks of the war in an attempt to further undermine the civilian morale. "Soviet Panzers head for Berlin — Call it a day!" it exclaims, exploiting the Germans' greater fear of retribution from the advancing Russian armies rather than falling into the hands of the Western Allies.

91BG's *Sweet Freda* (43-38772), with wingmen fore and aft, unloads over Berlin on 26th February 1945 as skymarker smoke trails mark the target. (USAF)

"...whereas the 28 raids during the evening and night (1 Jan – 28 Feb 45) did not on the whole cause heavy damage, the two daylight raids on 3rd Feb and 26 Feb were the worst to which the Reich capital has hitherto been subjected. Entire business districts were completely destroyed, transport and telephone connections interrupted..."

Extract from Situation Reports, Berlin Chamber of Commerce, February 1945

Fortresses. Seventeen other heavy bombers fell away from the formations from unknown causes, the majority probably flak-related, but made it safely to emergency fields on the continent or in nearby Russian held territory.

Solid undercast was experienced all the way to the target, over it and on the way home. Bombardiers relied on their H2X radar for target identification and unloaded almost 3000 tons of bombs and millions of leaflets onto the city. The total tonnage now dropped by the 8th Air Force made Berlin the most-bombed target of the war, surpassing even devastated Cologne.

The thick undercast, made thicker by the dense smoke from the fires below, made observation of damage impossible. But the rail sidings, goods yards, passenger terminal and rail repair shops at Schlesischer, the freight centre at Berlin-North and the Alexanderplatz passenger station were all seen to be heavily hit. RAF Mosquitos which followed up with yet another of their night raids hours later reported that fires were still burning as a result of the American daylight attack.

The air raid alert lasted some three and a half hours in the city and the areas sustaining the greatest damage included Mitte, where the Finance Ministry, Reichsbank and town hall were all severely damaged. In Schoneberg, the town hall and Stadtpark rail station were hit and air raid reports indicate considerable casualties. There was great disruption to the city's communications, public utilities and transport facilities. The gas works at Prenzlauer and Reinickendorf both received direct hits and the subway system also took a beating with the tunnels collapsed in at least 24 locations around the network. A number of local government buildings in Wedding, Tempelhof, Treptow, Lichtenberg and Weissensee were all reported to have sustained considerable damage during the raid.

The greatest loss of life occurred in the Horst Wesel district where another rail station was hit, but so too were three large school buildings and a hospital. Across the city more than 71,000 people were listed as being homeless as a result of the raid.

"The flak that had once made all combat crews fear Berlin was surprisingly absent as the mission turned out to be an absolute milk run."
Extract, 453BG 735BS's Operational Diary, 26th February 1945

Escorts claim one B17 destroyed!

In essence there was no fighter battle fought on the 26th February. Fifteen groups of escorts were allocated in three roughly equal forces to protect each of the bomber streams. Included were the 352FG and 361FG which were now based on the continent. The 726 P51 Mustangs and P47 Thunderbolts destroyed only six of the enemy's aircraft — all on the ground. Mustangs from 364FG caught four He111 bombers at Brockzetel airfield and fighters from other units destroyed two more aircraft on the tarmac at Varel.

Elements from the 2nd Air Division escorts found two abandoned B17s bellied in on the ground, strafed and destroyed them before Luftwaffe salvage teams could haul them away. Both Fortresses must have been shot down prior to the day's mission and 479FG pilots later lodged a claim for one B17 destroyed near Steenwijk.

The fighters had to make do with ground attacks for the day's action and even these seemed hard to find. Eleven locomotives were destroyed together with another loco and ten tank cars damaged. Eleven trucks were also claimed destroyed. Not a vast haul for the day.

Two 78FG Mustangs were lost when one of them developed engine trouble over Berlin. Forced to turn for home, the ailing Mustang named Green Eyes (44-11627), flown by Charles O'Brien, was escorted back by his wingman. Unable to continue for long, O'Brien had no choice but to belly land his fighter — whereupon Leonard Olson, who was accompanying him, promptly attempted to land to pick up his stranded colleague. The second Mustang unfortunately crashed into the soft ground and both pilots were captured. Lt O'Brien escaped captivity twice but was shot dead a few days later, 60 miles behind German lines.

".....On account of the loss of the production of the synthetic oil refineries, the operation of fighter defences is forbidden."
German High Command Directive to the Luftwaffe, 13th February 1945

Berlin's streets, like those in almost every other city across Europe, lost their identity as they were reduced to piles of rubble from the repeated air attacks. This was Potsdamer-strasse 500m west of Potsdamer rail station. (V Edwards)

26th FEBRUARY 1945

Bye bye, *Sweet Chick* – hello again, *Floogie!*

The 36 aircraft furnished by the 92BG began taking off at 0855 hours and assembled into the lead, low and high squadrons of the 40th 'A' CBW which led the entire 8AF to Berlin. PFF equipment in the lead ship failed on the bomb run. The deputy took over and succeeded in putting the bombs through the solid cloud onto the briefed target — the Schlesischer mainline rail station.

The briefed altitude for the wing's bombing was 25,000ft but one 92BG ship went over the target alone at just 15,000ft. An hour earlier, Lt John Paul Jr's 43-38969 had suffered a serious mechanical failure in its No.2 engine and was unable to maintain altitude. Rejecting the option of bombing a target of opportunity and turning for home, Lt Paul chose to keep heading for Berlin, falling further and further below the group's protection. Fortunately, the Luftwaffe were nowhere to be seen and they returned safely — another of the 92BG's planes did not and became one of three listed as missing.

Flak described as "meagre and generally inaccurate" over the target was still accurate enough to claim Robert Mason's *Sweet Chick* (44-6461) flying in the low squadron. Having feathered No.1 engine, Mason was forced to drop back from the formation and was last seen west of Wittenberg with a second engine out of action, some five miles behind the formation but escorted by two P51s. By 17.00 hours, *Sweet Chick* had crashed in a blazing wreck, seven of the crew were prisoners of the Germans and two men were dead.

452BG Fortress *Flatbush Floogie* (42-32083) had already force landed once in Russian-held Poland, 20 miles from Krakow. That was back in June 1944 flying a shuttle mission from Poltava to Italy. Repaired and flown back to England the plane was, once again, headed towards Poland.

2Lt Allen Marksian had taken his ship over Berlin but shortly after bombing received a burst of flak which put the No.4 engine out of action. Forced to feather the prop and with fuel streaming back from ruptured gas lines, *Flatbush Floogie* dropped out of the formation. It was last seen near the Rally Point, raising the bomb doors, still under control but still losing altitude. Fifteen miles short of Krakow in Poland, Marksian brought the plane down in a belly landing to be greeted for a second time by wary Russian soldiers.

The third B17 to be listed missing was 384BG Jack Barnett's 43-38823. Berlin flak also caught them over the city and they were last seen trailing the formation with two engines feathered. All on board were destined to spend the rest of the war as prisoners of the German authorities.

A number of other damaged bombers also made it over the Russian lines but were not listed as missing in action. A Liberator from 93BG (41-29456) crash-landed and another from 491BG (42-50680), piloted by Frank Jensen, was abandoned by its crew. They had lost their No.3 engine on the bomb run and then No.4 engine also. Dropping at the rate of 400 feet per minute they went into cloud at 15,000ft. At 5,000ft the crew began to abandon the plane, still in dense cloud. At 300ft their parachutes popped out into clear sky and all landed safely in Russian occupied Poland.

2Lt Perkins' 303BG Fortress (44-6316) also headed into Russian territory suffering from engine trouble and fuel shortage. It made a wheels up landing near the Poltava HQ of Eastern Base Command USSAFE with no casualties.

A far greater tragedy overwhelmed the 388BG crew flying in *Star Dust* (42-102559). The plane was a survivor of many Berlin raids starting as far back as 7th May 1944. About 20 minutes prior to bombing, Lt Ramsel was forced to abort and pull his bomber out of formation. The No.1 prop was feathered as a result of a flak splinter. Making its way back to the coast and home, *Star Dust* crashed in France killing all but the tail gunner.

The continuous raids by the USAAF and RAF wrecked Berlin's rail stations. At one time 448 trains left the city daily; by March 1945 it was reduced to less than 40 per day. Over 50,000 workers were kept busy constantly trying to restore even this meagre service. (USAF)

> **"I believe the Fuhrer was not much elated at the loss of efficiency of our air force."**
> Post war interrogation of Field Marshal Kesselring

The aerial photo at right shows central Berlin and the location of Friedrichstrasse Station, the Air Ministry and Foreign Office. Although the primary targets on 26th February were designated as Berlin Nord rail yard (in centre on top edge), Alexanderplatz and Schlesischer Stations (middle of right edge) the thick cloud cover meant that the bulk of the bomb load was dropped, yet again, into the centre of the city and spread over a wide area. (USAF)

A

6(d)(V)17

C

B

6(d)(V)70

A. FRIEDRICHSTRASSE MAIN LINE AND UNDER-
GROUND STATIONS

B. AIR MINISTRY.

C. FOREIGN OFFICE, MINISTRY OF PROPA-
GANDA, THE CHANCELLERY, AND
GESTAPO H.Q.

Almost one thousand Flying Fortresses with 347 Liberators were airborne on the 18th March to strike at tank production factories, munitions plants and two major rail stations in Berlin. The first force was 450 B17s from twelve groups of the 1AD, a second force comprised 530 B17s from fourteen groups of the 3AD and finally the third force of B24s was drawn from all groups of the 2AD.

Me262 jets made an attack on the 1AD as it led the stream over the target and two B17s went down as a result. Fifteen to twenty jets from the newly operational JG7 used contrails as cover and launched their assault after the bombers had turned at the IP. The attacks were mainly by groups of two to four

jets, well-coordinated, pressed aggressively and in one case closed to within 50 yards. Using superior speed with great skill the jets avoided the escorts by taking full advantage of the hazy conditions and persistent contrails which dogged the bombers throughout the mission.

The 3AD also received the attention of Me262s west of Salzwedel and although the attacks were not continuous they were aggressive. Again contrails were successfully used in the interception. The first attack came 20 minutes prior to the target when enemy jets singled out the low squadron of the second group in the formation (457BG), which had swung away from the main stream.

Kentucky Winner
– lost to friend or foe (?)

Bomber crews were briefed to expect contact with their Russian allies as they supported ground forces moving in towards beleaguered Berlin in the closing months of the war. Recognition signs and procedures in the event of such contact were often inadequate or ignored and both sides were wary of their 'friend or foe' allies.

385BG's *Kentucky Winner* (42-102481) had been assigned to the group almost a full year before and was a true combat veteran. Passing over Berlin and turning off the target, flak ripped into the No.3 engine and bomb bay starting fires. 1Lt William Cocke pulled the plane to one side and dived down into the clouds. Some observers in the group thought they saw chutes pop from the plane but in fact all the crew stayed with the damaged ship.

Sgt Robert Crider, the nose gunner, recorded what occurred soon after. "After we left the formation, we were attacked by Russian fighters. Whether they were piloted by Russian or German pilots we never found out but we did fire green green flares and rock our wings as we were told to do in briefing — and they still attacked. Our waist gunner was hit in the

left leg by what we thought was a 20mm shell... there were, I believe two of these planes. Our tail gunner, while trying to help the wounded man, was hit in the right arm..." Radio man, Sgt Figini, agreed "Although positive identification was difficult, it was generally agreed that we were shot down by two Russian fighters while making for Russia to land (our) damaged plane."

The crew were ordered to prepare for bail out but the pilot realised that, with two wounded on board and the low altitude they were then at, a crash-landing was the only option. *Kentucky Winner* struck the ground about 3 miles from Grodzisk, Poland with all the crew still on board.

Jack Leon's 487BG crew also fell foul of their allies' tactics when they bailed out of their flak-hit B17G, 44-8276. Russian Yaks strafed them in their chutes and killed two of the crew.

Other American planes also encountered the Russians and identification was not always easy. Some 359FG escorts were intercepted by Yak- 9s and Lagg-3s, reported to be "painted blue exactly like identified German aircraft". Another force of Lagg-5s dived on the same

group northeast of Berlin but did not attack. In a melee over Zackerick between German, Russian and American planes, Mustang pilots waved hands and US flags at the Russians. One waved back — another fired, fortunately without effect. In another dogfight, a P51 closed on and identified a Yak-9 but did not fire. His wingman came closer and identified it as an Me109G and attacked, getting some hits. 353FG also received an attack from the rear by two Lagg-5s northeast of Berlin. The flight rocked

their wings but was still attacked a second time, at which point the P51s broke into them and fired warning shots. The Russians were then reported to have "headed due east, after firing upon a straggling B17" — possibly Cocke's *Kentucky Winner*. A flight of 357FG Mustangs, escorting a lone B17 north of Stettin was also fired on by three Yaks, but they broke away upon realising the mistake. 352FG encountered six Yaks near Zielenzig but here, again, recognition signals were successful.

Smoke markers streak down from 100BG Fortresses over the allotments of Hohenschonhausen on their way towards the Berlin-Nord rail yards. (D. Rock)

The B24s bringing up the rear of the bomber column faired best and reported seeing only two jets near Luneburg. They lost none of their aircraft to fighters but one Liberator went down directly over the city as a result of flak.

The moderate to intense flak thrown up by the Berlin defenders had lost none of its potency. Six bombers reportedly received directs hits and others were also lost from the formation. In all thirteen heavy bombers were lost, at least eight of them to flak, but another ten crashed or force-landed in Russian held territory. Eight jets were claimed shot down by the bomber crews but surviving Luftwaffe records indicate only two were actually lost from JG7 that day.

The weather conditions were fair with slight to moderate cloud cover allowing radar assisted visual bombing. The higher flying formations were hampered by the persistent contrails which had been used with such effect by the Luftwaffe.

Almost 3200 tons of bombs were dropped through cloud and thickening smoke. The 1AD's target was the Brandenburgische Motorenwerke plant at Spandau and the main Schlesischer rail station and sidings. Several groups of bombs also fell onto the Tempelhof airfield, marshalling yards and the Gorlitzer rail station. A flak battery in the Friedrichshain Park was also hit. The 3AD, following, blanketed the west end of the Berlin North freight yards and adjacent built up areas although the majority of the bomb load fell an average of two miles from the aiming point. The gas works received two direct hits and a concentration extended into the Stettiner rail traffic centre. The district of Hohenschonhausen to the north east of the city centre was unfortunate enough to receive a massive concentration of over 100 high explosive bombs.

In central Berlin the Tiergarten area was heavily hit with considerable casualties reported. The townhall, Lehrter freight yards and station, as well as a hospital, received notable damage. The Mitte, Wedding and Kreuzberg districts took another pounding with hits reported on many of the government buildings located there and a police barracks. The districts northwest of the centre also took heavy casualties with hits on a number of rail stations, gas works, a police station and school buildings.

The final attack by the 2AD Liberators was aimed at two tank factories located at Henningsdorf and Tegel in the northwest. The Rheinmetall Borsig plant in Tegel was severely damaged with seven of its ten major buildings suffering structural damage. Three quarters of the entire target was blanketed with strikes. The Borsig Lokomotiv works in Henningsdorf had the majority of its important buildings severely damaged, with the main concentration falling on the southern half of the target. At least 40 high explosive bombs from this force fell into the residential area east of the Oranienburger marshalling yard.

The Russians are coming!

Four groups of Mustangs escorted the 1st Air Division at the front of the bomber column. Around Berlin, P51s from 359FG made contact with tactical enemy aircraft opposing the nearby Russian front at Zackerick. After being led away by two Russian aircraft, later identified as Yak-9s, the Mustangs attacked and destroyed one of four Fw190s that were strafing the Russian held airfield. A similar number of Me109s were encountered near Joachinsthal Lake and there were numerous other encounters with Russian fighter aircraft during the mission.

A composite He111 with its Fw190 astride its back was caught by 364FG just as it took off near Schwerin. The Fw190 successfully broke away from its mother ship but both planes were quickly shot down by the escorts. Later about ten German jets were engaged a few miles northwest of Berlin. In all, four victories were claimed for the loss of one P51 to engine failure.

The second bomber force was escorted by 220 Mustangs from five groups and these too succeeded in finding the Luftwaffe and scoring seven victories. Six long-nosed Fw190s near Kassel, an Me262 and twenty Fw190s at Wreizen, as well as a twin-engine jet over Dummer Lake, were all engaged.

Five fighter groups also escorted the B24s with more than two hundred and fifty Mustangs. North of Berlin, 339FG tangled with twenty Fw190s and claimed four shot down in a quick dogfight. One of the Fw190s was brought down without even being fired upon. As Capt Francis Gerard got into position and within firing range the German pilot immediately slid back his canopy and bailed out, giving Gerard his tenth, and easiest, victory. Gerard's Mustang was then hit by another Fw190 and he was almost forced to bail out himself but made it back to an emergency field at St Trond to crash-land safely. Eight Me262 jets were also sighted over Ludwigslust but they avoided combat using cloud cover and slipped away.

4FG covered the withdrawal of the B24s and, while most of them remained with the bombers, one flight dropped down to strafe Neubrandenburg airfield. As the first P51 streaked across the field at low level to test for flak it was hit, forcing the pilot to pull up and bail out just west of Prenzlau. His wingman, Captain George Green flying *Suzon* (44-14137), followed him down and landed in the same ploughed field, threw out his chute and took the stranded pilot aboard.

The scene was reminiscent of that played out by two Mustangs from 78FG almost one month earlier, on the last raid to Berlin. This attempt however achieved greater success. After a very short takeoff run they pulled up over trees and headed back to Debden to celebrate their lucky return.

"Heavy to unbearable flak, flak cut my shoe, cut my oxygen on the right side, holes in No.4 engine.... bombing was strictly visual – rough mission!

Diary extract, S/Sgt Charles Lubicic, gunner 385BG

Hide and seek amongst deadly contrails

Thick haze and high cirrus severely limited visibility and unusually heavy contrails exacerbated the problem, as did cockpit windows constantly icing up in the extreme temperatures. Over the Zuider Zee, the 1AD caught their first sight of Me262s but it was not until they were just sixty miles from Berlin did the jets begin their attack, sweeping in as three or four plane waves.

Turbulence and the dense contrails had caused the 457BG formation to swing fifteen miles north of their briefed course, forcing them to make an acute 90° turn onto their bomb run. In so doing,

in spite of the intense and accurate flak. Marauding jets also joined in and made intermittent attacks from out of the persistent contrails. Two Me262s were claimed by gunners of the 457BG, with another

dropping away. His later report detailed the attack, "The first fighter pass knocked out our vertical stabilizer and the ball turret, killing the gunner."

The other three jets continued on and one fired a rocket which penetrated the left wing root of the PFF lead ship (44-8717) setting the No.2 engine ablaze. Pilots, Capt Swain and 1Lt DeWeerdt, held the ship steady while the crew bailed out. An explosion blew DeWeerdt clear and killed the engineer, Capt Swain having jumped only seconds earlier. DeWeerdt later recorded, "The ship was tumbling to the ground some 70 miles east of Berlin." Bill Thompson was also on board the PFF, in the tail position as formation commander. He commented, "I was a little slow in getting out because I went back to the tail twice. Once to get some fruit drops and an orange, and again to get my chest pack. I delayed opening for at least 25,000ft because we had been told of guys who shot at chutes. The low clouds were estimated at 2,000ft and that's when I opened my chute. I landed in a pine tree and had to unhook and drop 20ft."

Another attack by three Me262s minutes later resulted in *Sweet Nancy II* (43-38861) diving away with two engines blazing. It nosed up and the tail section snapped away sending the plane spinning down. Rollie King's *Skyway Chariot* also took more hits, "On the next pass we received a great deal of damage to the plane and practically all of the controls were knocked out..." The jets lurked behind the formation until

> **"We got everything over Berlin today, flak, fighters and jets. Every place we looked there were fighters and flak"** After Action Report, Capt Rollins, 457BG

four aircraft from the low squadron lost contact and became dangerously isolated and exposed.

Choosing the moment with great skill, four Me262s swept in from the rear. The first Fortress to be hit was 43-38203, taking 30mm cannon hits in the No.3 engine, catching it on fire and sending the doomed plane plunging down into the undercast. *Que Up* (42-98024) was the next to suffer with cannon hits in the left wing which punctured the fuel cell and disabled No.2 engine, smashed the oxygen system and damaged the rudder controls. Pilot Lt Greason now had to use the dense contrails, previously so troublesome, as his saviour and he slid his B17 into their protective shroud. The other two Forts followed to save themselves from fatal damage.

The main 1AD formation began its run on to the target with fighters harassing it continuously

reckoned as a probable, and the group had been lucky to lose only one of their B17s.

1AD's second loss to the jets was 401BG's *Lady Jane* (43-38607), hit under No.4 engine and in the waist. David Vermeer kept with the formation until bombing then soared up and fell away. All except the pilot jumped clear but he and three others died.

The 3AD also encountered the jets west of Berlin and again the contrails were used to excellent effect by the attackers. The six Me262s, commanded by Oblt. Wegmann of 9/JG7, each carried 24 R4M rockets and were about to launch them for the first time in combat. In the initial attack, just 20 minutes from the target, the jets singled out the 100BG's low squadron which was badly strung out. The Me262s used a formation similar to that of the escorting P51s to approach — targeting the low squadron's low

element.

The ruse was successful and closing to almost point-blank range they severely damaged three bombers in their first pass. Copilot James Lantz, flying in the Purple Heart Corner position, recalled, "I got out of my seat just momentarily to retrieve my flak jacket and, then as I started to get back, all the guns began to chatter and someone yelled 'Fighters!' over the interphone. Then began the mad chase.... we were falling behind.... being attacked by four jet jobs, Me262s. Johnnie Greenlee and I both struggled with the controls to try to get the last bit of power to keep up with the formation. We knew once we fell out we were lost. A jet attacked at 4 o'clock and came up under our nose, but the chin turret went to work on him and we saw tracers hitting him... he kept going. A jet dived down on us with a P-51 on his tail and the B17 gunners were shooting at both of them... a ship above blew up and parts came floating back."

The leading fighter closed to point blank range and Rollie King's *Skyway Chariot* (43-37521) had most of its left stabilizer shot off before

> **"I was a little slow in getting out because I went back to the tail twice. Once to get some fruit drops... then to get my chest pack."** Bill Thompson, 100BG formation officer, 44-8717

> "A touch of the old Hun cunning and aggressive spirit was apparent today in the advantage taken of cloud and contrail cover for launching attacks and in directing his attention to a vulnerable strung out formation."
>
> Extract, 8AF INTOPS Summary No. 322

two Me262s made another pass on the high squadron. "On the third pass", continued Rollie, "we received a burst near the front which knocked out all of our controls and put the plane... into a violent spin... unable to get the plane out of the spin due to lack of control... told everybody to bail out." Navigator in *Skyway Chariot*, John Spencer, recorded, "Up until we received this last attack everyone in the ship reported they were all right. As soon as we were hit... I looked up through the astro-dome into the cockpit and my first pilot nodded for me bail out." The radio man, Archie Mathosian, wrote "The plane was in flames. I had to bail out through a hole made by a 30mm cannon shell... I was told that the plane blew up in mid-air." Three men from the rear of the ship were killed.

Seven other 100BG aircraft were damaged in the attack, including Merrill Jensen's *White Cargo* (44-6295). Five feet of its left wing was blown away, the No.4 prop split and control cables severed before it fell from the formation and limped away towards Russian lines. Me410s then picked off stragglers and in all 3AD lost four Forts to the fighter attack with others heading towards Russian territory and emergency fields on the continent.

The battle was not all one-sided, however. Doug Wright was the tail gunner in 100BG's *Quittin Time* (42-31530), a veteran of more than 90 missions. He recalled, "We encountered four Me262 jets that came in at 5 o'clock, slightly

high.... I was devastated, the sky was full of broken bodies and B17s as they zoomed through us. One Me262 returned and dropped back to finish off a smoking Fort... I started firing at him long out of range but must have gotten his attention for he forgot about the other B17 and came after us. Both my guns quit on short bursts so I quickly hand charged the right one, settled down on the sight... he blew up in a cloud of smoke. I was so relieved I kind of fell against my armor plate and said a quick prayer."

The Me262 shot down by Doug Wright was most probably that of Oblt Wegmann, 9/JG7, who claimed two of the B17s shot down that day bringing his total to six victories. Wegmann was severely wounded and had a leg amputated after he had bailed out near Wittenberg. Another JG7 Me262 pilot was killed when his jet was shot down and crashed near Perleberg. Two JG7 jets collided in the clouds but both pilots bailed out and survived. By the end of the day, pilots of the German jets submitted claims for 15 Fortresses destroyed and three P51 Mustangs shot down.

Many B17 crews later remarked at debriefing on the superb performance of the German jets over Berlin and commented that only the sheer number of defenders had saved them from disaster. The returning crews were beginning to realise that their B17s, which had been dubbed by the press in 1935 as the "Flying Fortress", were no match for these new weapons.

Naughty Virgin's men hit the silk – then the vodka

Oil leaking from No1 engine forced 305BG's Roy McCaldin, flying in *Naughty Virgin* (43-38014), to feather the prop shortly before the target. With a full bomb load still filling the bomb bay, the plane could not maintain its position in the formation and began to trail behind, gradually losing altitude. The crew contemplated the possibility of turning back after jettisoning their load, miles short of the primary target, but they decided to press on towards Berlin.

Alone and vulnerable the plane soon became the target for a lone German fighter which streaked in and poured 20mm cannon fire into the plane. One third of the right wing was blown off completely and fire began to eat away at the remains. Expecting the plane to explode at any moment, two men in the front of the ship bailed out immediately over Berlin to become prisoners. Thinking he was left alone the pilot also prepared to abandon the plane but made one last check on the intercom. To his surprise he discovered all but two of his crew were still on board and awaiting his instructions.

Checking the damage, McCaldin decided to try to reach the safety of Russian held territory to the east of the city. Most of the crew lined up in the waist in preparation for an

immediate exit should it become necessary.

Constant messages were relayed along the line of waiting men, keeping them informed about the progress towards the Oder river. One update was misinterpreted and in the confusion four men quickly leapt from the plane. A few minutes later, and still losing altitude, the three remaining crew abandoned *Naughty Virgin* to her fate.

Fortunately, all but the first two men to leave the plane came down in Russian territory. After some tense moments of confrontation with heavily armed Russian soldiers, the Americans were warmly welcomed by their allies and taken to their headquarters. Confusion abounded as neither party spoke the other's language, not helped by the consumption of tumblers of Russian vodka which left the Americans hardly able to stand. Taken on to a local Polish town, yet more vodka was consumed in yet more toasts of friendship with local dignitaries. From there the seven men were transported to the military headquarters at Lesno — and another seemingly endless round of vodka toasts. Eventually they reached Warsaw and began the journey back to American control — and relative sobriety.

> "Seeing the English coast was like seeing home again. None of us could deny that he had not been scared to death.... back at the hardstand the ground crew gave us the high sign and big smiles. Those boys really sweat out a mission like that... When I went back to my barracks I discovered three of my roommates had been in the planes shot down that day. They had only four more missions to go. Yes, Berlin was still a rough target!"
>
> James Lantz, co-pilot 100BG

18th MARCH 1945

Miss Lace goes East

Just as the bomb doors closed on the 303rd's *Miss Lace* (42-102411), flak sliced through the ship and damaged the No.1 engine's prop control. Lt Robert Krohn, flying on only his fourth mission having joined the group just a month earlier, slipped the plane from the formation as a windmilling prop vibrated violently at some 3400 rpm.

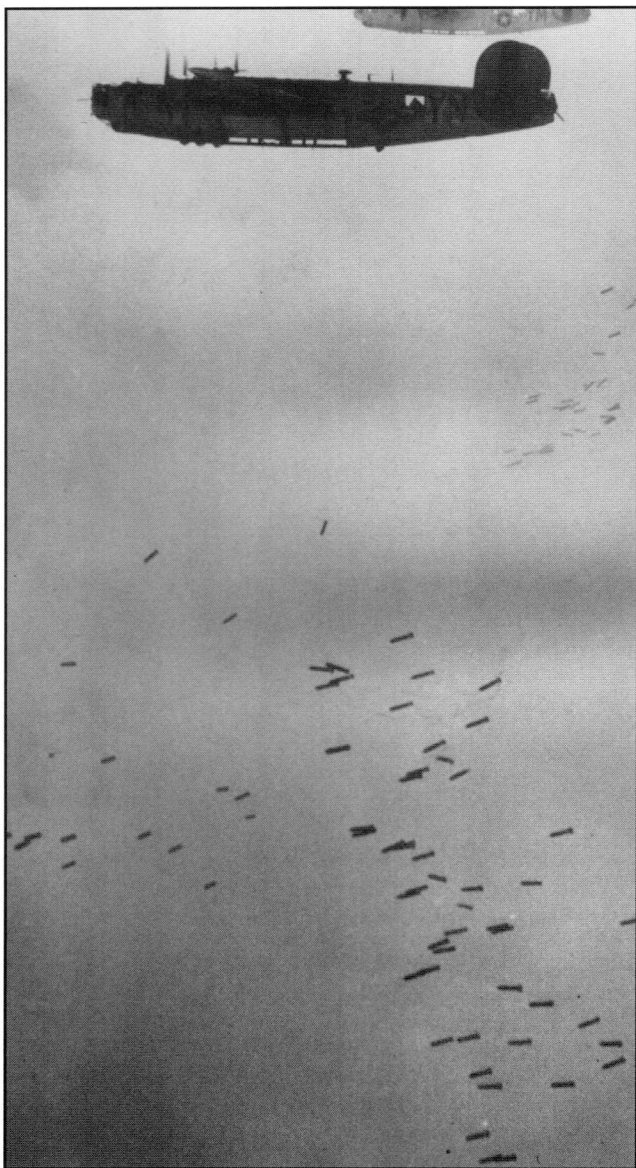

Mac McKenzie, radio man, recalled, "We went down in a tight spiral, almost a spin. I don't know if we could have bailed out or not because the centrifugal force was terrific. The plane was brought back under control by the pilots after the runaway engine finally burned out."

Soon after, No. 3 engine was also lost and, with German Me262 jets racing through the formation, Krohn had little choice but to turn *Miss Lace* east and head for the safety of Russian held territory just beyond the Oder River. "Our maps only took us as far as Berlin", continued Mac, "So we dead-reckoned our navigation. We threw everything we could overboard and destroyed vital equipment like the IFF (Identification Friend or Foe) and bomb-sight."

Two Soviet Yak fighters intercepted the ailing Fort and Mac McKenzie recalled one of them put a few rounds through the stabilizer of their plane. Then, while one held off to the rear, the other pulled in close. Crewmen aboard *Miss Lace* could see the pilot sketching their tail insignia on his note pad. Soon after he was gone.

As the weather worsened and an undercast formed, Lt Krohn dropped *Miss Lace* lower to 1000ft to get below the cloud deck. Finally locating a small airfield about two miles from Warsaw, the crew watched small biplanes practising touch-downs until a red flare gave them

(Above left) *Miss Lace* with 15 mission markers and an unauthorised crew member – a dalmatian hound! (McKenzie)

(Left) B24s from 93BG add their load to the Tegel armoured vehicle and tank plants below (USAF)

the all-clear to land.

Expecting a smooth landing, the crew were suddenly shaken by a roller-coaster ride along the ground as the wheels of the heavy Fort sank into recently filled craters left by the retreating Germans. With brakes shot out, the violent pitching did however serve to slow their pace until they came to rest with the right main gear sunk deep into a hole and the wing nearly touching the ground.

Almost immediately, a Russian staff car pulled up and Soviet officers warily eyed the crew. The name tag bearing the title "Krohn" was viewed with considerable suspicion at first until the Soviets were persuaded that the Americans were indeed their allies and friends. "I remember no one was frightened until we were on the ground outside Warsaw," said Mac McKenzie. "The Russians 'liberated' everything on the plane that was not nailed down. I recall seeing one Russian female soldier wearing our 8-day clock as a wrist watch, even though it was 2 inches thick!"

A shuttle-veteran aircraft was sent from Poltava to collect the crew, jointly operated by American OSS and the Russians. Three weeks later, after travelling through Russia, Iran, Egypt, Italy and France, the Krohn crew returned to Molesworth to continue their combat tour. Flying a further seven missions, they completed the group's last mission of the war on 25th April, to Pilzen, Czechoslovakia. *Miss Lace*, a veteran that had joined the 303BG at the end of April 1944, was left in Poland and declared salvage on 28th March 1945, the date of the 8th Air Force's final raid on the city of Berlin.

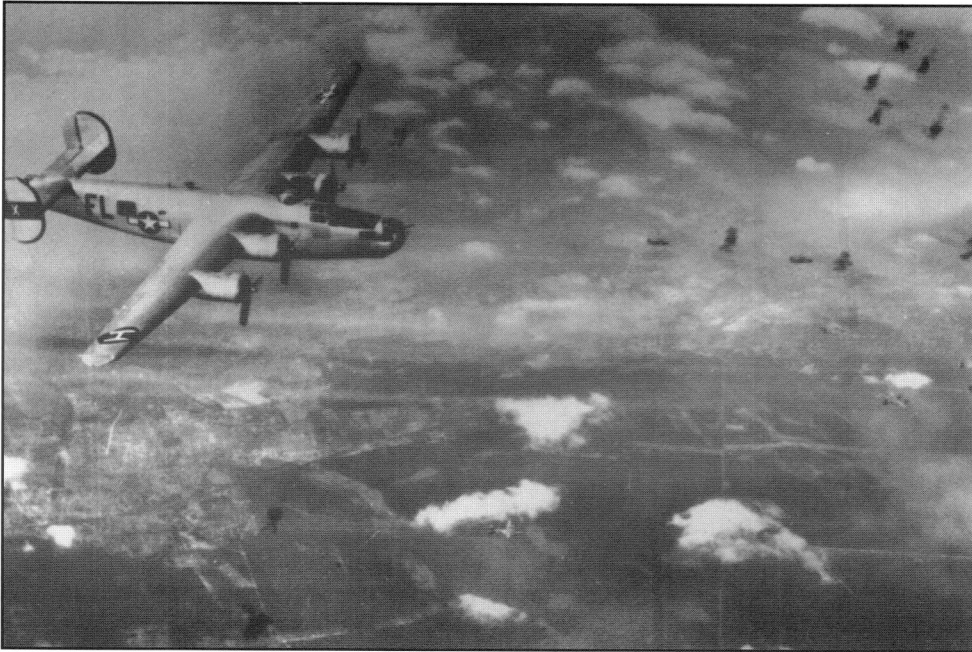

Liberators from 446BG plough on through the Berlin flak to strike at the tank factories in the west of the city. Only one B24 was lost on the mission but 128 others were damaged by the flak. 2nd Air Division's top five squadrons averaged 99% of their bomb load within a 2000ft circle, 81% within 1000ft of their aiming points. (USAF)

> **"Never expected a milk run to Berlin!"**
> Crew comment from 453BG's 735th Sqn history

Zig-zagging the 'Flag' to Sweden

Harry Culver was on his 33rd mission and had expected to be home in April, having completed his tour. He had written to his sweetheart to tell her so but Berlin changed all that! There had been an ominous warning of what was about to come when, flying his favourite 92BG plane *Flagship* (42-97288), the No.1 cylinder head had overheated on the 14th March mission and then again on 17th March. Ground crew checks had failed to find any problem.

Harry recalled, "We were approaching the Initial Point when the prop ran away on No.1, screaming like a siren. The RPM soared to 3,800 rpm... the plane shook and vibrated like it was being torn apart by the wild propeller." The co-pilot punched the feathering button but the windmilling prop continued to spin, increasing the drag.

As the plane lost altitude, the pilots decided to try to make the target. "Due to movements on the ground, advancing Allied troops or Allied prisoners of war, we were under strict orders to drop our bombs only on the target",

commented Harry. "We dropped to 15,000ft and were trailing behind the formation at an airspeed of about 110mph.... the flak batteries singled us out for the kill so we did a sweeping 180° turn to head back. We still had three engines running, but there were worse problems ahead. We flew a zig-zag course, making a sharp 45° turn every 15 seconds and watching the flak shells burst directly where we would have been."

"After what seemed like an eternity, we spotted open countryside and got rid of our bomb load. We were now headed west, flying at a reduced airspeed due to the windmilling prop. We considered diving the plane to make the prop shake loose but were fearful it might rip through the fuselage or destroy the wing... a near flak burst had caved in the bomb bay doors, adding to the drag."

As Harry Culver contemplated the options the No1 engine burst into flame and boiling black smoke. The co-pilot succeeded in putting it out with the CO2 extinguisher but there was now the

constant risk of another flare up as the shaft rotated red-hot against the oil-starved bearings. With fuel dwindling, the decision was made to head for Sweden and over the Baltic everything possible was ejected from the plane. Out went guns, flak suits, helmets, ammunition. The ball turret was unbolted and plummeted down into the icy waters below.

Harry picked up the story, "Shortly thereafter we sighted the coast and two Swedish J-22 fighters who had come up to escort us in. Suddenly someone shouted 'Fighter!' A lone German fighter made a pass directly below our plane, coming so close our crew could hear the swish of the bullets or possibly rockets as his tracers streaked by." Later Swedish airmen told them it had been a Ju88 but togglier Ray Weislar insisted it was an Me262 jet fighter. He stated that the jet shot past, started to make a sharp turn for a second pass, reached the apex of that turn and exploded. One of the Swedish escorts, piloted by Lennart Smith, had caught it. "Years later," Harry

added, "Smith's wingman, Sven Brise, called me and said that Smith had only fired tracers across the nose of the German fighter to warn him to leave Swedish air space and had not shot him down. I have always wondered what really happened."

"The airport at Malmo was located in a flat valley just below a hill at one end. We approached just high enough to clear the hill, made a quick short dive and pulled out to land on the grass field. Two truck loads of Swedish soldiers armed with automatic rifles surrounded our plane... I came out first, holding my .45 pistol by the barrel and handed it to the nearest Swede.... Yarbro and Schafer dipped into stocks of candy and gum and tossed them on to the ground. The soldiers dropped their guns and scrambled for the treats."

Crew members helped to patch flak holes in *Flagship* and Harry later flew four ferry flights taking B17s, including *Flagship*, back to England when the war was over. It was July before he made it home to the States to marry his girl.

For what would be the last major daylight raid on the German capital itself by the 8th Air Force, 446 Fortresses from the 1st Air Division set out to bomb an armament plant and a tank factory in the west of the city. The Second Air Division was not committed to action but 3AD Forts were sent to strike at the Hanomag armoured vehicle plant and the oil refineries and rail yards at Hannover.

Once again the weather proved to be the greatest enemy, disrupting the assembly and continuing to interfere with the cohesion of the force en route to target. Multi-layers of cloud, almost solid and very dense, combined with persistent contrails had forced the B17s to climb 9000ft higher than the briefed assembly altitude of 14,000ft. Many pilots were unable to locate their formations and were forced to return to their bases early or join other formations in the bomber stream.

The flak defence over Berlin was still punishing, bringing down one B17 and damaging a further 133 of the heavy bombers, 26 of them seriously, and causing another five to be scrapped on landing back in England.

Once again, Luftwaffe aerial opposition was non-existent. The desperate fuel shortage was now keeping those planes and pilots that could still be mustered securely on the ground in an ever-shrinking Fatherland. It was probably just as well

Belly landings, wet feet and a day trip to France

Only two Fortresses were listed as missing in action on this day. One of them was a 303BG plane named *Jigger Rouche II* (43-38248) which had joined the group back in August 1944.

After struggling up through the adverse weather over Molesworth, *Jigger Rouche II* made it to the target without problems. Immediately after 'bombs away' the leading aircraft made a right turn off the target towards the Rally Point. The co-pilot on *Jigger Rouche II*, Flight Officer H Goetz, was then heard on the radio reporting they had been hit on the underside by flak. Some of the control cables were shot away and three engines went out. Worse still, the pilot 2Lt Frederickson, navigator and engineer had been wounded.

With only one engine operating, F/O Goetz had to apply full rudder and heavy aileron control to keep the ailing plane in the air, but still lost altitude as each minute went by. Heading for the nearest Russian lines, Goetz spotted a small clearing near the Oder River in Poland and made a belly landing into it. Hitting trees, both wings were sheared clean away sending the slender fuselage snaking on, narrowly missing other trees and obstacles until finally coming to a stop. *Jigger Rouche II* was down but it had not made the safety of the Russian front lines and the entire crew were taken prisoner by the Germans. Although cared for by German doctors, the engineer died soon after.

Other 303BG Forts also had trouble. *Queenie* (42-97281) left the formation over France with two engines running rough. The No.2 engine eventually had to be feathered and with dense cloud making visibility very limited the pilot, 2Lt F Miller, was forced to drop down to 500ft to search for an airfield. With wheels up, *Queenie* finally slithered onto pasture land near Sandwich in Kent. There were no crew injuries but the plane was declared category 'E' and salvaged.

A third 303BG ship in trouble was un-named (43-38451). With fuel running desperately low, the pilots calculated they had just over half an hour's flying left as they crossed the English coastline. Ground controllers instructed them to head for the emergency field at Manston but the weather there was very restricted and the pilot picked up a VHF message saying conditions were clearer towards Rye. Upon reaching the area, however, the cloud base had dropped to zero forcing the plane into a belly landing on the beach near Rye harbour. Fortunately there were no casualties here either, but the plane's ball and chin turrets had buckled up and twisted the airframe — another category 'E'.

An un-named 306BG plane (44-6466) was also in trouble by the time it reached the coast. Ditching in shallow water just off Dungeness, the crew waded ashore. Cold, wet but otherwise unhurt, they left their plane to the sea.

> **"It was my 30th and final mission. I wasn't going to get off easy, as I drew the dreaded Berlin as a target."** Arnold Moselle, Pilot 303BG (44-8439)

Unable to even make it as far as the English Channel, another 303BG pilot, Arnold Moselle, was also experiencing problems in 44-8439. "It was my 30th and final mission," he recalled, "and I wasn't going to get off easy, as I drew the dreaded Berlin as a target." On the bomb run over Berlin, flak knocked out both engines on the starboard side. Forced to leave the formation, Lt Moselle found that the fuel tanks had also been hit and the fuel transfer system was inoperative, adding to his troubles. On reaching France, the navigator gave a heading for the nearest emergency field which was at Laon (A-26, occupied by 416BG's twin engine A20s). The now critical fuel situation demanded immediate clearance for landing and Lt Moselle carefully trimmed the ship, no easy task on a 28-ton heavy bomber with two engines out on the same side. Skilled piloting brought the plane and crew in to a perfect landing. In Moselle's words, "I got lucky and greased one in."

That evening Arnold celebrated his impending combat tour completion with his crew. The following day saw the fuel system repaired, along with one of the damaged engines. "Taking off on three engines presented no problem as far as I was concerned," commented Arnold, "but many of the A26 airmen turned out to watch us leave. I am sure that we created more than a few B17 fans when we did our fly-by salute as we left. That evening, at Molesworth, we were toasted again — this time having truly completed our tour."

since escorting pilots from 355FG reported the bomber boxes as "scattered, not in proper order and flying in poor formation." A few months earlier and a similar formation would almost certainly have been ravaged by the Luftwaffe, then so adept at exploiting such situations.

The bombing of the primaries at Spandau and Falkensee, with more than a thousand tons of bombs, was by H2X radar guidance through an almost solid undercast. Results were largely unobserved although radar scope photos did confirm lead bombs were on target at Spandau with others falling to the left into a built up area.

The fighter battle ???

There was virtually no enemy air activity reported on 28th March. The six groups of fighter escorts assigned to accompany the Berlin bomber stream despatched a total of 272 aircraft. One German jet was sighted in the vicinity of Mulhouse and two others were seen heading east from Goch.

There were no claims, either for aerial victories

or strafing, and no losses to enemy action. The 339FG however salvaged two of their P51s after one crashed on take-off and another came down near Colchester. Seven fighters were forced to land on the continent at emergency fields. It was a stark contrast to the aerial battles which had begun the campaign more than a year ago, in March 1944.

"...I think that to capture Berlin might cost us a hundred thousand casualties. A pretty stiff price for a prestige objective, especially when we've got to fall back and let the other fellow take over."

General Omar Bradley to the Supreme Commander, General Eisenhower, 28th March 1945

In fact, the old town of Spandau was completely blanketed by bombs during the attack, killing 300 people and injuring an unknown number. The rail freight marshalling yard at Rummelsburg, a frequent target of the RAF night attacks, was also heavily hit. A concentration of high explosive and incendiaries fell in the vicinity of the primary targets of the BMW Flugmotorwerke plant, Brandenburgische Motorenwerke factory and Auto Union works. Scattered bursts also hit the machine gun factory of the Deutsche Industrie Werke, as well as several component workshops and stores buildings in the immediate area.

The Charlottenburg and Westkreuz passenger rail stations both took direct hits when an estimated 200 high explosive and 6000 incendiary bombs fell into the Charlottenburg district. At Reinickendorf, the Schonholz rail station was also severely damaged by the 100 HE and 3000 incendiaries that fell into that area. A similar amount of ordnance was reported to have scattered across the residential area and marshalling yards in Tempelhof.

Cafe and restaurant signs on the corner of Friedrichstrasse and Dorotheenstrasse reveal that life goes on even amidst the devastation of Berlin. Work crews attempt to repair some of the damage. (Bundesarchiv)

General "Ike" turns away from Berlin

91BG's *General "Ike"* was christened in a blaze of publicity by the great man himself, at Bassingbourn on 11th April 1944. The renowned painter of some of the finest nose arts of all, Cpl Tony Starcer, painted a superb picture of Dwight Eisenhower onto both sides of the aircraft's nose. Ike was delighted with the likeness that had been achieved in the painting but criticised the choice of blue-grey for the eyes. He duly christened the plane using a bottle of pure Mississippi River water. A pilot had brought this to England intending to celebrate the completion of his tour, but had failed to return from a mission.

General "Ike" (42-97061) paid many visits to the German capital as part of the 8AF's campaign to support the Allied crusade against Hitler, starting with a lead role on 18th April 1944. The Supreme Commander, General Eisenhower, had no doubts about the importance of Berlin. Writing in a memo to his British ally General Montgomery on 15th September he noted, "Berlin is the main prize.... there is no doubt what-soever, in my mind, that we should concentrate all our energies and resources on a rapid thrust to Berlin."

This resolve however was not sustained. Six months later on 28th March 1945, just as the 91st's *General "Ike"* raided the city yet again and turned away for home, Eisenhower wrote to his Russian ally, Stalin. This letter stated his intention to halt the Anglo-American drive towards Berlin and, instead, turn south for Leipzig. Stalin was delighted. Generals Montgomery and Patton were not!

Perhaps politics, an awareness of the high casualties that could be anticipated in the assault on a city the size of Berlin, not to mention the enormous administrative problems that would be involved in feeding and caring for the millions of inhabitants of the city, had much to do with the decision. Writing to General Marshall in an attempt to pre-empt criticism, Ike noted, "May I point out that Berlin itself is no longer a particularly important objective." And to Montgomery he wrote, three days later, "That place (Berlin) has become, so far as I am concerned, nothing but a geographical location, and I have never been interested in these."

Prime Minister Winston Churchill was furious and responded to Ike's decision, "Nothing will exert a psychological effect of despair upon all German forces of resistance equal to that of the fall of Berlin." But the momentous decision was made. Ike turned his advancing forces away from Berlin and the map of Europe was redrawn for the next 45 years.

Bassingbourn's *General "Ike"* never again returned to Berlin, nor any of the other 8AF heavies. It, just like its illustrious namesake, completed the war in Europe and returned to the USA.

Tony Starcer painted this fine portrait of General Eisenhower, based on a 'Time' magazine cover, on to both sides of the nose. (J McPartlin)

A little extra help for the 8th

The plans for the 21st June 1944 raid on Berlin initially included the involvement of both the RAF heavy bombers and the US 15th Air Force based in Italy. Not until 24th March 1945 did 15AF heavies actually take off and head for the German capital — it was one of their longest missions and their only strike on Berlin.

Rare differential winds permitted the attack on the city which was almost 800 miles from some of the bases in Italy. Flying at one altitude on the way in and a different altitude on the return, giving tail winds in both directions, meant that the 15AF could make the trip — just!

169 B17s escorted by 289 fighters struck the Daimler Benz tank assembly factory at Berlin. Target photos indicated an effective strike with the majority of buildings in the target area damaged as well as rail tracks and marshalling yards west of the plant. Me262 jets were active against the strike and nine Forts were lost as a result of them and the flak, although three of them managed to get as far as the Mediterranean before ditching. Five P51 escorts were also lost, all from the 332FG. Gunners on the bombers claimed six jets and two other fighters destroyed and their escorts added a further seven jets to the tally. These victories were to be the last jets claimed by 15AF heavy bombers during WWII.

The mission was claimed by some as a publicity exercise but others, in 15AF, insisted that the 8th needed all the help it could get!

A windmilling prop sheared off and sliced into the side of *General Ike's* beautiful nose art painting on 16th February 1945, its 65th mission, fortunately without causing casualties in the crew. Tony Starcer had to repaint his damaged masterpiece. (D Wellings)

Outhouse Mouse sports an impressive array of mission marks. (Odenwaller)

Outhouse Mouse sneaks to Paris

The 91st Bomb Group took delivery of 42-31636 over a year before the final Berlin raid, on 12th March 1944. Since that date it had clocked up 130 combat missions to every major target in Germany and safely brought home many different crews. Tended and cared for by M/Sgts Rollin Davis and C.B. McGara, and the ground crew, *Outhouse Mouse* sported a cute piece of nose art based on the famous 'Tom & Jerry' cartoon. The 'Mouse' had been shot at by flak and fighters, patched and repainted more than once, and it was no stranger to Berlin, having paid a first visit on 22nd March 1944.

Flying with Joe Harvey's crew, tucked into the ball turret, was George Odenwaller. His terse diary notes record: "Ship No: 636... Name: Outhouse Mouse... Temp: -38°... Flak: very intense... Damage: some... " George recalled, "After bombing we flew into total cloud cover. Flew blind through 10/10 clouds and became lost and disorientated. Let down or bail out? We decided to stay and eventually came out of the cloud over France."

Outhouse Mouse had in fact made its way through the murk towards Paris. George continued, "There was a heavy fog over the area. We almost hit the Eiffel Tower as we flew round — twice! Then a tiny L-3 Grasshopper liaison plane appeared out of nowhere and we narrowly missed flying into that as well." Finally Joe Harvey located an airfield at Villa LaRoche and put the 'Mouse' down for repairs. As they landed they became aware of groups of French workers filling in recent bomb craters and only narrowly avoided cracking up on the potholed runway. "Crazy Americans!", they shouted.

"While on the ground," continued George, "We took the chance to visit Paris. We only had our flight gear with us, no dress uniform, no cap, no tie and not even any proper shoes — just our thick fur lined flight boots. We were very lucky not to have been picked up by the MPs — very lucky! On return to Bassingbourn we found we had been listed as 'MIA'. Personal lockers had been cleared out — including my scotch, uniform and (a prize possession) my piece of the painted *General Ike*, cut from the damaged B17 when it was hit by a runaway prop!"

Outhouse Mouse continued on to complete a further nine missions before the end of hostilities and a return to the USA.

Berlin claims its last victims

Joseph McCullough's 401BG crew were unlucky enough to draw the last strike on Berlin for their baptism of fire. Sgt Lawrence Genauer, the radar spot jammer, recorded later, "The crew were flying for the first time out of the 401st Bomb Group at Deenethorpe. I was an RCM operator and flew with a different crew each time."

Passing over the target, McCullough's un-named 43-37551 was hit by flak and dropped away but continued to shadow the formation with its left wing smoking. The radio man, wounded by splinters, was given first aid by Sgt Genauer. About 30 minutes later, at 11.20hrs and northwest of Magdeburg, observers saw a "big puff of smoke from the left wing and the aircraft went into a spin, down through the clouds at about 15,000ft."

McCullough sounded the bail out bell and six of the crew were able to exit the plane as it spiralled down. German salvage and recovery teams later found the bodies of four men still in the wreckage which crashed 40 miles west of Berlin, at Grasleben — Sgts McGurn, Winterburn, Tish and Jacobson. It was a cruel inaugural mission and they would prove to be among the last USAAF casualties to be claimed by the city's defences.

The final strikes around Berlin

The 8th Air Force launched two further assaults around Berlin but were not directed again to strike the city itself. On 10th April, the 1AD sent 417 Fortresses and 273 Mustangs to attack the munitions storage area, airfield and aviation industrial targets at Oranienburg, north of the city. They lost nine heavy bombers and four Mustangs. The 3AD despatched 138 bombers to Brandenburg/Briest airfield to the west as part of a strike against the Luftwaffe's jet bases and lost two B17s. Luftwaffe Me262 jets put in an appearance and four were caught by 56FG attacking the B17s en route to the target. One was shot down.

Marauding fighter escorts, for all the participating task forces, returned with the staggering tally of over 300 victories, almost entirely from ground strafing attacks. One third of these victories (105) were scored by 339FG in strafing runs on the densely packed dispersal area north of Neuruppin airfield, one of the other targets for the 3AD. Forty-one Me410s and thirty-seven Ju88s were among the burning wrecks left by the group. 56FG also had a field day and left 47 enemy planes burning on the ground after their attacks. The 357FG arrived on the scene just as the 339FG were withdrawing and submitted claims for a further 23 aircraft destroyed, including two Me262s.

Oranienburg and Brandenburg marshalling yards were the targets for the final aerial thrust into the Berlin area. The forces involved were eighty-two Forts from 3AD and 137 from 1AD respectively. All available fighter groups were involved in escort duties but the Luftwaffe made scant appearance and claims for the day amounted to only seven enemy aircraft destroyed. The only loss to the 8AF was a 401BG Fortress from the Brandenburg force.

THE RAF's CAMPAIGN AGAINST BERLIN

The first RAF bombers to fly over Berlin did so just one month after war was declared. On the night of 1st October 1939, Whitley bombers made the 1000 miles round trip to shower leaflets on the city. It would be almost a year before bombs would follow.

After air raids on London and several other major towns in England, the British War Cabinet authorised the first Berlin raid. The RAF despatched 103 aircraft on the night of 25th August 1940, about half of them headed for Berlin. Cloud prevented accurate bombing by the force of Hampden and Wellington bombers and strong winds on the return leg forced three Hampdens, at the limit of their range, to ditch in the sea. Three others were lost over Germany and France. The strike was hardly a success and Berlin archives record just one wooden summer house destroyed. But it was the start of, perhaps, the longest battle of the war.

Raids followed throughout the year, involving between ten and eighty bombers. However, on the night of 23rd September 1940 RAF Bomber Command took the decision to concentrate its forces against Berlin and despatched 129 aircraft to strike rail yards, power stations, gas works and aero engine plants. For three hours aircraft bombed their targets from 16,000ft down to as low as 4,600ft. The results of the raid are not known because the relevant air raid records were removed, possibly for fear of bad propaganda.

1941 saw sporadic raids on the city, the largest being on the night of 7th September when 197 bombers were despatched with a loss of 15. The final raid of the year came two months later on 7/8th November with a force of 169 Wellingtons, Whitleys, Stirlings and Halifaxes. Less than half of them actually

reached the city area and caused relatively little damage for their effort. It was the last major raid on Berlin until January 1943, fourteen months later.

Over two hundred Lancaster and Halifax bombers were despatched on the night of 16th January 1943. It was the first raid to use only four-engine bombers. It was another disappointment. Heavy cloud made navigation difficult and the city was shrouded by a thick haze resulting a scattered bombing. An unusually high number of casualties was incurred when the Berlin air raid warning system failed. The sirens sounded only as the first bombs began to fall and there was considerable panic. The largest assembly hall in Europe, the Deutschlandhalle with 10,000 seats, was hit and burnt out by incendiaries just after the last person had been evacuated. Berliners referred to the 'miracle' which had saved so many lives.

The following night 187 Lancasters and Halifaxes returned but again failed to score any appreciable hits on their primary targets. Sadly for the air crews, planners had scheduled them to follow the routes of the previous night and German fighters destroyed 22 aircraft, 11.8% of the force.

On 30th January 1943, two formations of RAF Mosquitoes made runs over the city to disrupt major rallies being held by the Nazi heirarchy. These raids were the first time daylight bombing had occurred on Berlin. At precisely the moment that Goering was due to begin his speech in mid-morning, three Mosquitoes roared overhead and dropped their bombs, forcing a postponement and much embarrassment. Then, in the afternoon, three more Mosquitoes again roared over just as

Goebbels was due to speak but this time German flak caught one of the raiders and shot it down, killing both men on board.

No further attempts on Berlin were made until March when three major raids were despatched, totalling 1029 aircraft — forty seven failed to return. Mosquitoes made diversionary raids on the city in July and August but on the night of 23rd August 1943 the RAF launched its biggest force to date, 719 aircraft. It was a disaster and brought the

RAF its greatest loss of aircraft in a single night so far, 57 bombers (7.9%). Although most of the bombs fell outside the city area, Berlin records reported it as the most serious raid of the war with more than 850 persons killed and 2,600 buildings destroyed or seriously damaged.

One week later, another large force of more than 600 bombers was despatched. It was another disaster and 47 more aircraft failed to return (7.6%), about two thirds being shot down over or near Berlin by night fighters. Pathfinders dropped their markers well south of the centre and the main force pulled the bombing back 30 miles along the approach route. Another raid followed on the night of 3rd September and 7% was lost from the force of 316 Lancasters. However, significant damage was caused to industrial and utility targets.

Mosquitoes flew a series of nuisance raids during the rest of September, October and November, sending a handful of aircraft over the city on each occasion. The greatest effect probably

being the loss of sleep to Berliners and aircrew alike.

On the night of 18th November 1943, the RAF launched the Battle for Berlin — an all-out effort to crack the city and its morale. Sir Arthur Harris had finally won his argument and was given a free hand to mount his campaign against the capital. It would last four and half months and involve fifteen major raids on the city, each using between 380 and 890 heavy bombers. Casualties would prove to be horrendous

---

"Berlin was the target of almost 40% of the sorties flown by (RAF) Bomber Command in Nov 1943 and over 50% of the sorties flown in Jan 1944.... US Bombing Survey

---

and the Luftwaffe's night defences reached the peak of their performance, with almost 400 twin-engine, radar-equipped night fighters available.

The Battle for Berlin opened on the night of 18th November 1943 when 440 Lancasters were despatched and bombed across the city. On 22nd November, the largest force so far, 764 aircraft comprising a 2-1 mix of Lancasters and Halifaxes, made a most effective raid on Berlin. Widespread destruction of Ministry and Embassy buildings was recorded as well as factories and the Imperial Guard barracks at Spandau. More than 2000 lives were lost including 500 persons caught in an air raid shelter located at Wilmersdorf. On 26th November, another large force of Lancasters headed for Berlin in clear skies. This was the raid which saw Hitler order every available fire appliance to the Alkett plant to fight the fires there while other parts of the city were allowed to burn. Most bombers escaped the fighters over the city but flak claimed several. As they streamed home the fighters caught up with them, 28 were shot down and a further 14 crashed in England. In the whole of November, the RAF had despatched 2030 aircraft to Berlin — 83 had failed to return.

December saw another four major raids on the city involving 2043 aircraft. 100 were lost and a further 29 abandoned over England. On 2nd December, Luftwaffe controllers correctly identified Berlin as the target twenty minutes before zero hour and vectored in many fighters to await the force. Forty bombers were shot down and one squadron, 460 (Australian) Sqn, lost 20% of its number. Hits were scored on two Henschel aircraft plants, also on a Daimler Benz factory and rail yards, but much of the night's effort fell on open countryside to the south.

Almost five hundred Lancasters returned on the night of 16th December and, yet again, the Luftwaffe fighter controllers accurately predicted the course. Fighter attacks began over the Dutch coast and continued along the approach and over the target but the losses were not as high as might have been expected (5%). Little damage was done to industrial targets and most of the bombs fell onto housing. Over 700 persons were recorded killed, at least 70 of them caught on a train at Halensee which received direct hits. On the 23rd December, another 390 heavies were despatched to Berlin. Fifteen of them failed to

return.

The last raid on the city in 1943 was on the night of 29th December with over 700 Lancasters and Halifaxes. Bad weather prevented the German night fighters from locating the bomber stream but still twenty aircraft were lost. Little significant damage was caused.

The new year of 1944 was heralded in on the night of 1st January, with a force of 420 Lancasters aimed at Berlin. Fighters took a heavy toll and 28 bombers failed to return. Most of the bombing fell into the Grunewald woods to the southwest. The following night 360 Lancasters returned to Berlin and were caught by fighters over the city, losing ten pathfinder aircraft and 16 others. It was another ineffective raid. A lull of almost three weeks followed but on the night of 20th January a large force of Lancasters and Halifaxes was back over Berlin. Thirty five bombers failed to return.

Thirty three more Lancasters were lost from the force of over 500 despatched on the night of 27th January. Extensive diversionary raids, including dropping imitation 'fighter flares' helped to draw off the fighter attacks. Even so another 33 bombers failed to return. The following night 46 more were shot down when controllers concentrated their night fighters over the city itself. The force of 677 bombers lost 6.8% of its strength but claimed the raid as the most concentrated attack

on Berlin so far. Damage and casualties were not recorded, the Berlin authorities were becoming overwhelmed by their

---

---

task. Two nights later, at least one thousand people died when another raid struck the city from 528 aircraft. It was the third raid on the city in four nights. Although they made a late interception of the bomber stream, the night fighters harried them on the return flight and 33 aircraft failed to return.

January 1944 had seen over 2,884 bombers despatched to Berlin. More than one hundred and seventy had not made it back home. The Battle for Berlin faltered and February saw only one major raid. The regular bombing squadrons were exhausted and had been withdrawn for two weeks to rest and re-equip. Then on the night of 15th February, the RAF launched its biggest raid on Berlin by sending more than 560 Lancasters and 300 Halifax bombers in a force totalling 891 aircraft. Night fighters and flak claimed 43 victims and cost Bomber Command another 324 aircrew. Large scale evacuation from the city began finally to reduce the enormous numbers of casualties sustained, but even so over 300 were killed. Considerable damage was done to important industrial targets and a thousand major fires were reported.

The last major raid undertaken by the RAF on Berlin came three weeks after the USAAF began its daylight attacks on the city. On the night of 24th March, over eight hundred

bombers struggled through high winds to reach the target. The strong wind forced the bombers south along their

approach, scattering the force and leaving it highly vulnerable to flak and night fighters. Fourteen bombers were shot down over Berlin and another 58 elsewhere along the route, almost 9% of the force. The high winds also scattered the markers and bombs fell over a huge area, including on more than 100 small towns and villages around Berlin. The Waffen-SS depot at Lichtefelde was badly hit, perhaps more by luck than judgement, and several industrial plants.

The Battle for Berlin was over. It had not cracked the morale of the Berliners or their masters. Since the major offensive began on 18th November 1943 RAF Bomber Command had lost 485 heavy bombers out of 8710 sorties to Berlin, almost 4000 trained aircrew. Up to a further 285 aircraft of various types had been lost on previous raids. However, an RAF target assessment on 21st March 1944 did claim that of the 60 priority targets in the city, 40 had been seriously damaged.

In the remaining months of the war, RAF Mosquitoes continued to strike at the city, usually in small numbers although as many as 122 were despatched on the night of 1st February and 142 on 21st March 1945. A total of 5662 sorties were flown by Mosquitoes to Berlin on 114 separate night raids between 31st March 1944 and 21st April 1945, forty-nine failed to return.

8TH AIR FORCE BOMBER LOSSES IN THE BATTLE FOR BERLIN

3 March 1944

1BD	**1CBW**	**91BG**	**B17s**	
42-37965		2Lt W Pickard		*My Desire*
		381BG	**B17s**	
42-37986		2Lt R Rogers		
	40CBW	**92BG**	**B17s**	
42-40014		1Lt W Lansford, Jr		
2BD	**14CBW**	**392BG**	**B24s**	
42-7491		1Lt R Smith		*Pregnant Peg II*
	96CBW	**458BG**	**B24s**	
41-29298		1Lt F Herzik		
3BD	**4CBW**	**94BG**	**B17s**	
42-38075		1Lt D Ahlwardt		
		447BG	**B17s**	
42-31112		1Lt F Graham		
42-31148		1Lt D Ralston		(Ditched)
	13CBW	**100BG**	**B17s**	
42-38017		1Lt J Gossage		
42-39817		1Lt R Vollmer		*Murderer's Row*
42-31970		Capt R Lohof		

4 March 1944

1BD	**1CBW**	**381BG**	**B17s**	
42-30151		2Lt D Keyes		*Spare Parts*
	41CBW	**384BG**	**B17s**	(bombed Cologne)
42-31606		Lt H Lovvorn		
42-32007		1Lt G Cosentino		
42-39991		1Lt W Carpenter		
3BD	**4CBW**	**94BG**	**B17s**	
42-38169		2Lt D Pollock		*Hey Mable!*
42-39801		2Lt J Blake		*Northern Queen*
		385BG	**B17s**	
42-39925		••••		
		447BG	**B17s**	
42-31165		2Lt P Geyer		
	13CBW	**95BG**	**B17s**	
42-31565		2Lt R Roehm		
42-31734		1Lt M Worthy		
42-31785		1Lt M Dunham		*Slightly Dangerous*
42-31910		1Lt W Brownlow		
		100BG	**B17s**	
42-38016		1Lt S Seaton		*Seaton's Sad Sacks*
	45CBW	**96BG**	**B17s**	
42-30412		1Lt P Herring		*Mischief Maker II*
		452BG	**B17s**	
42-31341		Lt A Mittman		*Breaks of the Game*

6 March 1944

1BD	**1CBW**	**91BG**	**B17s**	
42-97483		2Lt B Evertson		
42-31079		1Lt P Coleman		
42-31578		1Lt B Tibbets		*My Darling Also*
42-31869		1Lt C Mason		*Hell and High Water*
42-31911		1Lt D Harding		
42-38118		2Lt B Fourmy		
		381BG	**B17s**	
42-31448		2Lt M Fastrup		*Half Breed*
42-3215		2Lt R Cole		*Linda Mary*
42-31553		1Lt E Haushalter		
42-37983		2Lt H Cahill		(Ditched)
	40CBW	**92BG**	**B17s**	
42-97527		1Lt R Townsend		
42-31503		1Lt F Krizan		
42-31680		1Lt E Cooper		
42-40052		1Lt W Upson		
		306BG	**B17s**	
42-40006		1Lt C Smith		*Liberty Lady* (Sweden)
	41CBW	**379BG**	**B17s**	
42-31555		1Lt W Hendrickson		

	94CBW	**401BG**	**B17s**	
42-38136		2Lt C Kolb		
		457BG	**B17s**	
42-31595		2Lt E Whalen		
42-31627		2Lt R Graves		
2BD	**2CBW**	**389BG**	**B24s**	
42-100424		1Lt K Griesel		
		445BG	**B24s**	
42-7586		1Lt G Lymburn		*God Bless This Ship*
42-109796		1Lt N Serkland		*Balls of Fire*
		453BG	**B24s**	
42-64457		1Lt E Crockett		(Ditched)
42-64460		1Lt P Tobin		*Shack Rabbit*
42-52191		2Lt H Meek		*Lillie Belle/Little Joe* (Ditched)
42-52226		1Lt H Cripe		
	14CBW	**392BG**	**B24s**	
42-7598		1Lt E Hestad		*Flak Ducker*
	20CBW	**93BG**	**B24s**	
42-109832		1Lt J Harris		*De-Icer*
		446BG	**B24s**	
42-100288		1Lt Paltz		*Major Hoopo*
		448BG	**B24s**	
42-29191		2Lt C York		*Hello Natural* (Sweden)
	96CBW	**458BG**	**B24s**	
41-29286		Capt J Bogusch		
41-29299		2Lt T Hopkins		
42-52306		2Lt J McMains		
42-52450		2Lt B Ballard		
42-52515		2Lt G Clifford		*Ford Follies*
3BD	**4CBW**	**94BG**	**B17s**	
42-38022		1Lt C Johnston		*Lil Opportunity*
	13CBW	**95BG**	**B17s**	
42-97495		1Lt J Conley		
42-31251		1Lt T Keasbey		
42-31299		1Lt G Lloyd		*Junior/She's My Gal*
42-32002		2Lt T Barksdale		*Berlin First*
42-38024		1Lt M Russell		
42-39793		1Lt R Read		
42-29943		2Lt A Mailman		*Situation Normal*
42-3529		2Lt F Frantz		
		100BG	**B17s**	
42-97491		1Lt D Radkte		*Ronnie R*
42-30170		1Lt C Montgomery		*Pride of the Century*
42-97482		1Lt W Terry		*Terry and the Pirates*
42-30278		2Lt Z Kendall		*Sly Fox*
42-31051		2Lt R Koper		*Goin Jessies*
42-31731		1Lt A Amiero		
42-31735		1Lt G Brannen		*Lucky Lee*
42-31800		2Lt S Barton		
42-38011		1Lt E Handorf		*Kinda Ruff*
42-38044		1Lt M Rish		*Spirit of '44*
42-38059		Capt D Miner		
42-38197		1Lt J Lautenschlager		*Half and Half*
42-39872		1Lt F Granack		*Rubber Check*
42-39994		1Lt S Barrick		*Barrick's Bag* (Sweden)
42-30799		1Lt W Murray		*The BigAss Bird II*
		390BG	**B17s**	
42-31935		1Lt R Starks		*Stark's Ark*
	45CBW	**388BG**	**B17s**	
42-31135		1Lt M Givens		*Suzy Sagtitz*
42-31163		2Lt C Wallace		*A Good and Happy Ship*
42-31194		1Lt C Grindley		
42-31240		2Lt J McLaughlin		
42-37886		1Lt L Watts		*Blitzin Betsy*
42-40054		Capt P Brown		
42-38177		2Lt A Christiani		*Shack Rabbits*
		452BG	**B17s**	
42-31337		2Lt H Sweeny		
42-31373		2Lt C Wagner		*Flakstop*
		482BG	**B17s (PFF)**	
42-3491		Brig. Gen. R Wilson		

8th March 1944

1BD	**1CBW**	**91BG**	**B17s**
42-39892	2Lt C Williams		
		381BG	**B17s**
42-38029	Lt T Pirtle		
	41CBW	**303BG**	**B17s**
42-31471	1Lt L McGrath		*Doolittle's Destroyers*
	94CBW	**401BG**	**B17s**
42-31488	2Lt D Peterson		*Shade Ruff*
2BD	**2CBW**	**389BG**	**B24s**
42-99975	Lt J Kendrick		*Yankee Rebel Harmony*
42-100375	Lt J McArthur		
		453BG	**B24s**
42-52175	1Lt E Ehrman		*Portland Annie*
	20CBW	**446BG**	**B24s**
41-29292	1Lt J Merriman		
42-100231	1Lt C Helfer		
42-7595	1Lt H Bohnet		*Shif' Lus Skonk!*
		448BG	**B24s**
42-100342	Capt J Grunow		
42-100122	2Lt J Daley		*Twin Tails* (Ditched)
	96CBW	**458BG**	**B24s**
41-28720	2Lt J Adamson		
3BD	**4CBW**	**94BG**	**B17s**
42-5950	Lt Babington		*Peter's Pride*
42-31141	Lt Scott		
	13CBW	**95BG**	**B17s**
42-37929	Lt F Fagan		*Dianna*
		100BG	**B17s**
42-40056	Lt N Chapman		*Katie's Boys*
		390BG	**B17s**
42-30713	2Lt M Quakenbush		*Phyllis Marie*
42-31717	1Lt P Quillin		
42-37812	Lt S Branum		*Heavenly Body*
	45CBW	**96BG**	**B17s**
42-30847	1Lt D Kasch		*Pegasus*
42-39988	1Lt G Pond		*Iron Ass*
42-31403	2Lt C Ross		
42-31576	1Lt H Lemanski		
42-31716	2Lt J Swendiman		
42-31912	Capt N Thomas		
		388BG	**B17s**
42-30829	2Lt M Moran		*Princess Pat*
42-30340	2Lt A Amann		*Screamin' Red Ass*
42-38138	1Lt W Lentz		
42-31214	2Lt H Pou		*Return Engagement*
42-37819	1Lt L Tobias		
		452BG	**B17s**
42-31331	2Lt G Butterworth		*Tangerine*
42-31354	2Lt D Sorenson		
42-37954	1Lt H Wilson		
42-38211	2Lt T McDonald		*Sleepy Time Gal*
42-97525	2Lt F Stephens		*Invictus*

9th March 1994

1BD	**40CBW**	**92BG**	**B17s**
42-31564	1Lt D Floyd		(Landed Sweden)
42-31772	2Lt W Payne		
	41CBW	**384BG**	**B17s**
42-37781	Lt M Reed		*Silver Dollar*
3BD	**4CBW**	**447BG**	**B17s**
42-31208	1Lt J Jurneka		(Ditched)
42-31210	Lt McGuire		(Ditched)
	45CBW	**388BG**	**B17s**
42-37839	F/O B Dopko		*Little Willie*

22nd March 1944

1BD	**1CBW**	**91BG**	**B17s**
42-97125	Capt C Phillips		*The Buccaneer*
	40CBW	**305BG**	**B17s**
42-37957	1Lt E Whipple		
42-97523	2Lt H Burnett		
	94CBW	**351BG**	**B17s**
42-39849	2Lt W Slossen		
2BD	**20CBW**	**446BG**	**B24s**
41-29151	1Lt J Jaslofsky		*Joker*
42-100306	1Lt G Shafer, Jr		*War Goddess* (Sweden)
	96CBW	**458BG**	**B24s**
41-28678	2Lt M Dunlevie		
		466BG	**B24s**
41-29434	Lt W Terry		*Terry & the Pirates* (Sweden)
41-29416	2Lt G Brand		*Rebel Yell*
3BD	**4CBW**	**94BG**	**B17s**
42-31637	1Lt B Carlson		*Athenian Avenger*
		447BG	**B17s**
42-107038	2Lt E Stull, Jr		
	45CBW	**96BG**	**B17s**
42-6099	2Lt N Young		*Winnie C*

18th April 1944

1BD	**1CBW**	**381BG**	**B17s**
42-37733	1Lt H Souder		*Patches 'n Prayers*
	41CBW	**303BG**	**B17s**
42-97552	1Lt L Holdcroft		*The Road Back*
	94CBW	**351BG**	**B17s**
42-31955	1Lt E Apperson		
2BD	**14CBW**	**392BG**	**B24s**
42-52704	1Lt D Tiefendal		*Son of Satan II*
	96CBW	**458BG**	**B24s**
42-52382	1Lt W Schuman		*Wurf'less*
3BD	**4CBW**	**94BG**	**B17s**
42-31407	Lt G Craig		*Chief Chilletaccux*
42-31401	Lt A Gordon		*Old Hickory*
42-31874	Lt W Williams		
42-107019	Lt Schommer		
42-37797	Lt Brinkmeir		*Wolverine/Gin Mill Special*
42-37852	Lt Dillard		*The Payoff*
42-31650	Lt McMeekin		*Impatient Virgin*
42-38139	Lt I Pomerantz		*Lonesome Polecat*
42-97545	1Lt G Rieder		(96BG PFF a/c)
42-97569	Lt Campbell		(PFF a/c)
		447BG	**B17s**
42-97597	Capt M Easterline		(96BG PFF a/c)
	13CBW	**390BG**	**B17s**
42-30332	2Lt B Procopio		*Short Stuff* (Sweden)
42-37902	2Lt J Harrison		*Hell's Belles/Sure Thing*
42-97242	2Lt R Wassel		

29th April 1944

1BD	**1CBW**	**91BG**	**B17s**
42-31353	1Lt J Purdy		*Queenie*
	40CBW	**92BG**	**B17s**
42-3513	2Lt R Munson		
42-97319	2Lt J Langfeldt		
		306BG	**B17s**
42-31556	2Lt W Lutz		
	41CBW	**303BG**	**B17s**
42-31241	2Lt H Bohle		*Spirit of Wanette*
42-3158	2Lt J Fisher		*Max*
		384BG	**B17s**
42-102448	2Lt J Bouvier		
	94CBW	**401BG**	**B17s**
42-31116	2Lt J Singleton		*Cawn't Miss*
42-31226	2Lt D Butterfoss		
42-31521	Capt G Gould		*Badland Bat*

2BD 2CBW   389BG   B24s
| 41-28676 | Capt J Higgins | |
| 41-28784 | 1Lt A Locke | (Ditched) |

453BG   B24s
| 42-52301 | 1Lt M Davison | (Ditched) |
| 42-50322 | 2Lt F Tye | |

14CBW   44BG   B24s
42-100279	2Lt K Schuyler	*Tuffy*
42-29471	2Lt G Sweigert	
41-29513	2Lt R Hruby	(Ditched)

392BG   B24s
42-110062	2Lt L Ofenstein	
42-100371	2Lt W Kamenitsky	
42-100100	2Lt G Rogers	*Double Trouble*
41-28759	2Lt F Sheres	
42-110105	2Lt R Bishop	
42-7510	2Lt B Wyatt	*El Lobo* (Ditched)

20CBW   446BG   B24s
| 42-100360 | 1Lt W Jones | *Luck and Stuff* |

448BG   B24s
41-29523	1Lt M Turpin	*Miss Happ*
42-99988	2Lt W Pouge	*The Sad Sack*
42-7683	2Lt W Rogers	*Sweet Sioux*
41-29479	2Lt O Howard	*(Big Bad Wolf)*
42-52435	2Lt J Cathey	
42-7655	1Lt J Clark	*Chubby Champ*

96CBW   458BG   B24s
| 42-28718 | 2Lt R Morris | *Bo* (Sweden) |

466BG   B24s
| 41-29399 | 2Lt F Cotner | *Playboy* |
| 41-28754 | 1Lt C Hitchcock | *Tell Me More* |

467BG   B24s
41-28730	1Lt J Gavin	*Blonde Bomber*
41-28749	1Lt F Prokop	
42-52506	1Lt B Moore	

3BD 4CBW   94BG   B17s
| 42-102520 | 2Lt J McClurkin | |
| 42-31498 | 2Lt K Chism | *Passionate Witch* |

385BG   B17s
42-107045	2Lt L Sexton	
42-31133	1Lt H Garza	
42-31174	1Lt F Hart	
42-31773	1Lt C Johnston	
42-97078	2Lt W Henry	
42-97226	2Lt R Huntingdon	
42-97559	1Lt R Barney	

447BG   B17s
42-31124	2Lt W Davidson	
42-31144	1Lt H Hughes	
42-31161	2Lt A Peper	
42-31217	2Lt H Paris	
42-37866	1Lt W Donahue	
42-37868	2Lt C Blom	
42-97135	1Lt C Marcy	*Hey Mabel! (?)*
42-97501	2Lt E Johnson	*Gum Chum*
42-102421	2Lt C Dowler	
42-102479	2Lt E Farrell	*Mississippi Lady*
42-31519	••••	(Ditched)

13CBW   95BG   B17s
| 42-31320 | 1Lt E Leaser | *I'll Be Around* |
| 42-37988 | 2Lt J Vilberg | *Flagship* |

390BG   B17s
| 42-102526 | 1Lt R Rayburn | |

45CBW   388BG   B17s
| 42-31393 | 2Lt D Walker | |
| 42-37980 | 2Lt J Covner | |

452BG   B17s
42-31784	2Lt Suckow	(Ditched)
42-39920	2Lt H Nelson	*Karen B*
42-39981	2Lt G Haakenson	*Section Eight*

7th May 1944

1BD 1CBW   91BG   B17s
| 42-31580 | 1Lt N Kovachevich | *Merry Widow* |

41CBW   379BG   B17s
| 42-38161 | 1Lt C Darnell | *Sarah Jane* |
| 42-37791 | 2Lt T Smith | *Blues in the Night* |

384BG   B17s
| 42-31235 | 1Lt T Goller, Jr | *Goin Dog* |

94CBW   351BG   B17s
| 42-37714 | 2Lt R Presley | *Ronchi* |

401BG   B17s
| 42-39943 | 2Lt B Grimmett | *Lassie Come Home* |

3BD 4CBW   385BG   B17s
| 42-5879 | 2Lt S Hoffman | |

45CBW   96BG   B17s
| 42-3324 | 2Lt N Behrens | *Rikki Tikki Tavi* |

8th May 1944

1BD 40CBW   92BG B17s
| 42-31277 | 1Lt T Fishburn | |

40CBW   306BG   B17s
42-97259	Lt Smith	
42-37942	Lt Jacobs	*Four Leaf Clover*
42-97239	Lt Lambert	
42-38008	2Lt L Matichka	
42-31969	Lt Schlecht	

94CBW   401BG   B17s
| 42-30855 | 2Lt J Lenkeit | *Ol' Massa* |

3BD 4CBW   385BG   B17s
| 42-31786 | 1Lt A Drobysh | *Gin Rickey* |

13CBW   100BG   B17s
| 42-31710 | 2Lt D Riggle | *The Savage* |

390BG   B17s
42-31603	1Lt O Miller	*Belle of the Brawl*
42-31913	1Lt T Hammond	*ETO-itis / Shy Ann*
42-3498	2Lt J Son	*Red Head / Hap's Hazard*
42-39911	2Lt W Simmons	*Mary Lou*

45CBW   96BG   B17s
42-102482	2Lt H Eye	
42-38190	1Lt J Fitzpatrick	
42-102444	F/O L Green	*Smilin Thru*
42-97403	2Lt M Fancher	
42-38062	2Lt F King, Jr	*Laura Jane*
42-102451	1Lt G Sterler	
42-97782	1Lt H Niswonger	
42-102525	1Lt C Birdsey	
42-97631	1Lt J White	
42-39998	Capt M Shoesmith	

388BG   B17s
| 42-39907 | 2Lt T Pittman | *Nasty Nellie* |
| 42-107061 | 2Lt S Pickett | *Peg of My Heart* |

452BG   B17s
| 42-97220 | 2Lt H Morehouse | *Kickapoo Joy Juice* |

19th May 1944

1BD 1CBW   91BG   B17s
| 42-97455 | 1Lt R Wylie | *Keystone Mama* |

381BG   B17s
| 42-32088 | 1Lt H Blog | *Dry Gulcher* |
| 42-97454 | 1Lt E Sharp | |

398BG   B17s
| 42-97339 | 2Lt I O'Neal | |

41CBW   303BG   B17s
| 42-31386 | 1Lt E Roth | *Sky Duster* |

379BG   B17s
| 42-39783 | 2Lt M Wilson | *Blues in the Night* |

94CBW   401BG   B17s (Bombed Kiel)
| 42-38026 | 1Lt M Hagen, Jr | *My Day* |

457BG   B17s
| 42-97481 | 2Lt P Birong | |

3BD	4CBW	94BG	B17s
42-31540		Lt Reid	Miss Donna Mae II
	13CBW	95BG	B17s
42-97290		Lt W Waltham	Smiling Sandy Sanchez
		100BG	B17s
42-38191		2Lt M Rupert	
42-37807		Lt J Rogers	(Rogers Raiders)?
42-97607		2Lt R Horne	
		390BG	B17s
42-102532		2Lt R Tannehill	
	45CBW	388BG	B17s
42-107160		2Lt W White	Little Joe
		452BG	B17s
42-39990		2Lt S Gaal	Junior

24th May 1944

1BD	1CBW	91BG	B17s
42-107178		2Lt W Nee	(Sweden)
		381BG	B17s
42-31698		1Lt C Wainwright, Jr	
42-97214		1Lt J Wardencki	Carolina Queen
42-39890		2Lt C Dasso	Return Ticket
42-38010		1Lt C Ezzell	
42-31878		2Lt W Higgins	Spam Can
42-31291		1Lt C Gardon	Avengress
		398BG	B17s
42-107231		Capt U Brodin	
42-107132		1Lt J Ingram	
	40CBW	92BG	B17s
42-31635		2Lt W Reuther	
		305BG	B17s
42-39949		2Lt J Brown	
		306BG	B17s
42-32113		1Lt R Ehrler	
	41CBW	303BG	B17s
42-97787		1Lt J Worthley	
		379BG	B17s
42-39828		2Lt T Kunda	
42-38082		Capt L Shumake	
42-37784		2Lt W Gease	The Old Fox
		384BG	B17s
42-31364		2Lt G Seamon, Jr	Nuttall's Nut House
	94CBW	351BG	B17s
42-38005		Capt R Clay	Stormy Weather
		401BG	B17s
42-31619		2Lt J Whiteman	BTO in the ETO
		457BG	B17s
42-102965		1Lt H Stafford	(Ditched)
3BD	4CBW	94BG	B17s
42-31252		2Lt J Whorton	Sweaty Betty
		385BG	B17s
42-31742		2Lt R King, Jr	
		447BG	B17s
42-102494		2Lt R Simon	
	13CBW	95BG	B17s
42-39924		2Lt W Sheehan	Tornado
		100BG	B17s
42-31534		1Lt F Malooly	Powerhouse
42-97845		Maj M Fitzgerald	
42-31941		1Lt L Williamson	(Big Stoop)?
42-97095		1Lt D Pearson	
42-31306		1Lt E Siewert	Nelson King
42-102635		1Lt M Hoskinson	
42-102648		2Lt R Roeder	BTO in the ETO
42-102528		1Lt H Jesperson	Times Awastin
42-102624		2Lt C Johnson	

21st June 1944

1BD	1CBW	91BG	B17s
43-37626		2Lt J Paskvan	
44-6117		2Lt R O'Bannon	
42-97891		1Lt J Follet	
42-102527		1Lt E Waters	Sleepy Time Gal
		381BG	B17s
42-31980		2Lt R Dassault	
42-97174		1Lt R Pendergist	Joanne
42-38194		1Lt A Bailey	Baboon McGoon
		398BG	B17s
42-97686		1Lt R Rohrer	(PFF - part 398BG crew)
	41CBW	303BG	B17s
42-97096		1Lt C Allen	
42-32037		1Lt H Way	
42-107002		2Lt T Morningstar	Mairzy Doats
		384BG	B17s
42-107221		F/O F Finch	(Sweden)
	94CBW	351BG	B17s
42-97144		2Lt J Walters	
		401BG	B17s
42-31496		2Lt Atherton	
		457BG	B17s
42-107015		1Lt R Crumm	
42-31656		2Lt H Wilson	
2BD	2CBW	389BG	B24s
42-52579		1Lt E Patterson	Fightin Sam (!I)
42-95044		2Lt A O'Steen	
42-95122		1Lt C Hartquist	The Magic Carpet
42-95145		1Lt W Core	
42-109794		1Lt R McAuliffe	Nuff Sed
42-50371		1Lt G Schukar	
		445BG	B24s
42-95130		Capt J Salisbury	(Ditched)
42-50329		Capt R Plant	
		453BG	B24s
41-28591		1Lt M Williams	Inspector's Squawk
	14CBW	44BG	B24s
42-100411		2Lt N Howe	
		392BG	B24s
42-110027		1Lt H Belitz	(E for Easy)
	20CBW	93BG	B24s
42-109816		1Lt M Barkan	War Goddess (Sweden)
		446BG	B24s
41-29124		2Lt J Nicholson	Connie
		448BG	B24s
42-95186		2Lt C Howall	
42-95075		1Lt J Mercer	Happy Hangover
42-95089		2Lt R Fox	Dual Sack (Sweden)
	96CBW	466BG	B24s
44-40093		Lt L Mower	Lovely Lady's Avenger
		467BG	B24s
42-52525		2Lt E Rudowska	(Sweden)
42-52497		1Lt E Helton	
3BD	4CBW	94BG	B17s
42-97614		1Lt H Nichols	Nick's Place
		385BG	B17s
42-3490		2Lt M Totten	
42-38135		2Lt M Lohmeyer	
		447BG	B17s
42-97932		2Lt G Carter	
	13CBW	390BG	B17s
42-30715		2Lt M Dinsmore	Cincinnati Queen
	45CBW	452BG	B17s (Frantic Force)
42-31359		2Lt H Lerum	
42-102662		2Lt E Armm	
42-31810		2Lt M Anderson	
42-107036		2Lt J Sorenson	(Sweden)
42-38202		2Lt L Hernandez	BTO in the ETO

8TH AIR FORCE BOMBER LOSSES IN THE BATTLE FOR BERLIN

6th August 1944

1BD	1CBW	381BG	B17s	
44-6020		1Lt A Webb		Underground Farmer
		398BG	B17s	
42-102467		1Lt I Alhadeff		
	40CBW	305BG	B17s	
42-97674		1Lt D Farmer		
	94CBW	351BG	B17s	
43-37557		1Lt J Barieau, Jr		Hubba Hubba
42-107046		2Lt W Boyd, Jr		Screwball
42-102971		1Lt P Pattison		
42-31509		2Lt W Petty		Twinkle Toes (Sweden)
43-37920		1Lt G Uttley		
43-37533		2Lt W Strange		
		401BG	B17s	
42-31369		2Lt J Sauerwald		Round Tripper
		457BG	B17s	
42-97131		2Lt V Frost		Home James
3BD	4CBW	94BG	B17s	
42-97974		1Lt L Hicks		
42-107185		1Lt O Spenst		
		487BG	B17s	
43-37805		1Lt J Hatfield		
	45CBW	388BG	B17s	
44-6088		1Lt D Kluth		Fortress Nine
		452BG	B17s	
42-32087		2Lt L Graber		(Sweden)

6th October 1944

3BD	4CBW	94BG	B17s	
42-31599		1Lt J Brashers		Filthy Hag/Boots & her Buddies
43-37630		1Lt M Fausnaugh		Our Baby
42-38207		1Lt C Davis		(Ditched)
44-8143		Capt J Batty		(PFF a/c led 385BG)
		385BG	B17s	
43-38060		1Lt L Courcelle		Texas Bluebonnet
44-6159		1Lt R Noiseau		West Virginian (?)
43-37548		1Lt H Kaplan		Hell's Belles (?)
43-38217		2Lt R Tuley		
42-97079		1Lt E Isaacson		Dozy Doates
42-97275		1Lt B Leverett		Roger the Dodger
42-98010		2Lt D Taylor		
42-98016		2Lt R Funk		
42-102465		2Lt W Jens		Wee Willie Wilbur
43-38430		1Lt D Andreas		
		447BG	B17s	
43-37821		2Lt V Mateyka		Red Hot Mama (Ditched)
	13CBW	100BG	B17s	
43-37882		2Lt F Reed		
	93CBW	490BG	B17s	
43-38180		1Lt W McLennan		

5th December 1944

1BD	1CBW	91BG B17s		
43-38234		1Lt D Freer		Easy Does It
43-38360		2Lt R Blanton		Bride of Mars
43-38693		1Lt Mitchell		
	40CBW	305BG	B17s	
42-39947		Lt C Todd		Chiquita
42-37827		Lt R Pounds		Sweet Seventeen
43-38074		Lt R Funkhouser		
		306BG	B17s	
42-39963		Lt Stetler		Little Lulu
42-32099		Lt Manning		Fightin' Carbarn Hammerslaw
	94CBW	351BG	B17s	
43-38432		Capt H Williamson		
3BD	45CBW	96BG	B17s	
43-38644		2Lt M David		Green Weenie
		452BG	B17s	
44-8518		1Lt C Wagner		
	93CBW	34BG B17s		
44-8140		Capt R Gregory		(PFF a/c from 490BG)

3rd February 1945

1AD	1CBW	91BG	B17s	
42-97632		1Lt F Adams		
42-32085		1Lt G Miller		Yankee Belle
		381BG	B17s	
42-102873		2Lt J Anderson		The Joker II
43-38898		2Lt P Pucyleuski		Hitler's Hoe Doe
		398BG	B17s	
43-38697		1Lt P Powell		
42-97387		1Lt J McCormick		Maude an' Maria
	40CBW	92BG	B17s	
43-38364		2Lt B Morrow		
		305BG	B17s	
42-102555		Lt D Shoemaker		(Ditched)
43-38102		Lt J Gordon		
		306BG	B17s	
42-102547		1Lt V Daley		Rose of York
43-38407		2Lt G Luckett		
42-97658		2Lt R Lissner		The Jones Family
	41CBW	379BG	B17s	
42-97678		1Lt W Webber		Birmingham Jewell
		384BG	B17s	
42-102501		2Lt R Long		The Challenger (Ditched)
42-97960		1Lt C Molder		
44-6592		2Lt G Ruckman		Stardust

95BG's *Smilin' Sandy Sanchez* (42-97290) joined the group in mid March 1944 and flew a total of 22 missions by the time of its loss over Berlin on 19th May. The plane had been named just six days earlier in honour of S/Sgt Sator (Sandy) Sanchez who, on 13th May 1944, held the record for ETO heavy bomber missions – a staggering total of 44. It was the first B17 in the 8th to be named after an enlisted airman serving in that Air Force. Although *Smilin' Sandy Sanchez*, the plane not the man, failed to return on 19th May it did make it to Sweden and put down at Akesholm where Lt

Waltman's crew were interned. Unfortunately, the plane hit a tree while landing which severely damaged the nose area and it was scrapped in 1945.

S/Sgt Sanchez, who had been the tail gunner on Lt Overstreet's crew, was not flying in the ship that day, having returned to the USA for a five month break. He volunteered to fly a second tour of combat and was posted to the 15AF's 301BG in Italy where he completed a further 31 missions before being shot down and killed on 15th March 1945 on a raid to Ruhland refinery, just 25 miles Southeast of Berlin. (S. Markz)

3AD	4CBW	487BG	B17s
42-98014	2Lt A Rothstein		*Mutzie B*
	13CBW	95BG	B17s
42-102951	2Lt R Morris		
43-38899	1Lt J Taylor		
		100BG	B17s
44-8379	Capt J Ernest		
42-102958	2Lt R Beck		
44-6092	2Lt W Oldham		
44-6500	2Lt O Cotner		
	45CBW	96BG	B17s
44-6170	2Lt L Wyman		*Sittin' Pretty*
		452BG	B17s
43-38358	1Lt W Fry		*Slightly Dangerous* (Sweden)
	93CBW	490BG	B17s
43-38150	1Lt S Spiege		
		493BG	B17s
43-38242	2Lt H Sherman		

26th February 1945

1AD	40CBW	92BG	B17s
44-6461	2Lt R Mason		*Sweet Chick*
	41CBW	384BG	B17s
43-38823	Lt J Barnett		
2AD	14CBW	491BG	B24s
42-50680	Lt F Jensen		*Big Un*
3AD	45CBW	452BG	B17s
42-32083	2Lt A Marksian		*Flat Bush Floogie*

NOTE: Many other aircraft were forced to divert and/or force-land in Russian or Allied held territory while flying Berlin missions. Some of these were later repaired and eventually returned to their bases, others were salvaged. They were not considered as Missing in Action and are, therefore, not included in the above listing.

NOTE: Other heavy bombers were listed as Missing in Action on the above dates but are not listed here because they were flying on alternative missions, to targets other than Berlin.

Victory claims on Berlin missions

Date	Bomber claims	Fighter claims
3/3/44	3-1-1	8-1-3
4/3/44	6-2-3	9-3-4
6/3/44	97-28-60	82-8-33
8/3/44	63-17-19	87-12-32
9/3/44	1-0-0	0-0-0
22/3/44	0-0-0	1-0-0
18/4/44	13-5-6	20-0-13
29/4/44	73-26-34	22-7-14
7/5/44	0-0-0	0-0-0
8/5/44	76-16-16	22-0-13
19/5/44	0-0-0	49-0-19
24/5/44	0-0-0	30-7-6
21/6/44	29-23-22	20-0-12
6/8/44	0-2-6	25-0-6
6/10/44	3-9-5	15-0-5
5/12/44	0-0-0	90-7-25
3/2/45	0-0-0	29-1-11
26/2/45	0-0-0	6-0-0
18/3/45	7-1-1	14-0-4
28/3/45	0-0-0	0-0-0
TOTAL	371-130-173	529-46-200
GRAND TOTAL	900-176-373	

Destroyed - Probable- Damaged. Extracted from Intops Summaries and includes ground strafing claims.

18th March 1945

1AD	40CBW	92BG	B17s
42-97288	1Lt H Culver		*Flagship* (Sweden)
		305BG	B17s
44-6564	2Lt W Schultz		
43-38014	2Lt R McCaldin		*Naughty Virgin*
	41CBW	379BG	B17s
43-37855	2Lt D Mohr		
	94CBW	401BG	B17s
43-38607	2Lt D Vermeer		*Lady Jane*
		457BG	B17s
43-38203	2Lt J Schwikert		
2AD	96CBW	467BG	B24s
42-52546	1Lt W Shinn		*Southern Clipper*
3AD	13CBW	100BG	B17s
43-37521	1Lt R King		*Skyway Chariot*
43-38861	1Lt E Gwin		*Sweet Nancy I!*
44-8717	1Lt P DeWeerdt		
		390BG	B17s
44-8265	2Lt S Mroz		
43-37564	1Lt E Freeman		*Little Moron*
	45CBW	452BG	B17s
43-38879	2Lt W Bishop		(Ditched)
	93CBW	385BG	B17s
42-102481	1Lt W Cocke, Jr		*Kentucky Winner*
44-6944	1Lt H Bloom		

28th March 1945

1AD	41CBW	303BG	B17s
43-38248	2Lt C Frederickson		*Jigger Rouche II*
	94CBW	401BG	B17s
43-37551	2Lt J McCullough		

The cost to the 8th Air Force

(Estimated no. of aircrew)

1505	Killed or Missing in Action
2568	Prisoners of War
257	Interned
340	Returned wounded
141	Returned dead or died soon after

4811	TOTAL *(Approx. 3.2% of the manpower deployed)*

229	Rescued from sea or Returned via Russians
88	Evaded through enemy lines

373	B17s MIA	81	B24s MIA
201	P51s, P47s & P38s MIA		

15th Air Force losses
24th March 1945

		2BG	B17s
44-6718	1Lt R Tappen		
44-8162	2Lt R Rapelyea		(Ditched)
		463BG	B17s
44-6283	1Lt T Tubman		*Betty Lou*
44-6640	1Lt W Wilson		*Iaetitia* (Ditched)
44-6686	2Lt G Giacopuzzi, Jr		
44-6702	1Lt W Foster		*Umbriago*
44-6761	1Lt J Swan		
44-8498	1Lt W Hatcher		
		483BG	B17s
44-8159	2Lt J Dailey		(Ditched)

CASUALTIES IN BERLIN FROM 8AF AIR RAIDS

The following casualty statistics were supplied by the Landesarchiv from official documents compiled during 1944 and 1945 for the administrative districts of Berlin. Some Berlin air raid reports are missing entirely from the official files — presumably destroyed, either accidentally or deliberately. Although many town halls and local government buildings were hit during raids, with the undoubted loss of many documents, it is curious that even partial records do not remain for certain dates.

It should also be noted that even those records which are detailed here may not be complete, especially in the closing months of the war. Huge numbers of refugees flooded into the city as the Allied and Russian armies advanced towards Berlin. Although everyone in Germany had to carry identity papers, hundreds of casualties may have been missing but un-missed simply because no one knew they were there. It is not clear from these Landesarchiv records whether or not casualties from the armed forces, police, etc, are included — or those from the tens of thousands of forced labourers and prisoners working in the city in the factories, repairing the damage or involved in bomb disposal. It must also be remembered that additional casualties were inflicted in areas lying outside the city limits. Numerous small towns and villages received concentrations of bombs on many occasions. With less sophisticated air raid protection, these locations may well have suffered considerable casualties as a result.

6th March 1944

District	Killed	Injured	Missing
Spandau	4	3	2
Zehlendorf	30	11	10
Steglitz	27	20	4
Kopenick	2	-	-
Lichtenberg	5	10	-
Weissensee	5	8	-
Reinickendorf	13	5	1
TOTAL	86	57	17

7th May 1944

District	Killed	Injured	Missing
Mitte	? (42) 25	? (53) 35	10
Prenzlauerberg	11	139	32
Horst Wesel	15	10	104
Kreuzberg	4	14	-
Schoneberg	4	17	22
Tempelhof	2	-	-
Kopenick	-	1	-
Lichtenberg	1	9	-
Weissensee	67	10	-
Pankow	33	14	-
TOTAL	? (179) 162	? (267) 249	168

8th May 1944

District	Killed	Injured	Missing
Mitte	6	4	-
Tiergarten	1	5	-
Wedding	55	15	52
Horst Wesel	6	26	2
Treptow	74	42	-
Kopenick	-	2	-
Lichtenberg	53	125	-
Pankow	-	1	1
TOTAL	195	220	55

24th May 1944

District	Killed	Injured	Missing
Mitte	3	2	-
Tiergarten	2	4	-
Wedding	-	1	-
Horst Wesel	80	-	-
Kreuzberg	31	4	-
Spandau	2	-	-
Zehlendorf	14	23	-
Schoneberg	1	4	-
Steglitz	-	1	-
Tempelhof	17	-	-
Neukolln	4	1	-
Treptow	1	1	-
Kopenick	-	-	1
Lichtenberg	-	30	-
Weissensee	2	-	-
Reinickendorf	1	1	-
TOTAL	158	71	1

6th August 1944

District	Killed	Injured	Missing
Tempelhof	45	36	2
Treptow	2	62	-
Kopenick	-	19	-
TOTAL	47	117	2

6th October 1944

District	Killed	Injured	Missing
Wedding	1	2	-
Charlottenburg	5	9	-
Spandau	185	160	-
Schoneberg	7	12	15
Reinickendorf	95	74	20
TOTAL	293	257	35

5th December 1944

District	Killed	Injured	Missing
Spandau	9	5	-
Neukolln	44	58	-
Weissensee	20	31	1
Pankow	79	20	4
Reinickendorf	172	159	1
TOTAL	326	273	6

3rd February 1945 (revised as of 15th Feb 1945)

District	Killed	Injured	Missing
Mitte	791	388	339
Tiergarten	36	24	1
Wedding	52	132	1
Prenzlauerberg	7	2	-
Horst Wesel	294	269	132
Kreuzberg	863	530	180
Charlottenburg	-	5	-
Wilmersdorf	53	99	33
Schoneberg	204	78	4
Tempelhof	51	16	-
Neukolln	34	29	20
Treptow	67	18	2
Lichtenberg	54	51	2
Weissensee	23	7	-
Pankow	10	5	-
Reinickendorf	2	15	-
TOTAL	2541	1668	714

26th February 1945

District	Killed	Injured	Missing
Mitte	45	38	17
Tiergarten	1	-	-
Wedding	1	5	10
Prenzlauerberg	25	35	57
Horst Wesel	200	80	100
Kreuzberg	30	?	50
Schoneberg	139	64	-
Tempelhof	24	15	-
Neukolln	8	16	23
Treptow	28	22	25
Kopenick	19	13	17
Lichtenberg	27	71	190
Weissensee	3	10	30
Pankow	84	16	-
Reinickendorf	2	4	-
TOTAL	636	389	519

"...When the attack came... it quickly became apparent that the ARP (Air Raid Precautions) was seriously disorganised and short of staff... the undermanned fire brigade had great difficulty in fighting the gigantic fires... the greatest damage was caused in the areas round the Tempelhof railway stations... Many Berliners were so shocked by this last visitation that they refused to emerge from their shelters..."

Swedish press dispatch, 4th February 1945

18th March 1945

District	Killed	Injured	Missing
Mitte	20	29	39
Tiergarten	88	45	31
Wedding	14	25	70
Prenzlauerberg	26	13	-
Horst Wessel	28	70	51
Charlottenburg	9	30	-
Kreuzberg	6	-	29
Neukolln	8	28	-
Treptow	10	4	-
Lichtenberg	23	17	31
Weissensee	59	13	-
Pankow	19	23	13
Reinickendorf	26	60	2
TOTAL	336	357	266

28th March 1945

District	Killed	Injured	Missing
Wedding	2	2	-
Charlottenburg	30	44	-
Spandau	300	?	?
Tempelhof	5	11	-
Lichtenberg	-	3	-
Reinickendorf	3	2	5
TOTAL	340	62?	5?

BERLIN - 31st March 1944	Official German Estimates
Seriously Damaged Buildings	
18% of all buildings	11% of all industrial buildings
Totally Destroyed Buildings	13.17% of all houses (196,035)
Heavy & Total Damage	20.91% of all houses (311,419)

"...big bunkers had been built and a feeling of renewed confidence was apparent. Nevertheless, living in an atmosphere of smoke and foul air caused by the severity of the fires was very upsetting and disturbing to morale... by then the flak defences of the city were under severe criticism and the jibe was made 'Flak is not a weapon, but an article of Faith'..."

Extract from Berlin survivor interview, made by British Intelligence in 1945, referring to bombing during 1944 and 1945

"...What I remember best is the whistling sound made by the bombs as they fell. During a lull I quit the cellar to see what damage had been done and I had just reached the entrance when another bomb fell and blew me back. I remember crawling into the cellar again on all fours..... on the whole I think that the women in Germany, particularly in Berlin, showed themselves to be more stouthearted than the men."

Frau Lint, German teacher to General Sir Brian Robertson

Dust, smoke and soot swirl through the streets of the Mitte District of Berlin after the raid on 24th May 1944. Parochialkirche, 1km east of Friedrichstrasse station, looms out of the devastation.

"... we scrambled out of the shelter with wet cloths over our mouths but at street level it was no better... soot and smoke everywhere, we choked on it... I have never seen such devastation, it was like some hellish gothic painting I had studied at school... broken timbers, masonry, rubble piled everywhere... smashed street cars... I did not even recognise the street I had worked in for four years."

Gerda Laumann, Berlin survivor

BERLIN — Extract from TARGET SUMMARY (compiled in 1945)

Target	Date	Sighting	Effective Sorties	Bomb Tonnage HE	IB	Frag	Total
AIRCRAFT PLANTS							
Marienfelde — Daimler Benz	21/ 6/44	H2S/Vis	30	44.5	31.8		76.3
aero engine & tank factory	6/ 8/44	Vis	82	151.5	42.5		194.0
Spandau — BMW aero engine & tank	6/10/44	Vis	140	224.5	57.6		282.1
Spandau — BMW plant, Auto Union plant							
and Deutsche Industriewerke tank plant	28/ 3/45	H2X	403	694.2	344.5		1038.7
TOTAL Aircraft Plants			**655**	**1114.7**	**476.4**		**1591.1**
AIRFIELDS							
Staaken	6/ 3/44	H2X	6	15.0			15.0
INDUSTRIAL AREAS	6/ 8/44	Vis	4	10.0			10.0
	12/ 9/44	Vis	13	32.5			32.5
	5/12/44	H2X	13	19.5	13.0		32.5
	3/ 2/45	Vis	1	1.5	1.0		2.5
TOTAL Industrial Areas			**31**	**63.5**	**14.0**		**77.5**
MARSHALLING YARDS							
Spandau	6/ 3/44	H2X	19	47.5			47.5
Unidentified (now known to be Rummelsberg)	18/ 3/45	H2X	34	20.2	67.7		87.9
TOTAL Marshalling Yards			**53**	**67.7**	**67.7**		**135.4**
MILITARY & CIVIL GOVERNMENT AREAS							
	6/ 3/44	H2X	366	638.5	237.0		875.5
	9/ 3/44	H2X	332	528.8	239.8		768.6
	22/ 3/44	H2X	621	512.0	862.2		1374.2
(also hit Tempelhof Airdrome)	29/ 4/44	H2X	581	711.5	712.0		1423.5
	7/ 5/44	H2X	525	812.2	450.7		1262.9
	8/ 5/44	H2X	384	768.2	146.6		914.8
	19/ 5/44	H2X/Vis	493	404.0	662.5		1066.5
	24/ 5/44	H2X	493	461.2	643.0		1104.2
	21/ 6/44	H2X/Vis	560	1100.3	270.7		1371.0
	3/ 2/45	H2X/Vis	932	2028.8	250.6		2279.4
TOTAL Military & Civil Government Areas			**5287**	**7965.5**	**4475.1**		**12440.6**
MISCELLANEOUS INDUSTRIAL PLANTS							
Robert Bosch AG (?)	4/ 3/44(?)	H2X	31	45.0	24.3		69.3
MOTOR TRANSPORT, ARMOURED VEHICLES & ARMAMENT WORKS							
Niederschoneweid-Nordbau	21/ 6/44	H2X/Vis	54	102.1	13.0		1 15.1
Nordeutsche Motorenbau (tank)	6/ 8/44	Vis	45	73.0	35.0		108.0
Tegel - Altmarkischen Kettenwerke (Alkett)	6/10/44	Vis	89	166.5	46.0		212.5
Tegel - Rheinmetall Borsig AG	5/12/44	H2X	388	762.3	171.2	9.1	942.6
Locomotive and armaments works	18/ 3/45	H2X/Vis	225	225.8	185.0		440.8
TOTAL Motor Transport, AFV & Armament Works			**801**	**1359.7**	**450.2**	**9.1**	**1819.0**
ORDNANCE DEPOTS							
Spandau - Neustadt	6/10/44	Vis	68	83.5	27.2	51.3	162.3
Spandau - Military Depot	6/10/44	Vis	69	105.0	59.2		164.2
TOTAL Ordnance Depots			**137**	**188.5**	**86.7**	**51.3**	**326.5**
RAIL STATIONS							
Friedrichstrasse Station	8/ 3/44	Vis	30	23.8	51.3		75.1
Schlesischer Station	26/ 2/45	H2X	374	538.3	356.7		895.0
	18/ 3/45	H2X/Vis	387	441.1	541.0		982.1
Stettiner (Berlin -Nord)	26/ 2/45	H2X	291	402.7	249.1		651.8
	18/ 3/45	H2X	498	745.9	688.8		1423.7
Alexanderplatz	26/ 2/45	H2X	424	623.7	607.5		1231.2
TOTAL Rail Stations			**2004**	**2764.5**	**2494.4**		**5258.9**
GRAND TOTAL			**9005**	**13584.1**	**8088.8**	**60.4**	**21733.3**

HE = High explosive   IB = Incendiary   Frag = Fragmentation   H2X = Radar   Vis = Visual

The statistics reproduced in this table are as officially compiled in 1945. In some cases, there is a discrepancy between these figures and data accumulated from other official sources and from later research. For example, it is now known that the Robert Bosch plant took no hits during the raid on 4th March 1944, although the table indicates 69.3 tons of ordnance dropped on this location. Total effective sorties does not always tally with information gleaned from individual group reports or later documentation.

Target	Date	Sighting	Effective Sorties	Bomb Tonnage HE	IB	Total
BASDORF	22/3/44	Vis	32		80.1	8C.1
	21/6/44	H2X/Vis	81	124.2	60.9	185.1
TOTAL Basdorf			**113**	**124.2**	**141.0**	**1265.2**
GENSHAGEN	6/3/44	H2X/Vis	51	33.8	99.6	133.4
Grossmotoren Genshagen Gmbh	21/6/44	Vis	152	234.0	144.9	378.9
Daimler Benz	6/8/44	Vis	172	280.5	115.0	395.5
TOTAL Genshagen			**375**	**548.3**	**359.5**	**907.8**
ERKNER						
VKF Ball Bearing Plant	8/3/44	Vis	468	300.4	761.0	1061.4
ORANIENBURG	18/4/44	Vis	129	97.6	145.9	243.5
Heinkel Germandorf	18/4/44	Vis	106	34.2	170.5	204.7
Heinkel Annahof	18/4/44	Vis	34	50.5	24.0	74.5
Airfield Annahof	10/4/45	Vis	139	379.0	37.2	416.2
TOTAL Oranienburg			**408**	**561.3**	**377.6**	**938.9**
RATHENOW						
Arado Flugzugwerke	18/4/44	Vis	162	103.8	287.8	391.6

Geographical distribution of output of ball bearings

Location	No. of plants	Percentage of total production
Schweinfurt	3	45.0%
Stuttgart	1	18.3%
Berlin	**2**	**13.0%**
Steyr	1	10.2%
Misc. other	35	13.5%

Total forces deployed against Berlin

Aircraft sorties		Estimated aircrew
B17s	11622 (inc 15AF)	110,409
B24s	2591	24,615
P38s	1881	1,881
P47s	5216	5,216
P51s	7487 (inc Frantic escort)	7,487

Aircraft sorties against Berlin (inc 9AF escorts, scouting forces and RAF support)

Date	Despatched	Effective	% MIA (Bmbrs)
3rd March 1944			1.47%
B17	555	--	1.62%
B24	193	--	1.04%
P38	89		
P47	484		
P51	130		
4th March 1944			2.99%
B17	502	31	
P38	86		
P47	563		
P51	121		
6th March 1944			9.59%
B17	504	474	10.71%
B24	226	198	7.08%
P38	86		
P47	615		
P51	100		
8th March 1944			5.78%
B17	414	353	6.52%
B24	209	183	4.31%
P38	104		
P47	613		
P51	174		
9th March 1944			1.14%
B17	361	339	1.66%
B24	165	—	—
P38	88		
P47	572		
P51	177		
22nd March 1944			1.74%
B17	474	460	1.48%
B24	214	197	2.34%
P38	125		
P47	496		
P51	196		
18th April 1944			2.45%
B17	501	439	3.39&
B24	275	159	0.73%
P38	119		
P47	296		
P51	236		
29th April 1944			9.43%
B17	446	368	8.52%
B24	233	212	11.16%
P38	117		
P47	468		
P51	263		
7th May 1944			1.06%
B17	600	514	
P38	152		
P47	317		
P51	413		
8th May 1944			3.97%
B17	500	386	
P38	155		
P47	233		
P51	285		
19th May 1944			2.72%
B17	588	495	
P38	154		
P51	518		
24th May 1944			5.36%
B17	616	464	
P38	224		
P47	178		
P51	381		
21st June 1944			4.30%
B17	703	639	3.70%
B24	368	238	5.43%
P38	310 (+ 72 Frantic escort)		
P47	323 (+ 38 Frantic escort)		
P51	335 (+ 122 Frantic escort)		
6th August 1944			2.82%
B17	568	397	
P51	339		
6th October 1944			4.07%
B17	418	382	
P51	414		
5th December 1944			2.66%
B17	451	404	
P51	711		
3rd February 1945			2.69%
B17	1003	937	
P51	613		
26th February 1945			0.34%
B17	823	781	0.36%
B24	361	285	0.28%
P47	20		
P51	706		
18th March 1945			1.13%
B17	980	916	1.43%
B24	347	314	0.29%
P51	733		
24th March 1945 (15AF)			5.33%
B17	169	148	
P51	289		
28th March 1945			0.45%
B17	446	389	
P51	272		

Stark testimony to the ferocity of the aerial bombardment of central Berlin. The Kaiser Wilhelm Palace situated at the junction of Friedrichstrasse and the Unter-den-Linden. (V. Edwards)